AF600690

RUSSIAN MODERNISM IN THE MEMORIES OF THE SURVIVORS

THE DUVAKIN INTERVIEWS, 1967–1974

RUSSIAN MODERNISM IN THE MEMORIES OF THE SURVIVORS

THE DUVAKIN INTERVIEWS, 1967–1974

Edited by Slav N. Gratchev, Margarita Marinova, and Irina Evdokimova

Translated by Slav N. Gratchev and Margarita Marinova

UNIVERSITY OF TORONTO PRESS
Toronto Buffalo London

© University of Toronto Press 2021
Toronto Buffalo London
utorontopress.com

ISBN 978-1-4875-2725-9 (cloth) ISBN 978-1-4875-2727-3 (EPUB)
ISBN 978-1-4875-2726-6 (PDF)

Library and Archives Canada Cataloguing in Publication

Title: Russian modernism in the memories of the survivors : the Duvakin interviews, 1967–1974 / edited by Slav N. Gratchev, Margarita Marinova, and Irina Evdokimova ; translated by Slav N. Gratchev and Margarita Marinova.
Other titles: Duvakin interviews, 1967–1974
Names: Duvakin, V. D., interviewer. | Gratchev, Slav N., editor, translator. | Evdokimova, Irina, 1976– editor. | Marinova, Margarita (Margarita D.), editor, translator.
Description: Includes bibliographical references and index.
Identifiers: Canadiana (print) 20210157933 | Canadiana (ebook) 20210158131 | ISBN 9781487527259 (cloth) | ISBN 9781487527266 (PDF) | ISBN 9781487527273 (EPUB)
Subjects: LCSH: Authors, Soviet – Interviews. | LCSH: Artists – Soviet Union – Interviews. | LCSH: Authors, Russian – 20th century – Interviews. | LCSH: Soviet Union – Intellectual life – 1917–1970. | LCSH: Soviet Union – History.
Classification: LCC DK266.4.R87 2021 | DDC 947.084–dc23

Title page and chapter opener illustration: Detail from Georgi Yakulov, *The Spring Salon of Poets*, 1918.

This project is presented with financial assistance from the West Virginia Humanities Council, a state affiliate of the National Endowment for the Humanities. Any views, findings, conclusions or recommendations do not necessarily represent those of the West Virginia Humanities Council or the National Endowment for the Humanities.

University of Toronto Press acknowledges the financial assistance to its publishing program of the Canada Council for the Arts and the Ontario Arts Council, an agency of the Government of Ontario.

Canada Council for the Arts Conseil des Arts du Canada

Funded by the Government of Canada | Financé par le gouvernement du Canada | Canada

To my dear son, Sancho, whose incredible energy and love of life remind me that we all were children once. And it was the best time ever.

S.G.

Contents

Illustrations

Acknowledgments

Our sincere gratitude goes to our colleague and friend Professor Victor Fet, whose incredible intelligence, love of literature, and suggestions for revisions and corrections made this book immeasurably better.

We also express our gratitude to the staff of the Mayakovsky State Museum in Moscow, Russia, especially its director, Alexey Lobov, and Yulia Sadovnikova, Dmitry Karpov, and Ekaterina Snegireva. They all were instrumental in the preparation of the unique photograph gallery that appears in this book.

We thank Professor Caryl Emerson, who dedicated time to reading our manuscript, suggested insightful revisions, and, most important, wrote a brilliant afterword to the volume. The final product of our efforts has benefited enormously from her generous participation in and attention to this project.

Special thanks go to Dr. Dmitry Sporov, the head of the Department of Oral History at Moscow State University. Without his help this book would not have been possible. The translation was done directly from the Russian interview audio files provided by Dr. Sporov. Some of those were independently transcribed and published in Russian as Duvakin, V.D., *Besedy s Viktorom Ardovym.* ([*Conversations with Viktor Ardov*] Moscow, 2018). All translations of poems in the book are ours, unless otherwise noted.

We want to express our gratitude to our home institutions, Christopher Newport University and Marshall University, and specifically Dr. Mary Wright, Dean Lori Underwood, and Dean Robert Bookwalter whose financial assistance contributed greatly to the timely publication of our project.

Last but not least, we are very thankful to the anonymous reviewers and our wonderful editors at University of Toronto Press, who helped us improve our book in every possible way.

All translations in the book are ours unless otherwise noted.

RUSSIAN MODERNISM IN THE MEMORIES OF THE SURVIVORS

THE DUVAKIN INTERVIEWS, 1967–1974

Introduction: The Revolution of the Word and Its Context

Dmitry Sporov

Moscow State University holds a relatively small collection (about three thousand interviews) of recorded conversations about the history of science, the arts, and everyday life in Russia during the twentieth century. The collection has grown significantly since 1967, the year Victor Duvakin (1909–1982) began his original recordings of conversations – which were always marked by informality and a certain fluidity in terms of the representation of the conveyed information – with such notable figures of Russian culture as Mikhail Bakhtin, Viktor Shklovsky, Nikolay Timofeev-Resovskii, and Vyacheslav Ivanov. Moscow State University has spent the last ten years adding to Duvakin's treasure trove of oral history. As with any oral history documents, what matters most is not so much the pre-existing prominence of the interviewee but the ability of the two interlocutors to find common ground and a shared language in the conversation. The interviews about Russian culture from the beginning of the twentieth century collected in this book are perfect examples of that kind of successful communication.

In the context of the Russian historiographic tradition, oral history as a form of recording private memories has developed its own special characteristics. The official state directive to create a "new Soviet man" with a "clean memory," though executed with varying degrees of success, demanded the complete restructuring of both national memory and public history. Only the history of the revolutionary party of the Bolsheviks, the victory of the young republic, the heroic military triumphs of the past, and the revolutionary struggle for freedom were deemed worthy of inclusion in the national memory repository. In that grand historical narrative there was hardly any place for the regular private citizen. Any personal connection to the pre-revolutionary period or familial history was interpreted as a dangerous relic of the bourgeois past. Private memory, including familial memory, was seen as one of the markers of individuality and of estrangement from the collective work of building the socialist state. Consequently, private memory became the locus of free will and play during the reign of authoritarian "great history." Thus, "kitchen conversations," we might say, enabled the formation of new kinds of relationships to the past and created the possibility of their humanization and acceptance during the Soviet period. Oral history was transformed into an act of political resistance. Even when the conversation followed the accepted norms of ritualistic Soviet parlance, it was impossible not to slip and avoid subversion. That is the nature of live speech: like water, it always finds a way to seep through.

This particular characteristic of oral history was embraced and celebrated by the founder of the university's archives, the philologist Victor Duvakin, who devoted his life to the study of poetry, especially the new Soviet language of Vladimir Mayakovsky. His initial involvement with oral history began in the aftermath of the first show trial to be held in the post-Stalin era, of those Soviet authors who had dared to publish their work abroad. One of them, Andrey Sinyavsky, was a student of Duvakin. As a witness for the defence at the trial, Duvakin recited poems and offered interpretations of literary metaphors. Much like his student, he had serious disagreements – especially aesthetic in nature – with the Soviet regime. The trial inaugurated the emergence of serious resistance, a new dissidence that had already begun in literary language, in a return of the forgotten, and in publications of the forbidden. Naturally, he had to be punished for his independent thought and willingness to stand up for fellow intellectuals: in 1966 Duvakin was fired from his position as a professor at the Moscow State University. Yet he found a way to be productive even under those difficult circumstances. He finally had the long-desired freedom to accomplish something that no one in the Soviet Union had ever tried to achieve: the creation of an oral collection of reminiscences by leading figures in the arts and sciences from the first half of the twentieth century.

The life of each of his interlocutors included three revolutions, two world wars, famine, repressions, flight, and, finally, a miracle – the only way one can explain their survival. They almost never talk about that directly, however, and seem to glide over the diabolical context of their conversations. Duvakin's interviews with his colleagues can be seen as formally and ideologically unconstrained and intimate conversations, marked by their own narrative logic, a response deliberateness, and a striking sense of "outsidedness" experienced by all the participants. From the very beginning of the project, the taped dialogues strove to capture the multitudinous aspects of human existence that were not covered in the public discourse of the times: from gender and nationality to repression to emigration and to resistance to power, though for the most part such topics were not addressed directly but in roundabout ways through hints and insinuations.

Victor Duvakin envisioned the interviews as part of a larger corpus of personal recollections about the poet Vladimir Mayakovsky and saw his work on this project as a service to Russian culture generally and to the "cult of Mayakovsky" in particular, which is worthy of a separate discussion. The fifteen years he laboured on this task (1967–82) coincide with the period of great stagnation in the Soviet Union known as "the long 1970s." The Duvakin phenomenon and his collection represent one of the most important documents of the times, as they reveal a crucial feature of this period: a new focus on literature and the importance of cultural memory in everyday life (and I would venture to suggest not just for the intelligentsia but for Soviet society as such). The life, creative endeavours, and memory of Duvakin's interviewees sought to balance between the realities of the revolution (a momentous breaking point in the past) and the realities of art and science as they were experienced in practice after the revolution (the times of political oppression and uniformity). As a result, private memory underwent a transformation that allowed an escape from the publicly accepted norms and "facts" in order to focus on the literal and the specific as counterweights to the collective work in which all were expected to participate. The unprecedented freedom of Duvakin's undertaking, and his hagiographic explorations of Mayakovsky's biography, revealed a completely different culture, another sociality, and different microhistories. The importance of this archive and the conversations published in the present book, therefore, can be found not only in the covered topics but also in the formal features of the recorded speech acts, which create narratives with such an unusual degree of freedom, especially when compared to other existing private memory repositories that are still shackled by the language of Soviet conventionality.

This latest (third) publication in English of materials from the oral history archives at Moscow State University, edited and annotated by three outstanding scholars – Slav Gratchev, Margarita Marinova, and Irina Evdokimova – presents conversations from the 1960s and 1970s with the popular writer-satirist and caricaturist Viktor Ardov, the eminent linguist Roman Jakobson, and the husband-and-wife literary scholar team of Vladimir and Ariadna Sosinsky. Their memories are centred on the literature and culture of the 1910s and 1920s – that is, the time of the symbolic birth of a new language, a new word. Viktor Ardov was one of the bright, young, and slightly arrogant builders of the intellectual foundations of the Soviet state, who inaugurated constructivism and boldly criticized anything that did not comply with the ideals of the new social order. Roman Jakobson was one of the leaders of the new approach to artistic language, and his work contributed significantly to the development of structuralism and psycholinguistics. His primary focus of study was the literature of the Russian avant-garde. For example, Jakobson's ideas about Velimir Khlebnikov's phonoscript masterpieces laid the foundations for his theories about glottogenesis and the origination and development of languages. Vladimir and Ariadna Sosinsky were apostles of classical Russian literature and should be seen as literary scholars in the traditional nineteenth-century sense of someone devoted to the understanding and celebration of literary language. For this reason, the heroes of their story happen to be the best Russian writers of the first half of the twentieth century: Tsvetaeva, Remizov, Babel. In their conversations with Duvakin the interviewees come across as modest and wise, but in their youth, during the times to which their oral memoirs transport us, they resembled a magnificent lightning strike across the skies above Europe and beyond, both running away from the idea of the grand utopia attempted by the new Soviet social order, and forever carrying it within.

These conversations are an expression of Russia's other voices, which are needed and much appreciated today not only at home but also, I trust, in America. I am very grateful to the translators and editors of this book and for the serious work they have done in decoding and encoding the original language and providing meaningful commentaries, as well as visual illustrations, to help the non-Russian reader imagine and understand better the world remembered in these pages. Without any one of those constituent parts the results would not have been the same, and I am already looking forward to future publications that will continue our conversation about the artistic and intellectual revolutions of the early twentieth century.

DIALOGUE 1
With Viktor Ardov on 6 August 1974*

My immediate task is to save what can still be saved.

Victor Duvakin[1]

Victor Duvakin first interviewed Viktor Ardov in 1967,[2] and then again, seven years later, in the taped conversation translated here. During those intervening years Duvakin managed to expand significantly his collection of primary phono-documents, with the goal of recording "the history of Russian culture of the first quarter of the twentieth century." Naturally, the content of the first interview had been forgotten by 1974, so Ardov recounts several stories concerning Mayakovsky.[3]

The main subject of this conversation is Sergei Yesenin.[4] Ardov recalls, and even tries to imitate, how Yesenin read his poems. He insists that Yesenin's often

* Length of interview – 62 minutes

1 *Arkheograficheskii ezhegodnik za 1989 god* (Moscow: Nauka, 1990), 308.

2 Viktor Ardov (1900–1976) was a Soviet writer and a renowned satirist and cartoonist. He was a close friend of all the major literary figures of the Soviet era, many of whom (Joseph Brodsky, Alexander Solzhenitsyn, Boris Pasternak, Anna Akhmatova, Marina Tsvetaeva, and Andrey Tarkovsky, to name a few) spent time living – for various reasons – in his large, comfortable apartment in Moscow.

3 Vladimir Mayakovsky (1893–1930) was one of the most celebrated poets of the early Soviet era and the foremost representative of Russian futurism. He was one of the few Soviet writers who were allowed to travel freely in the West and write about his experiences abroad. After his suicide (or, as some still assert, assassination by the secret police, NKVD) in 1930, Mayakovsky was canonized by the Soviet authorities.

4 Sergei Yesenin (1895–1925) was a prominent Russian poets of the early twentieth century. A peasant by birth, he was able to obtain a decent education and then moved to Saint Petersburg, where he was welcomed by the artistic Bohemia. In 1921 he married Isadora

1.1. Sergei Yesenin with Isadora Duncan and her daughter, Irma Duncan, Moscow, 1922. Photographer unknown.

outrageous behaviour and, perhaps, even his presumed suicide were the result of the poet's constant need for attention. Ardov also talks about one of Yesenin's public appearances at a poetry reading at the Polytechnic Museum,[5] which he attended wearing a top hat and carrying a cane.

Duncan and travelled with her to Europe and the United States. He returned, very disappointed with his family life and what he had seen in the West. The NKVD never forgave Yesenin for this trip abroad, and in 1925 he was forced into a psychiatric clinic. He escaped to Leningrad, but, a few days later, he was found dead in a room at Hotel Astoria. Many scholars believe that Yesenin was murdered by the NKVD, but the official version was that the poet had committed suicide.

5 The Polytechnic Museum in Moscow is one of the oldest science museums in the world. Founded in 1872, it was designed and built by the fashionable nineteenth-century Russian architect Ippolit Monighetti (1819–1878). Now the museum's collection contains more than 190,000 rare items, including the first achromatic telescope. Its impressive scientific library holds more than three million volumes. The grand hall of the museum has always been used for public lectures, debates, and poetic evenings, and the poetry readings of the 1960s were particularly noteworthy.

Duvakin: Victor Yefimovich, we meet with you again seven years later.

Ardov: Time flies, it's true!

Duvakin: Yes. Well, my collection since then has become huge, about four hundred tapes. You may recall that in the beginning I was mainly recording people who could tell me about Mayakovsky, but now my main goal is to create a collection of original phono-documents that capture the history of Russian culture of the first three decades of the twentieth century. That is, up until the middle of the 1930s.

Of course, these conversations are about people of the 1920s, who made the twenties what they were. I am mainly interested in the period preceding the First Symposium of Soviet writers,[6] the one that ends at the same time as the first *pyatiletka* [five-year plan].[7]

I'd like to ask you to tell us the history of *Krokodil* (*Crocodile*).[8] It was founded in 1923, wasn't it?

Ardov: No, in 1922.

Duvakin: You could tell us about the people who ran it – their habits and characters – and then (we don't have to finish everything today; I can come again another time) we could talk about some of your personal acquaintances. We already discussed Mayakovsky in our previous conversation, but if you want to add something, we can start there. Besides Mayakovsky, I would like

6 The First Soviet Writers Congress, officially presided over by Maxim Gorky, took place in August of 1934. It established the guidelines for socialist realism. All major and minor literary figures of Soviet literature, including Boris Pasternak, Mikhail Zoshchenko, Boris Pilniak, Mikhail Privshin, Il'ia Ehrenburg, Isaak Babel, and Iurii Olesha, were in attendance. Out of the almost five hundred writers in attendance, more than two hundred would be prosecuted, sent to labour camps, or shot during the following five years.

7 The first five-year plan was adopted by the Communist Party in 1928. It was a list of economic goals that were supposed to transform the country from being mainly agrarian to being truly industrial. Even though it was declared that the plan was fully realized in four years and three months, almost all the reported figures were fake. In fact, the years between 1928 and 1932 were perhaps the hardest in the history of the Soviet Union: more than eight million people died of famine (Holodomor, or the Great Famine) due to administrative mismanagement and to the total crop failure that struck the richest grain-producing areas of Ukraine, Russia, and Kazakhstan in 1932.

8 *Krokodil* (*Crocodile*) was a Soviet satirical magazine founded in 1922. Its initial forays into uncompromising political satire were soon curtailed, and the magazine became an "official" satirical journal, allowed to exist in order to offer a gentle critique of specific aspects of socialist reality. The magazine ceased publication in 2000 due to a significant decrease in its audience.

to give you a list of people I want to ask you about. Yesenin is one. Marienhof is another.[9]

Were there any other notable or interesting people you met throughout your life that I might also know about?

Ardov: First of all, let me say that Yesenin had nothing to do with *Krokodil*.

Duvakin: Oh, that doesn't really matter!

Ardov: Fine. I will gladly start by telling you about Sergei Yesenin because we met a long time before the magazine *Krokodil* came into existence. He is a very important person, in fact, so important that he deserves to be discussed separately.

When someone like him dies, it always turns out that he had had ten times more friends than he realized when he was alive. This happened to Yesenin: as soon as he died, he became famous. As a matter of fact, everything happened exactly as his friend Marienhof had predicted in his novel, which was, in my opinion, overall too frank and cynical.[10]

But perhaps it was fair after all: while he was alive, the overwhelming majority of his audience saw him in a negative light. By the way, there were many who did not accept Mayakovsky either. One really had to hate both of these poets a priori in order not to see their greatness. In particular, Yesenin was considered no more than a literary hooligan because some lines in his poems were deemed indecent from a puritanical point of view. But Yesenin himself was very quick to respond to such labels. So why did it happen? I tried to explain this phenomenon in my short memoirs about Yesenin.[11] Neither the Imaginists[12] nor the

9 Anatoly Marienhof (1897–1962) was a Soviet poet, writer, and playwright and a principal figure in the Imaginism movement. Following the death of Yesenin, a close friend, Marienhof published two very controversial works, *Roman bez vraniia* (*A Novel without Lies*, 1926), which was a fictionalized account of Yesenin's life and of Russia's Bohemia; and *Tsiniki* (*The Cynics*, 1928), about the experiences of young members of the Russian intelligentsia during the revolutionary period and war communism. Marienhof was attacked severely by the Communist critical establishment because *The Cynics* was published in Germany. In order to save his life, he had to write a letter apologizing publicly for "daring" to print his works abroad.

10 Ardov refers here to *A Novel without Lies*.

11 In 1970 Ardov wrote a short essay about Yesenin, "Dva slova o Yesenine" ("Two Words about Yesenin"), but it was never included in his book *Etudy k portretam* (*Sketches for Portraits*). It can be found in the Russian State Archive of Literature and Art (RGALI).

12 Imaginism was a Russian avant-garde poetic movement that originated in 1918 in Moscow. Its main proponents were Anatoly Marienhof, Vadim Shershenevich, and Sergei Yesenin. To distance and differentiate themselves from the Futurists, the three men founded the Order of Imaginists and proclaimed that the main purpose of art was to create memorable *images*.

Futurists[13] were the first to invent this particular style of poetry, whose aim was to shock the audience, to provoke and tease the middle class, which was seen as very beneficial.

They rebelled against any kind of traditional civility and against such markers of politeness as the phrases "I had the honour," "I have the pleasure," "dear public," and so on. Instead, they wanted to stand out for their devil-may-care attitude towards people and their traditions.

Let me tell you a very interesting story. In Moscow, on Gorky Street (then it was called Tverskaya Street), there was a house, number 18. (Later, unfortunately, that house was demolished.) The first and second floors of that building housed several different little stores, but if you climbed up the stairs a bit higher, you would find yourself in a café called Domino. This café was given over to the local poets and became known as the Poets' Café.[14]

Duvakin: I see! So that's how it came to be known as the Poets' Café?

Ardov: Yes, the Poets' Café, but, before, it was called Domino. Anyway, it also served as the headquarters for the Poets' Union.[15] It was quite influential for a time. We must note that the union's chairman was Valery Bryusov,[16] that he frequently visited the café, and that he organized and participated in public poetry readings there.

So what did the café look like? It was on commercial premises. Everything – the tables, the buffet – was left over from the previous owner. The kitchen was run by Matvey Roizman's father, who was also a poet.[17] He died recently, after publishing his book about Yesenin. Do you know it?

---

13 Futurism was another Russian avant-garde movement, founded around 1910–11 by a group of young poets that included Vladimir Mayakovsky, David Burliuk, Aleksey Kruchenykh, Velimir Khlebnikov, and Vasily Kamensky. Proponents of anarchy, they repudiated the art forms of the past, sought to capture the experiences and feelings of the masses, and oriented their artistic creations and belief system towards the future.

14 The Poet's Café was established in 1917 thanks to the generous financial support of a rich merchant, Nikolai Filippov. Mayakovsky, Burliuk, and Valentina Khodasevich (niece of Vladislav Khodasevich) painted brightly coloured, exotic scenes on the café's walls. Mayakovsky, a genius of metaphoric expression, referred to it as "the great-grandmother of all literary cafes." The café existed for only one year, until 1918.

15 The Poets' Union, which hoped to unite poets of all movements and schools, was formed in Moscow in 1918. It organized public lectures and literary evenings for its members. The union was even able to publish an almanac, but the increasing censorship and control of the Communist Party over the arts resulted in the union's dissolution in 1929.

16 Valery Bryusov (1873–1924) was a principal member of the Russian Symbolist movement. A prominent poet, writer, playwright, translator, critic, and historian, he was one of the few of his circle who supported the Bolshevik government after the revolution. Later he obtained a prominent position in the Ministry of Culture of the new state, but in 1924 he caught pneumonia and died shortly thereafter.

17 Matvey Roizman (1896–1973) was a mediocre poet, writer, and memoirist who maintained a low profile during the years of repression. Later he wrote mystery novels and published

1.2. Vadim Shershenevich, Moscow (?), 1920s. Photographer unknown.

Duvakin: No. When was it published?

Ardov: Last year, in 1973. It's notable for its amazing integrity and accuracy. The book as such is not that great at all, because the author [Roizman] never had much talent, but his facts are all correct. Most importantly, he himself was a member of the group of Imaginists, and he really knew very well Yesenin, and Marienhof, and Kusikov,[18] and Shershenevich,[19] as well as other prominent Imaginists.

---

an interesting book about Yesenin: *Vse, chto pomnyu o Yesenine* (*All I Remember about Yesenin*), (Moscow: Sovetskaya Rossiya, 1973).

18 Alexander Kusikov (1896–1977) was an active member of the Order of Imaginists but a very mediocre writer. He was a close friend of the prominent figures of the times – Mayakovsky, Bryusov, Konstantin Balmónt, Yesenin, Kamensky – and even owned a publishing house, called Chikhi-Pikhi. In 1921, while abroad, Kusikov decided to defect, and he never returned to the USSR. He died in Paris. His later poetry is marked by themes of pessimism, solitude, and anticipation of chaos.

19 Vadim Shershenevich (1893–1942) was a Russian poet, translator, and theorist of Imaginism who left many interesting works about cinema and theatre. His poetry uses an excess of metaphors and neologisms, whose artistic goal was to shock, rather than to please readers.

The food at the café was bad, but it was the 1920s. However, the government allowed them to serve pastries, which were procured illegally. If someone was caught making such pastries out of precious flour (flour was very scarce in Moscow then), sugar, and butter, that person was immediately sent to the Cheka.[20]

But here, in the café, such things were allowed. Also it was possible to have some porridge; sometimes they even served *vobla*![21] It was a beggar's meal, to be sure, but at that time very enviable. We spent a lot of time there, eating and talking, while the poets read their works from a small stage. Yesenin also read his poems, as did other Imaginists. Sometimes, though quite rarely, Mayakovsky would make an appearance, too. Then, there was an endless line of poets and wannabe poets who belonged to all kinds of groups and associations (now nobody even remembers their names). For example, there was a group called Nichevoki [Nothing-ists].[22]

Duvakin: Oh, yes, of course! The Nichevoki became a part of literary history: Zemenkov,[23] Ryurik Rok.[24]

During the Second World War Shershenevich was evacuated from Moscow, but he died in 1942 from tuberculosis.

20 Cheka (in Russian, ЧК) was a special committee created in 1917 by Vladimir Lenin and headed by Felix Dzerzhinsky until his mysterious death. It was the first Soviet Bureau of State Security. Later, it was renamed MGB (sometimes called GPU), Ministry of State Security. In 1934 MGB was replaced by the NKVD, which became the principle vehicle of Stalin's terror. Essentially, it was the same organization, which was given different names as it grew.

21 *Vobla* (*Rutilus caspicus*) is a type of fish that lives exclusively in the Caspian Sea. When the fish has been brined in saltwater for three days, then carefully allowed to dry in a dark and dry place, it becomes very tasty and rich in flavour. In Russia it is served with beer.

22 The Russian avant-garde poetic group Nichevoki was formed in Rostov-on-Don around 1920. It became fairly well known in 1922 in Moscow when, after Mayakovsky had announced in one of his public lectures that he was going to "clean up" Russian poetry, the Nichevoki took to the stage and proposed that Mayakovsky go to Pushkin's monument right then and there and proceed to polish the boots of everyone who asked him to do so. This was their way of publicly renouncing anyone's right to decide what poetry is good and what poetry is bad. The group existed for about two years and dissolved after the death of its leader, Sergei Sadikov, in 1922.

23 Boris Zemenkov (1902–1963) was a Soviet poet, artist, and historian of the city of Moscow. As a poet, he was not significant, but his artistic talent flourished when he began work as an art restorer. He recreated the external appearance of buildings in Moscow, Moscow region, and Saint Petersburg; they all were related to the life and work of prominent figures of Russian culture such as Leo Tolstoy, Anton Chekhov, Alexander Pushkin, and Nikolay Gogol.

24 Ryurik Rok (b. Gering) (1900–1962) was one of the leaders of the poetic group Nichevoki. For a short time he worked with Vsevolod Meyerhold in his theatre. Rok did not accept the Bolshevik Revolution and in 1926 left the USSR for Germany. He later moved to Switzerland.

Ardov: Yes. Then Rok was charged with embezzlement and jailed, but that has nothing to do with what we're discussing now. I had just graduated from high school but had not started attending university yet. The times were such that one felt no desire to study. I was working in a Soviet government office, but I always dressed in the military style: pants, leggings, uniform jacket. And I often visited the café [the Poets' Café] to listen to poets. One day I saw Ippolit Sokolov there.[25] He is still alive, but he is now a film critic or something like that. Such a boring, hopeless man. Back then he was writing very bad, stupid poetry, often obscene and nonsensical, just so he could attract attention to himself.

Anyway, that day he started to read. But the audience didn't listen to him: they were making noise, rattling their spoons while eating their porridge, laughing, and so on. Sokolov stopped reciting and asked someone to call in a Poet's Union "member on duty." And when he emerged from the kitchen, this member on duty turned out to be Sergei Yesenin! He was completely sober, bored, and gloomy. He stood in the doorway and asked Sokolov from there, "What do you need?" "They are not listening, just making noise," complained Sokolov. In response, Yesenin shouted out: "Hey, you, *farmatsevty* [pharmacists]! Pay attention or get out of here! Or did you come here just to stuff yourselves full?" Then he yawned and left.

Farmatsevty at that time was a derogatory term used for people who didn't have anything to do with the arts. It was true, there were among them some self-proclaimed patrons of the arts, some vulgar people, and mediocre townsfolk. The term suited them well, I think.

The audience quieted down a bit. Sokolov went on with his recitation – and then they began to make noise again. He again stopped and asked for the member on duty. Yesenin, this time very angry, came out and yelled loudly: "Hey you, *farmatsevty*! Either listen, or get the f—out of here!" He really said that word, so crude!

You cannot imagine what kind of rage his words produced in the majority of those present.

Duvakin: But who were the majority? The *farmatsevty*, or the poets?

Ardov: There were people of different social backgrounds there.

Duvakin: I understand, but were there many poets present?

---

25 Ippolit Sokolov (1902–1974) was a leader of the Russian Expressionists. He became interested in the new art of cinema and devoted his professional life to it. Sokolov became one of the first professors at the State Institute of Cinematography (VGIK), worked with Sergei Eisenstein, and gave numerous lectures on the history of cinema at Moscow State University.

Ardov: No, the reading was meant for the normal visitors of the café, not for the poets. There were events, literary competitions specifically for poets, but that day there were mostly regular people who had come to the café to get a bite to eat. So, when those guys, the majority of the audience, got angry, something quite interesting took place. Among those present was a pince-nez-wearing Left SR–type[26] of intellectual with a black moustache, dressed in a military suit with red Hussar trousers.[27]

He was there with a very pretty woman, and, judging by their behaviour, they were obviously in the so-called lyrical stage of their romance. They kept cooing at each other and ignored everybody else. But when they heard what Yesenin said, the gentleman got very upset, stood up, and went somewhere – likely to make a phone call. A short time later a couple of officers from Lubyanka showed up and started to check everyone's documents.[28] Obviously, they wanted to arrest Yesenin for his inappropriate behaviour, but by then he had already gone home. All of us had to go through the process of showing our documents; we couldn't leave – they had placed guards by the door. I was able to return home only around 4:00 a.m., and some people were detained and taken to Lubyanka. This is how that situation turned out in the end.

Duvakin [*surprised*]: And you witnessed everything?

Ardov: Yes, I did.

Duvakin: You were in the audience that night?

Ardov: I was there, and I saw the gentleman who called the officers from Lubyanka to check everybody's documents, as it were, and I heard those wonderful words come out of the poet's mouth with my own ears.

---

26 SRs, or Eseri (эсеры), were the Socialist Revolutionaries. Theirs was the largest political party, going back to the pre-revolutionary period and comprising one million members after the February Revolution. But their success was short-lived, and for most party members the end was tragic: after the October Revolution the party leaders were systematically repressed and then killed; some members voluntarily went into exile to save their lives. In 1917 the SR party split into two: while the majority supported the provisional government, the Left SRs supported the Bolsheviks and, as a result, participated in their government from October 1917 to July 1918.

27 A Hussar was a soldier of the light cavalry. This type of military originated in Hungary in the fifteenth century. The etymology of the word is unclear, but it is thought to be connected with *Corsair*, that is, "someone who sits on a horse."

28 The most feared place in the USSR, the Lubyanka building was the main headquarters of Cheka, GPU, NKVD, and KGB between 1919 and 1991. Now it belongs to the Federal Security Bureau (FSB). The building is located in Moscow, not far from the Kremlin, on Lubyansky Square. It also housed a prison where some of the most famous prisoners were Alexander Solzhenitsyn, Vsevolod Meyerhold, and Osip Mandelstam.

Duvakin: And that happened in 1918? Before the uprising of the Left SRs, or later?[29]

Ardov: It was 1920.

Duvakin: Ah, already 1920. Then Blyumkin was there?[30]

Ardov: Yes, Blyumkin was a frequent visitor too.

Duvakin: But the SR-type intellectual was not Blyumkin, was he?

Ardov: Oh, no! Blyumkin was a Jew. He was a very ugly man, resembling a character by Sholom Aleichem.[31] In addition, he had a cleft lip.

Duvakin: Oh, I didn't know that.

Ardov: I didn't know Blyumkin that well. But, no, he was not at the café that evening. And he couldn't have been; in 1919 he had left Russia in order to save his life after the assassination of Count Mirbach.[32]

Duvakin: I think it was in 1918.

Ardov: Right. He left in 1918, then wrote a repentant letter to Dzerzhinsky,[33] and was allowed to return and continue to work for Cheka. Then he was sent

---

29 The uprising of the Left SRs (6 July 1918) was perhaps the most dangerous moment for the new Bolshevik government. The Left SRs, being in complete disagreement with the Bolsheviks, decided to remove them from power by assassinating the German ambassador, Count Wilhelm von Mirbach, whom they charged with conspiring with and financially supporting the Bolshevik government. The Left SRs proceeded to arrest twenty-seven members of the Bolshevik party (including Felix Dzerzhinsky, the head of Cheka), but then, suddenly, they stopped further activity. The Bolsheviks quickly regained their ground and, after a few hours of fighting in the streets of Moscow, were able to suppress the rebellion completely.

30 Yakov Blyumkin (1900–1929) was the first Soviet "special agent," so to speak. A man of incredible intelligence (he spoke fluently Hebrew, Turkish, Arabic, Mongolian, and Chinese), Blyumkin was a terrorist, cruel, mean, and treacherous. For some time he served as the personal bodyguard of Leon Trotsky. In 1929, after his return to Moscow following one of his deadly missions, Blyumkin was suddenly arrested and sentenced to death. It is interesting to note that he loved poetry, was interested in all contemporary aesthetic movements, and was a personal friend of Yesenin, Mayakovsky, Shershenevich, and Marienhof. They most likely never knew who he really was and what he did for the government.

31 Sholom Aleichem (b. Solomon Rabinovich) (1859–1916) was a Jewish writer and playwright. Often called the Jewish Mark Twain, he loved public appearances and, by giving lectures virtually all over the world, at a fairly young age became an internationally known figure. His last years were darkened by progressive tuberculosis, from which he eventually died at the age of fifty-seven.

32 Wilhelm von Mirbach (1871–1918) was a German ambassador in Soviet Russia. His unfortunate appointment started in April of 1918, and on 6 July he was assassinated by the Left SRs.

33 Felix Dzerzhinsky (1877–1926) was a close friend of Lenin. After the revolution he became the head of Cheka, where he wielded significant power and was feared by Stalin

to Mongolia where the Whites were fighting with the Reds.[34] While there, he arrested some colonel and sent him to Moscow where they immediately shot him, and the Mongolian government demanded that Blyumkin be removed from his post.

After that, he returned to Moscow. I met him a few times in the 1920s, just ran into him here and there. And then he *pogorel* [got burned], as they say. He brought a letter to Radek[35] from Trotsky.[36] Did you know that? He called Radek and told him that while he was abroad he had seen Lev Davidovich [Trotsky], who sent a letter with him. In response, Radek began to shout that he was tired of such provocations, and so on. A few days later Blyumkin was arrested and, soon after, executed.[37]

Duvakin: Was that in 1931?

Ardov: Yes, later, around that time. Blyumkin was an unpleasant man, a difficult man.

Duvakin: But very adventurous.

Ardov: That's true. But let's talk more about Yesenin. When I hear people talking about his poetry, I must say I understand why there is such fascination with

---

himself. In 1926, while reporting to party leaders about the all-pervading corruption and bureaucracy, Dzerzhinsky began to feel ill and died the same day from, presumably, a heart attack. Some scholars suspect, perhaps with reason, that Stalin ordered his poisoning.

34 The Whites, or the White Army, was a loose confederation of anti-Communist forces, which fought the Communist Bolsheviks, also known as the Reds, in the Russian Civil War (1917–22/3). Although defeated by the Reds, the Whites continued operating as militarized associations of insurrectionists both outside and within Russian borders in Siberia until the start of the Second World War.

35 Karl Radek (b. Karol Sobelsohn) (1885–1939) was one of the most unscrupulous Communist Party members. Vladimir Lenin did not respect him but valued his talent as a journalist. In 1936 he was arrested and expelled from the party. His wife and daughter were also arrested and exiled. Radek was sent to the labour camps, but in 1939 he was killed by a cellmate who, in reality, was a special NKVD agent who had been ordered to eliminate him.

36 Leon Trotsky (b. Leiba Bronshtein) (1879–1940) was the second most important figure in the Bolshevik government and the founder of the Russian Red Army. After Lenin's death in 1924, Trotsky's influence began to wane; by 1927 he had been stripped of all previous appointments and in 1929 was forced into exile. In 1936 Trotsky settled in Mexico, where he was welcomed by Frida Kahlo and Diego Rivera. In 1940 an agent of NKVD, Ramon Mercader, snuck into Trotsky's villa and killed him with an ice axe.

37 The arrest and execution of Blyumkin in 1929 were so reckless that Radek's reputation (which was already damaged because he was suspected of betraying his friends Karl Liebknecht and Rosa Luxemburg) was totally destroyed; everyone realized that Radek had turned in Blyumkin.

this bright and talented author. Indeed, he is a wonderful lyrical poet. Yesenin was extraordinarily charming.

He had one unusual feature. He had hair such as I've never seen in my entire life, neither before nor after: it was not just blonde, it was strawberry blonde. His hair was so thin, so curly, and the forelock above his forehead – it seemed to have a life of its own; it moved by itself. Do you understand what I mean? The air is completely still, and the person himself is calm, but his hair is alive and moving by itself. It was amazing!

Women loved him! That's understandable: he had such talent, such personality, such lyrical emotion.

Yesenin was absolutely amazing when he read his poetry. He was always incredibly charming, but when he began to read, the verses just poured out of him. This does not happen with every poet. Pasternak read his poems this way,[38] and the most complicated and confusing places in his work always became clear and simple when he read.

Yesenin became a different person when he read his poetry. When he walked onto the stage, he closed his eyes, like the Khlysts did when they fell into ecstatic fits.[39] Yesenin stretched his right arm forward, palm down, and one got the impression that he was trying to touch and feel the words he was pronouncing.

Like many poets, he preferred to exaggerate the rhythmic structure of the poems at the expense of their content. That is the way all real poets read poetry. They say Pushkin read this way, too,[40] and Lermontov,[41] and

---

38 Boris Pasternak (1890–1960) was a famous Soviet poet. In 1958 he received the Nobel Prize in Literature "for his important achievement both in contemporary lyrical poetry and in the field of the great Russian epic tradition." Pasternak became the second Russian writer to be given this prestigious award (after Ivan Bunin). During Stalin's reign, to save his life and to support his family, Pasternak focused on translation. His translations of Shakespeare, Goethe, Schiller and Calderon are still among the very best. The publication of *Doctor Zhivago* in 1957 in Italy (after it was refused for publication in the USSR) brought him universal fame but created serious problems for him in his own country. The atmosphere of open animosity displayed by the official authorities destroyed Pasternak's health and contributed to his premature death in 1960.

39 The Khlysts was one of the oldest Russian religious sects, which had seceded from the Orthodox Church in the sixteenth century. Although there are many differences among the groups within the sect itself, depending on the geographical location, their religious beliefs go back to traditional Slavic mythology or paganism that was dominant in ancient Rus' (before the tenth century). For more on the Khlysts see A. Etkind, *Khlysty: Sekty, literarura i revolyutsiya* (*The Khlysts: Sects, Literature, and Revolution*), (Moscow: Novoe literaturnoe obozrenie, 1998).

40 Alexander Pushkin (1799–1837) is considered the founder of modern Russian literature and one of the greatest Russian poets. He was also a talented literary critic, innovative playwright, and brilliant prose writer. His life ended tragically early in a duel with Georges d'Anthès, a suitor of his wife, Natalia Pushkina (b. Goncharova; 1812–1863).

41 Mikhail Lermontov (1814–1841) was the most significant Russian poet after Alexander Pushkin. Many scholars still believe that if he had lived longer, he could have bested

Tyutchev,[42] and Mayakovsky. But for Mayakovsky the rhythm prevailed, while Yesenin read in such a way that he hypnotized the audience. Let me try to recreate that. I'll read a few lines – the way I remember them. That day he [Yesenin] was reading his *Pugachev*.

[*Ardov reads, trying to recreate Yesenin's performance:*]

Ох, как устал и как болит нога! ...
Ржет дорога в жуткое пространство.
Ты ли, ты ли, разбойный Чаган,
Приют дикарей и оборванцев?

(Oh, how tired I am, and how my legs hurt!
The road mocks me with its terrifying endlessness.
Is it you, is it you – Bandit Chagan,
Haven for savages and vagabonds?)[43]

Well, mine is, of course, a poor imitation of Yesenin's reading.

Duvakin [*very excited*]: Excuse me, but ... did Yesenin pronounce *g* like more guttural *h*, as you did just now?

Ardov: Yes, he stressed the *o* over the *a*.

Duvakin: No, I am asking about his *g* and *h*.

Ardov: Ah. Yes, it is a little surprising that a *ryazanets* [someone from Ryazan][44] pronounced *g* like a soft guttural *h*.

Pushkin in his literary achievements, but at the age of twenty-seven Lermontov was shot and killed in a duel. A masterful prose writer as well as a poet, he wrote a brilliant novel, *Geroi nashego vremeni* (*The Hero of Our Time*), which inaugurated the Russian psychological novel.

42 Fyodor Tyutchev (1803–1873) was a prominent Russian poet, diplomat, and academician. He loved ancient poetry and conversed fluently in Latin. His poetry is often misunderstood or under-appreciated, although it would be fair to say that Tyutchev is one of the most refined, most philosophical Russian poets.

43 The poem "Pugachev" was written by Yesenin in 1921 after he had conducted careful research in the Russian historical archives. According to Yesenin, Pushkin, who first wrote about Emelyan Pugachev's rebellion (1773–5) in his novel *Kapitanskaya dochka* (*The Captain's Daughter*, 1836), significantly distorted the original events. Yesenin's poem was meant to express his own views on this important moment in Russian history. All poetry translations are ours, unless otherwise noted.

44 Ryazan is an old Russian city located about 150 miles west of Moscow. The phonetic differences in pronunciation between Moscow and Ryazan are insignificant. This is the reason Duvakin expresses surprise that Yesenin, who was born and raised near Ryazan, pronounced the phoneme *g* as a soft and guttural *h*, which is more typical of the southern regions of Russia and of Ukraine.

1.3. A Moscow street near the Arbat Square, 1925–30. Photographer unknown.

I have this guttural sound because I am from Voronezh,[45] where the influence of the soft Ukrainian *h* is quite prominent. You can also hear it in the region of the former Don Host Province.[46] The older I get, the more pronounced my accent seems to become. But why Yesenin, a pure *ryazanets*, sounded like that, I have no idea. But he did.

Duvakin: That's very important, indeed.

Ardov: Yes. That's how he sounded. Now, allow me to cite something from Marienhof's *Novel without Lies*. He describes, in my opinion, a very typical

45 Voronezh is a city in southern European Russia, about 350 miles south of Moscow. It is considered to be the cradle of the Russian fleet. During the time of Peter the Great's reforms (1689–1725) the first Russian modern ships (215) were built there. That was the beginning of future victories over the Ottoman Empire on the Black Sea.

46 The Province of the Don Cossack Host (1786–1920) was the official name of the territory of the Don Cossacks, corresponding approximately to the present Rostov Oblast of Russia, with its capital in Novocherkassk. During the civil war the Don Republic (1918–20) was an independent anti-Bolshevik state. When the Cossacks were defeated by the Red Army, the Don Republic ceased to exist. For many years afterwards the vindictive Bolshevik government pursued a policy of genocide against the Cossacks.

episode. In the 1920s, somewhere near Arbat,[47] on one of the nearby streets, there was a fire. People flocked to see it, as it is customary in Russia, you know. We even had "fire fans," so to speak. The late Zoshchenko was obsessed with fires.[48] He had even procured a special pass, issued to him by the city fire department, that gave him permission to attend any city fire. [*Duvakin laughs.*]

Yes, yes, it is true. Anyway, the two young poets – Yesenin and Marienhof – also came to see the fire. So, there they are, standing around, watching the fire. And not very far from them, away from the crowd, there is a tall, blonde, very handsome man with a haughty expression, about fifty years old, with some sort of attendants around him. And people started turning away from the fire and staring at this blonde man. There's a fire, but they turned their backs on it to look at that man – why?

Then you heard his name: Chaliapin![49] Sure enough, Chaliapin, who lived on Novinsky Boulevard, had also come to watch the fire.[50] And people stared at him instead. Yesenin turned to Marienhof and said, "Tolya! This is what I want: that people look at me instead of the fire!" I am paraphrasing, of course; I didn't hear him say that myself.[51]

---

47 About a mile long, Arbat Street is the central and perhaps best-known street in Moscow. Its name is first mentioned in documents from the fifteenth century. A number of notable people lived on Arbat Street, including Alexander Pushkin, Nikolay Gogol, Leo Tolstoy, Anton Chekhov, Alexander Blok, and Andrey Bely. Joseph Stalin liked to take this street when he travelled to Kremlin by car, so it was constantly monitored by the NKVD. In the 1980s Arbat Street became a pedestrian zone, and today it is lined with many stores, theatres, and museums.

48 Mikhail Zoshchenko (1894–1958) is now viewed as one of the most eminent Soviet writers of the twentieth century, but during his life, despite his heroic military service, he was humiliated, trampled, and morally destroyed by the Soviet government and betrayed by his friends and literary colleagues. His last and most important novel, *Pered voskhodom solntsa* (*Before the Sunrise*, 1943) was prohibited from publication. His very original short story "The Monkey's Adventures," published in a children's magazine, was proclaimed to be an anti-Soviet satire. As a result, the name of Zoshchenko was erased from the annals of Soviet literature, and his books were removed from all libraries for the next forty years.

49 Fyodor Chaliapin (1873–1938) was a Russian opera singer, famous for the depth and expressiveness of his bass voice. He is remembered not only as a genius opera singer but also as an accomplished performer, movie actor (in *Don Quixote*, 1933), talented artist, and sculptor.

50 Chaliapin bought a beautiful mansion on Novinsky Boulevard in 1910. He spent many evenings there with friends Sergei Rachmaninov, Maxim Gorky, Konstantin Stanislavsky, Ivan Bunin, and many others. The Bolshevik government nationalized the building in 1918 and housed ten different families there. Chaliapin, offended to the core, left Russia for good. Only in 1988 was the house repossessed by the Moscow city government and is now the Chaliapin museum.

51 In the *Novel without Lies* we read the following:

> Несколько поодаль стоял человек почти на голову выше ровной черной стены из людей. Серая шляпа, серый костюм, желтые перчатки и желтые лаковые ботинки делали его похожим на иностранца [...] Стоял он, как монумент из серого чугуна. И на пожар глядел, как монумент - сверху вниз [...] вдруг кто-то шепотом произнес его имя - Шаляпин! Оно обежало толпу, и через минуту тот, кто соперничал с

Duvakin: Is it in the *Novel without Lies*?

Ardov: Yes. Such a representative, important episode! Let me also tell you this: if you ever looked at any photograph of Yesenin that was not retouched – there was this stupid desire to make him look super handsome (which was completely unnecessary; he had tremendous success just as he was, more than any goofy-looking man ever did!) – you will see that his face was not completely symmetrical – its outline. By the way, did you see Yesenin's monument on the boulevard?[52]

Duvakin: The one that was installed recently?

Ardov: Yes. I can show you a picture of this monument. It's a real masterpiece. The sculptor[53] never saw Yesenin alive, but he did a splendid job: the figure of the poet is made to look very interesting – realistic, and symbolic at the same time. But, most importantly, he [the sculptor] captured the expression that always appeared on Yesenin's face when he read poetry. I would like to show you that picture. [*It seems that Ardov is looking for something and cannot find it. He returns.*] Anyway, I will get that picture if you need it.

Vulgar people believe that poets should all have a certain facial expression that resembles that of lambs, as the expression goes – as if they were always dreaming of something beautiful. That's how Philistines picture a poet. Yesenin had a cunning face, sometimes even a cynical one. He was never a simpleton but, rather, a very dynamic and, I would say, cunning man. He always looked at people with a tinge of irony, as if he were saying, "I understand why you're doing this, and why

---

чугуном, стал соперничать с пожаром [...] Я почувствовал, как задрожала рука Есенина. Его зрачки расширились, на матовых щеках от волнения выступил румянец. Он выдавил из себя задыхающимся от ревности, зависти и восторга голосом: "Вот это настоящая слава!" (A. Marienhof, *Roman bez vranya* [Moscow: Azbuka, 2016], 314–15)

(A bit to the side, there stood a man towering almost a whole head and shoulders above the black wall of people. His grey hat, grey suit, yellow gloves, and yellow leather boots made him look like a foreigner [...] He stood there like a monument made of grey cast iron. He even looked at the fire, like a statue from the top down [...] Suddenly someone whispered his name – Chaliapin! The whisper spread around fast, and a minute later the rival of cast iron now rivalled the fire itself [...] I felt the hand of Yesenin tremble. His pupils dilated; his pale cheeks flushed red from excitement. His voice choking from a combination of jealousy, envy, and delight, he uttered, "Now that is real fame!")

52 This monument, the bronze figure of Sergei Yesenin, was unveiled in 1972. With its natural pose and youthful lyricism against the background of birch and aspen trees, it quickly became a favourite attraction along Yeseninsky Boulevard.

53 This very talented and prolific Soviet sculptor was Vladimir Tsigal (1917–2013). During the Second World War he served in the special forces and participated in many important military operations. His war experiences greatly influenced his later work as a sculptor in terms of themes and stylistic expression.

you say what you're saying, so what do you really want?" It was difficult to look into his eyes: they were so deep – the eyes of a very cunning man.

But his poetry was a completely different matter. I have no intention of reducing the value of his work. His reputation as a poet keeps growing and growing. But his cunning, his ability to do his business successfully, to understand other people and to understand them, as it were, deeper and better than what's expected from a lyrical poet – he always had that gift. For example, from time to time he'd say, "We need to make some noise. They have already started to forget me." And immediately he'd think of something that nobody expected, that would either amuse or infuriate people.

Once, when the inebriated Yesenin was arrested by the Militsiya,[54] he wanted to prove to them that he and his friends were important literary figures, and so he told the officers, "Call Demyan Bedny.[55] He will tell you who I am!" When they did, Bedny responded in the following manner: "So he is acting up, behaving like a bully? Where? The Militsiya? Let him sit there then – enough of his horsing around!"

I also remember another episode. I went to another café, Stoilo Pegasa [Pegasus's Stall],[56] on Gorky Street (at that time, the Tverskaya Street). Now that building is gone, and in its place there's a glass store and, I believe, a fish shop. Anyway, at the corner there was another café, called Bom. Why Bom? Because it belonged to the famous pair of clowns – Bim and Bom.[57] Bim (Radunsky)

---

54 Militsiya was the proper name for the police force in the USSR that was created by Lenin's personal order in November 1917, right after the October Revolution. The Militsiya was meant to replace the regular police force that was still loyal to the Russian tsar, Nicholas II.

55 Demyan Bedny (b. Efim Pridvorov) (1883–1945) was a Soviet poet, a devoted Bolshevik, and a close friend of Stalin. More than two million copies of his poetry collections were sold during the 1930s. He was compared to Maxim Gorky and called an exemplary Soviet poet. Bedny lived in a huge Kremlin apartment and had an assigned personal Ford automobile and driver. When he became sick (from diabetes), Stalin sent him to Germany for treatment, with all expenses paid. Bedny had the biggest Soviet private library (more than thirty thousand rare volumes), which Stalin liked to use as well. Quite suddenly, however, he fell out of favour, lost his apartment, and could not publish his work any more. His last days were bleak and gloomy, though he was able to avoid further repressions.

56 Stoilo Pegasa was a literary café located on the famous Tverskaya Street in Moscow. It was owned by Yesenin and Marienhof and became a centre for Russian avant-garde artists, mainly Imaginists. The café existed between 1919 and 1922.

57 Bim Bom (in existence between 1891 and 1946) was a clown duo: Ivan Radunsky (Bim) and Mechislav Stanevsky (Bom). The duo was enormously popular for several decades, even though after the October Revolution they maintained a critical stance towards the Bolsheviks. In 1920 Stanevsky left the USSR, and Radunsky had to find another partner. In spite of difficulties, Stalin's repressions, and the Second World War, the duo continued to exist until 1946 when Radunsky, at the age of eighty, decided to retire.

died when he was almost a hundred years old, here, in the USSR. He was an entrepreneur and director of the circus on Tsvetnoy Boulevard.[58]

And the clown Bom (Stanevsky) was an amazing comedian: when he laughed, the whole circus answered with laughter. He was the red clown, this Bom, while Bim was the white one.[59]

Anyway, Bim and Bom opened a café called Bom. Sometime after the revolution this café was, of course, closed. They fled abroad, I think,[60] and Yesenin and Marienhof took over the café and called it Pegasus Stall. It was very similar to the Domino Café, that is, the Poets' Café, but now they were in charge. But they also participated in some public readings.

I remember one day when I was there, I misbehaved; I shouted something very loudly from my seat. Yesenin came over, very much the proprietor in appearance, and said reproachfully, "Hey, you are one of ours, and you make such a noise. Please stop it, or the Militsiya will fine us." Those were his words.

I have to say that vulgar people look at everything from one point of view only. I have to share one more interesting episode, told to me by my old friend Ivan Yefimov, the animalist sculptor. His works are in many museums in the USSR and in the West.[61] He was a friend and colleague of another sculptor,

---

58 Tsvetnoy (Цветной, Flower) Boulevard is located near downtown Moscow. It got its name in 1851 from the nearby flower market. The circus on Tsvetnoy Boulevard is the oldest stationary circus in Russia. It was built in 1880 by the Jewish entrepreneur Albert Solomonsky (1839–1913), who also was a rider, equestrian acrobat, horse trainer, and actor. It was known as the Solomonsky Circus for many years until the Bolsheviks expropriated it in 1936.

59 Radunsky left us an interesting note in his book:

> Я выходил в клоунском костюме, а он [Станевский] появлялся в ультрамодном смокинге, в цилиндре, надетом слегка набекрень, с огромной хризантемой в петлице. Грима мой партнер почти не клал, парика тоже не надевал. Я играл человека наивного, сохранившего как-бы детские черты, а Станевский изображал самоуверенного пшюта. На этом различии образов мы и строили наши номера. (I. Radunsky, *Zapiski starogo klouna* [*Memoirs of an Old Clown*], (Moscow: Iskusstvo, 1954), 67)
>
> (I came out in a clown suit, and he [Stanevsky] appeared in a super-fashionable tuxedo, in a top hat, worn slightly to the side, with a huge chrysanthemum in his buttonhole. My partner put on very little makeup; he didn't wear a wig either. I played a naive person who had managed to preserve some childlike traits, and Stanevsky portrayed a self-assured dandy. We built our success on this contrast of images.)

60 In 1920, while abroad on tour, Stanevsky, who had a Polish passport, decided to stay in Poland. Radunsky did the same, and they continued to work together. But in 1925 Radunsky returned to the USSR, and the famous duo never performed together again.

61 Ivan Yefimov (1878–1959) was a Soviet sculptor, painter, book illustrator, and puppeteer. Many of his works are now on permanent display in the State Museum of Russian Art, the Tretyakov Gallery, the Pushkin Museum, and elsewhere.

Anna Golubkina.[62] One day she went to Yasnaya Polyana,[63] to work on a sculpture of Tolstoy.[64]

When she came back, Yefimov asked, "So, what can you tell me about Tolstoy?" She responded, "What can I say? He is a wolf! He has the eyes of a wolf."[65]

Isn't that amazing! Any fool would have seen in Tolstoy his good will, righteousness, desire to be kind, not to offend anyone. But she saw beyond that: he had the eyes of a genius and noticed everything!

[*A long pause*]

Ardov: The same was true of Yesenin: he was also ambivalent, and all his mischievous deeds, his harsh language, his practical mind, the cynicism in his dealings with people – they were all part of who he was. But those characteristics

---

62 Anna Golubkina (1864–1927) was a Russian sculptor whose works determined the main tendencies of the future Soviet school of sculpture. While in Paris, she studied at the famous Académie Colarossi and became a friend of Auguste Rodin. In 1899 Golubkina returned to Russia, where her success and popularity were tremendous. Her works are now displayed in numerous museums all over the world.

63 Yasnaya Polyana is the name of Leo Tolstoy's family country estate. It is located 200 kilometres (120 miles) from Moscow. Tolstoy was born there in 1828, and his grave is there as well. Yasnaya Polyana became a national museum in 1921. During the Second World War the Nazis occupied Yasnaya Polyana for forty-five days and, upon retreat, tried to burn down Tolstoy's house, but the fire was extinguished quickly and did not leave much damage. The museum contains Tolstoy's personal effects and furniture, as well as his library of twenty-two thousand volumes.

64 Golubkina visited Tolstoy in Moscow, not at Yasnaya Polyana. Initially she did not have a plan to make his sculpture; she just wanted to see him and talk to him. There were a few other people there, too, some of whom were workers. Tolstoy, as always, talked about the need to change ourselves on the inside, to replace our self-love, self-interest, and malice with love, humility, and mercy. "При этих словах Голубкина вдруг вскочила и со словами: 'Это все пятачки какие-то!' – ушла. Лев Николаевич посмотрел ей вслед. – Какая странная женщина, – сказал он." (With these words, Golubkina stood up briskly. "But this is absolutely naïve!" she said and left immediately. Lev Nikolaevich looked after her and said, "What a strange woman.") The description of this visit (possibly in 1900) can be found in N. Gusev, *Letopis zhizni i tvorchestva L.N. Tolstogo* (*The Chronicle of the Life and Work of L.N. Tolstoy*), (Moscow: GIKhL), vol. 2, 341–2.

Golubkina went to Yasnaya Polyana once more, but she was told that Tolstoy could not see her. So, her famous sculpture of Tolstoy was made from memory, in 1927. It remained in wood because Golubkina was sick and did not have the time or energy to do it in bronze. She died that same year.

65 There also exists a different version of Golubkina's reported assessment. According to the painter and memoirist Alexandra Khotyantseva (1865–1942), Golubkina said, "Tolstoy is like an ocean …but his eyes! He has the eyes of a wolf." A. Golubkina, *Pis'ma. Neskol'ko slov o rabote skul'ptora. Vospominaniia o sovremennikakh* (*Letters: A Few Words about the Job of a Sculptor. Reminiscences of Contemporaries*), (Moscow: Sovetskii khudozhnik, 1983), 197.

easily coexisted with his talent as a lyrical poet and did not impede his artistic abilities at all.

I will tell you another story. It's not a particularly savoury one, but, I think, we may still want to record it. In Moscow, I believe it was around 1921, there was a poet, Ivan Aksenov.[66] Later he became a notable Shakespeare scholar. I think he wrote some kind of encyclopaedia of characters in all Shakespeare's plays, but I am not sure.[67] He worked with Meyerhold for quite some time and was also a translator. I think he translated *The Magnificent Cuckold,* a farce by Crommelynck.[68] That piece became a watershed moment for the Russian theatre and created a huge scandal in 1922.

No one could work with Meyerhold for a long time, though; sooner or later he drove everyone away and even declared Aksenov his enemy. But this is not important for now; the important thing to note is that Aksenov was a very short man and totally bald, with a skull that looked like an acorn, very similar to Purishkevich's.[69]

Duvakin [*with enthusiasm*]**:** I remember him [Aksenov]!

Ardov: He [Aksenov] had a long beard then, down to his chest.

Duvakin [*surprised*]**:** Really? He had a beard?

Ardov: His beard was so long that it covered half of his chest.

Duvakin: But in the 1930s he was already clean shaven.

Ardov: Let me tell you why he lost his beard. One day Yesenin, who was quite drunk, came to the [Poets'] Café and saw a short man who was wearing a

---

66 Ivan Aksenov (1884–1935) was a Russian/Soviet poet, literary critic, and translator. As an avant-garde poet, he was insignificant, but as a literary critic he is remembered for his book about Pablo Picasso (1917). Aksenov was also the author of the first scholarly essay about Sergei Eisenstein in Russia. See I. Aksenov, *Pikasso i okrestnosti* (*Picasso and Around*), (Moscow: Tsentrifuga, 1917); and I. Aksenov, *Sergei Eisenstein: Portret khudozhnika* (*Eisenstein: A Portrait of an Artist*), (Moscow: Kinocenter, 1991).

67 Ardov may be referring to Aksenov's book *Shekspir: Ocherki* (*Shakespeare: Essays*), (Moscow: Goslitizdat, 1937).

68 *The Magnificent Cuckold* (1921; in Russian, *Velikolepnyi rogonosets*), a play by the Belgian playwright Fernand Crommelynck (1886–1970), was staged by Vsevolod Meyerhold in his theatre in 1922. The play had a tremendous success and was hotly debated afterwards. In general, it was well received by critics, who noted the excellent staging and brilliant work of the leading actors, Igor Ilyinsky (1901–1987) and Maria Babanova (1900–1983).

69 Vladimir Purishkevich (1870–1920) was a notable Russian political activist, a monarchist. He participated in the plot to murder Grigori Rasputin (1869–1916) and was the one who shot Rasputin when the latter tried to escape. To his last day, Purishkevich continued fighting against the Bolsheviks. He died of typhus in 1920.

commissary trench coat, had a long beard, and was totally bald. Yesenin assessed his looks as follows: "His beard is like a forest, but there is no place to shit." The same evening, Aksenov shaved off his beard.[70]

[*Duvakin chuckles.*]

I will tell you more. From 1934 to 1937, I lived on Furmanov Street in a house that belonged to the Writers' Union.[71] I was one of the members of the house management group, and I lived on the first floor, off the same hallway as where

---

70 It should be noted that, when he was drunk, Yesenin was often rude verbally and sometimes even physically. However, in Roizman's book there is a different description of the same event:

> Четвертого ноября 1920 года в Большом зале консерватории состоялся вечер – Суд над имажинистами. В качестве литературного прокурора был Валерий Брюсов, а в качестве истца – Аксенов. Оба они подвергли имажинистов ироническим нападкам, а подсудимые выступали с острыми ответами.
>
> Очень умно говорил Есенин.
>
> – А судьи кто? – воскликнул он, припомнив *Горе от ума*. Показал пальцем на Аксенова, продолжил: – Кто этот истец? Есть ли у него хорошие стихи?
>
> И громко добавил: "Ничего не сделал в поэзии этот тип, утонувший в рыжей бороде!"
>
> Мало того, что все сидящие за судейским столиком хохотали, но в следующие дни стали приходить посетители и просили показать им гражданского истца, утонувшего в рыжей бороде. Число любопытных увеличивалось с каждым днем, и Аксенов, узнав об этом, сбрил бороду! (M. Roizman, *Vse, chto ya pomnyu o Yesenine* [Moscow: Sovetskaya Rossiya, 1973], 103–4)

> (On 4 November 1920 an event was held in the Great Hall of the Conservatory – a symbolic trial of the Imaginists. The literary prosecutor was Bryusov, and the plaintiff was Aksenov. Both men engaged in ironic attacks, and the defendants responded sharply to all accusations.
>
> Yesenin spoke very cleverly. "Who are the judges?" he exclaimed, remembering *Woe from Wit*. He pointed to Aksenov and continued, "Who is this plaintiff? Does he have good poems?"
>
> Then he added loudly, "This type, the one drowning in his red beard, has not accomplished anything in poetry!"
>
> Not only did everyone sitting at the judges' table laugh, but in the following days visitors started to come asking to see the plaintiff who was drowning in a red beard. The number of the curious increased every day, and once Aksenov found out about it, he shaved off his beard!)

71 The Union of Soviet Writers, or the Writers' Union, was created by the Bolsheviks in 1934 as a vehicle of state control and censorship. Becoming a member of the union meant gaining permission to publish books and earn money by writing. The union also financially supported its members in "good" standing by giving them nice apartments, country cottages, excellent medical service, and money. To lose one's union membership usually spelled disaster; the unfortunate writer would never be able to publish in the USSR and would also lose any previous perks. In 1934 the union included 1,500 writers; in 1991 (when the union was dissolved) it had about 10,000 members.

Mandelstam,[72] Máté Zalka,[73] and others also used to reside. Sergei Klychkov lived in the apartment across from mine,[74] which made us somewhat closer; sometimes we would get together and chat like good neighbours.

Klychkov was one of Yesenin's friends. With eyes brimming with tears, he told me that his [Yesenin's] death in the Angleterre Hotel[75] was a tragic accident caused by … He then quoted Yesenin's famous words: "иногда надо пошуметь, а то тебя забывают" [Sometimes you need to make some noise, or they forget you].

That is, he was certain that Yesenin only wanted to pretend to commit suicide in order to draw attention to himself, "make some noise." He [Klychkov] lived then with his friend, Vol'f – I forget – a poet. Do you remember his first name, by any chance? I knew him too, a mediocre poet.[76]

Some people believe that Yesenin waited to hear steps in the corridor – that was supposed to be Vol'f returning home – before putting his head through the

---

72 Osip Mandelstam (1891–1938) was one of the most influential Russian poets of the twentieth century. He dared to express openly his dissatisfaction with Stalin by writing his famous "Stalin Epigram" in 1933. Although he read it to only a dozen of his closest friends, someone informed the authorities of the event, and Mandelstam was arrested in 1934. After three years of exile in Voronezh, where his only friend was his wife who had followed him into exile, Mandelstam returned to Moscow but was soon arrested again. This time his health suffered terribly, and Mandelstam died somewhere near Vladivostok. His grave's location is unknown.

73 Máté Zalka (b. Béla Frankl) (1896–1937) was Hungarian by nationality. During the Second World War, in 1916, he was imprisoned by the Russian army and, while in a Russian prison, became fascinated by the ideas of Communism. Following his release, Zalka decided to stay in Russia, where he fought in the Red Army, participated in the Russian Civil War, and then became a writer. In 1936 he decided to take part in the Spanish Civil War under the nickname "General Lukas," and was killed in a battle. As a military officer he was notorious for his cruelty.

74 Sergei Klychkov (1889–1937) was a Russian/Soviet poet, writer, and translator. His poetry was not particularly original but rather an imitation of that of his more talented friends, Yesenin and Mandelstam. In 1937 he was arrested, falsely accused of counter-revolutionary activity, and shot on the same day, 8 October 1937.

75 Angleterre Hotel became famous following Yesenin's death in one of its rooms on 28 December 1925. Many famous visitors stayed at this hotel at different times, including Anton Chekhov and Isadora Duncan.

76 Ardov refers to Vol'f Erlikh (1902–1937), a Russian/Soviet poet. Like many others, he was arrested in 1937 and shot a few months later. In his book *Taina gibeli Yesenina* (*The Secret behind Yesenin's Death*), Vladimir Kuznetsov offers the following note about Vol'f Erlikh: "Есть предположение, что Эрлих был секретным агентом ГПУ и, выполняя соответствующее задание, принял непосредственное участие в убийстве поэта. Однако 4 апреля 1956 года Военный Верховный суд СССР отменил все обвинения в адрес Вольфа за отсутствием состава преступления." (*Taina gibeli Yesenina: po sledam odnoi versii* [Moscow: Sovremennik, 1998], 42–51; There was the idea that Erlikh was a GPU secret agent and that, following orders, he took direct part in the murder of the poet. However, on 4 April 1956 the USSR Supreme Military Court dismissed all accusations against Vol'f because of lack of evidence.)

noose, knowing that Vol'f was about to enter the room and save him. But it was a different person going to a different room. That was, presumably, the reason why he [Yesenin] died.

I can't say that I am sold on this version, not in the least, but it is plausible enough, considering everything we know about Yesenin and his behaviour.

I also want to tell you one more thing about Yesenin. Recently, an interesting book came out by Ilya Shneider.[77] He describes there how Yesenin met Isadora Duncan,[78] and everything that happened after that.[79] He was a professional ballet manager (he was always involved with ballet – as an administrator or as the husband of one of the ballerinas). Sometime at the beginning of 1920s, he was ordered by Lunacharsky to organize Isadora Duncan's Moscow tour and studio.[80]

For that reason, he [Shneider] was invited to a literary evening in the house of the artist Yakulov.[81] Yesenin also came, and, as Shneider notes, they [Yesenin and Duncan] were immediately attracted to each other, like a needle to a magnet.

They left soon.[82] Of course, their relationship didn't last long, and it couldn't have: they were both capricious geniuses, and there was the age difference, and so on. Yesenin soon returned to Moscow.

---

77 Ilya Shneider (1891–1980) was a Soviet theatre scholar and literary critic. He was instrumental in founding the Isadora Duncan Ballet Theatre (1922–46) in Moscow. Shneider became a victim of the last wave of Stalin's repressions (1948–52): in 1949 he was arrested and sentenced to ten years of hard labour. He started working on his book about Yesenin while he was in the Gulag.

78 Isadora Duncan (1877–1927) was an innovative American and French dancer who rebelled against the rigid principles of classical ballet. Today she is famous for being Yesenin's wife (1922–4) and for her tragic death: during a visit to Nice, France, her long silk scarf became entangled in the wheels and axle of the automobile in which she was riding; she was pulled from the open car and broke her neck.

79 Ardov refers to Ilya Shneider's book *Vstrechi s Yeseninym. Vospominaniya* (*Encounters with Yesenin: Memoirs*), (Moscow: Sovetskaiia Rossiia, 1965).

80 Anatoly Lunacharsky (1875–1933) was the first Soviet minister of education. Lunacharsky had a brilliant education and was fluent in many European languages. He served as a liaison between the new Bolshevik government and the "old" academia who, rightfully, did not trust the Bolsheviks. Understanding how important culture was to the new Soviet country, Lunacharsky did whatever he could to save academics and the intelligentsia from political persecution.

81 Georgy Yakulov (1884–1928) was a Russian avant-garde artist and a close friend of many Futurists and Imaginists. A real dandy, witty, and smart, Yakulov was the heart of any gathering. His nickname was "George the Wonderful." His large apartment in the centre of Moscow was always open to his friends – Mayakovsky, Yesenin, Andrei Bely, Meyerhold, Blok, Marienhof, Bryusov, Khlebnikov, and even Lunacharsky who at that time was not yet a Bolshevik.

82 Ardov refers to the trip (1922–3) to Europe and the United States that Duncan and Yesenin took together. Their brief marriage was stormy, and the trip was clouded by constant quarrels. In 1923 Yesenin returned to Moscow while Isadora started a new page in her life by entering into a relationship with the famous Broadway playwright and notorious lesbian Mercedes de Acosta.

1.4. Georgi Yakulov, *The Spring Salon of Poets*, 1918.

One day a special event honouring Yesenin was organized in the Great Hall of the Polytechnic Museum. As a journalist, I was back stage when Yesenin arrived. As always, in an attempt to impress everyone, he came in late, wearing an evening suit like they do in the West for a visit to the opera or for a ball: a dress coat, white vest, white tie, black cloak with white lining, a top hat, and a cane with a golden handle, without which one couldn't go to the Grand Opéra for an evening performance[83] – but the cane had to be checked in. But when he saw the rest of us – the modest visitors of the usual Moscow performances, debates, and literary evenings – he seemed enormously uncomfortable. That, too, was typical of him.

[*There is a break in the recording.*]

In fact, Sergei Alexandrovich [Yesenin] understood perfectly well that his dandy outfit was completely inappropriate for the Moscow Polytechnic Museum. One would only show up dressed like that if he wanted to show

83 Grand Opéra, often called Opéra de Paris or Opéra Garnier, is one of the most famous opera and ballet theatres in the world. In 1964 its ceiling was painted by Marc Chagall.

everybody that he was a member of the European civilization, not just a young man from Ryazan and Moscow, that he now moved in the best circles of the Western capitals. But, at the same time, he felt a little embarrassed because he was a sensitive person and understood very well how he looked in comparison to the humble, ordinary Moscow audience.

It must be said that every time Yesenin did something that he called *пошумим* [let's make some noise], he always felt a bit guilty and wanted to show that he was not serious.[84] But people, regular folk, and those who did not like him all got angry with him; that was perhaps the main reason why he never enjoyed the kind of popularity he craved so much while alive.

There's no doubt that Yesenin was correct in assessing his talents so highly, but, as always, the real fame came after he died.

Duvakin: Victor Yefimovich, but is such a categorical statement entirely true? Yesenin's popularity was at its highest in 1924–5, that is, the last two years of his life. I personally remember (I was a schoolboy at the time) that everyone was crazy about him, and everyone was trying to catch him wherever he went.

I was present when he recited his poetry in Pereval.[85] There were fantastic rumours, often rather uncouth, that Yesenin, like Nadson,[86] suffered from tuberculosis, as befits a true lyrical poet.

Yesenin, together with Mayakovsky, always occupied the centre of attention, but after his death his fame was brutally and almost instantly suppressed. His name became connected with the so-called *yeseninshchina,*[87] and after 1928 his

---

84 This is how Lev Nikulin described Yesenin's outfit during one of his public appearances: "Далеко за полночь пришел Есенин. Он почему-то был во фраке: очевидно, для того, чтобы поразить нас, но эта одежда скорее напоминала маскарадный костюм. Мне помнится, что он всячески старался показать пренебрежение к этой парадной одежде. Озорно, по-мальчишески, он вытирал фалдами фрака пролитое на столе вино." (*Lyudi i stranstviya. Vospominaniya i vstrechi* [*People and Travels: Memoirs and Encounters*], [Moscow: Sovetskii pisatel, 1962], 86; Sometime after midnight Yesenin arrived. For some reason he was in a dress coat: obviously, the goal was to impress us, but his clothes rather resembled a fancy masquerade costume. I remember that he tried his best to show how little he actually cared for his formal attire, and, like a mischievous child, he kept wiping the wine spilled on the table with the tails of his coat.)

85 Pereval, or the Union of Revolutionary Writers, was one of numerous literary groups that were formed in the 1920s in Moscow and Saint Petersburg and dissolved later, when the Bolsheviks decided to tighten their grip on the cultural life.

86 Semyon Nadson (1862–1887) was a Russian Romantic poet. His poetry, similar in tone and themes to Mikhail Lermontov's, though not very original, was well regarded during his short lifetime. He died from tuberculosis at age twenty-five.

87 *Yeseninshchina* (Eseninism) was a derogatory term in the Soviet Union, meaning a self-destructive behaviour among the young people allegedly influenced by Yesenin's poetry. It is now hard to believe, but in the late 1930s one could be expelled from high school or university for reading or reciting Yesenin's poetry at public or private gatherings.

books were not reprinted any more – until maybe the 1950s. I recall that in 1948 a little book of poems came out. Yes, they didn't publish him for a long time.

Ardov: I think you are mistaken. Maybe you don't quite understand what it really means to be famous. First of all, fame can be partial, so to speak: a certain artist, poet, or writer may be famous in some circles, but in other circles their popularity might be met with a steady resistance, sometimes even wrath. But we are now talking about national fame. Such a fame came to Yesenin only after his death.

Duvakin: Better to say that it happened not right after his death but thirty years later.

Ardov [*emotionally*]: Not at all! To destroy one's fame through administrative actions – not publishing their books, withdrawing their paintings from public display, and so on – that's really *not* possible! The years when, as you rightfully observe, Yesenin's books were not available did nothing to suppress his popularity. His poems were copied by hand; people were learning them by heart. He continued to live among the people, and no one could really control the dissemination of his poetry or destroy it completely. I don't believe that administrative actions can diminish someone's fame. That's just wrong.

Yesenin flourished in the 1930s, '40s, and '50s as a favourite national poet. His books were not published – so what? The problem was easily remedied by manuscripts produced by what is now known as Samizdat [self-publishing].[88]

I personally witnessed many times (I used to travel all over the country during that time) that people talked about Yesenin as if he were still alive. He was a most beloved and most famous poet who, for some reason, was not published by certain idiots and bureaucrats. That's what was really happening.

Now, about Mayakovsky … The situation with him was quite different: I think with him just the opposite happened. Because he was so glorified.[89]

---

88 In the USSR, *Samizdat* (from Russian *sam*, "self," and *izdatelstvo*, "publishing") was not just a word; it was a complex network. The term refers to literature that was secretly written, copied, and circulated in the former Soviet Union and usually critical of the Soviet government. From its inception the Samizdat movement and its contributors were subjected to surveillance and harassment by the KGB, the secret police. Copying, disseminating, or reading banned works – such as Alexander Solzhenitsyn's novels, Boris Pasternak's *Doctor Zhivago*, or, in this case, Yesenin's poetry – came with the serious risk of being found out, arrested, and sentenced to ten to twenty years of hard labour.

89 Ardov is referring to the comment that Stalin made in response to a letter from Lilya Brik. Lilya Brik had complained that Mayakovsky, the most important poet of the October Revolution, was being absolutely forgotten. Stalin made the remark, which amounted to an order, that Mayakovsky deserved to be celebrated as the best revolutionary poet. From that moment on, Mayakovsky was virtually canonized by the Soviet literary establishment. However, this attitude did not allow for a proper appreciation of Mayakovsky's art as being truly innovative and original.

Duvakin: But when it happened, it was already 1935.

[*There is a pause in the recording. Ardov is silent, trying to recall something.*]

Ardov: Yes, his glorification began in 1935. I think, last time I told you about the remark that Brik[90] made about the Mayakovsky Square. No? Then, I will tell you now. I was a friend of the Briks.[91] In 1935 they lived in Leningrad[92] because Lilya was married to General Primakov.[93] So, when I came to Leningrad, I called them, and they told me, "Come right away, Ardik (this is what they called me) – we have good news!"

I went, and Osip Maximovich [Brik] told me that they had written to Stalin, and Stalin had issued his famous resolution: "Mayakovsky was and remains the best and the most talented poet of our Soviet era."[94]

Duvakin: "Any indifference to his memory and his works is a crime."

---

90 Osip Brik (1888–1945) was the first husband of Lilya Brik. Born to a rich Jewish family, he never experienced any financial hardship, even after the revolution. He got to know Mayakovsky in 1915, who soon became the lover of his wife Lilya, and the three of them decided to move in together and live like a family. Osip joined the Bolshevik party and even worked for Cheka. Some historians believe that Osip never stopped working for Cheka and saved his life by doing so. He died from heart failure, on the staircase in front of his apartment, in 1945.

91 Lilya Brik (b. Kagan) (1891–1978), known as the muse of the Russian avant-garde, hosted one of the most famous literary salons of the twentieth century. Mayakovsky's long poem "Oblako v shtanakh" ("A Cloud in Trousers") was dedicated to her. Until her very last days Lilya Brik maintained close contacts with some of the most interesting people of the twentieth century: Alexander Solzhenitsyn, Mstislav Rostropovich, Pablo Neruda, Phillipe and Polina Rothschild, and Yves Saint Laurent. At the age of eighty-six, after breaking her hip and realizing that she could not continue the active lifestyle to which she had grown accustomed, Lilya committed suicide in Moscow.

92 Leningrad had a series of names. Petrograd was the name given to Saint Petersburg in 1914, rather than using a German-derived term. In 1924, it was called Leningrad to commemorate Vladimir Lenin, the leader of the Bolsheviks. The name Saint Petersburg was returned to the city in 1991. So, in three hundred years since 1703 when it was founded, the city has been named four times: Saint Petersburg (1703), Petrograd (1914), Leningrad (1924), and again Saint Petersburg (1991).

93 Vitaly Primakov (1897–1937) was a legendary and very talented Soviet military commander: he did not lose a single one of the sixty battles he led. A good historian, Primakov was the author of a few interesting books about Afghanistan, China, and Japan. In 1936 he was arrested, brutally tortured, and sentenced to death by the NKVD.

94 In response to Lilya's letter, Stalin reacted immediately by writing to Yezhov (the future attorney-general of the country and the force behind the first wave of repressions): "Товарищ Ежов! Очень прошу Вас обратить внимание на письмо Брик. Маяковский был и остается лучшим, талантливейшим поэтом нашей советской эпохи. Безразличие к его памяти и его произведениям - преступление." (Comrade Yezhov! I beg you to pay attention to the letter by Brik. Mayakovsky was and remains the best and the most talented poet of our Soviet era. Any indifference to his memory and his works is a crime.)

Ardov: Then I said, "Please give me some kind of a document testifying that I loved him [Mayakovsky] before this resolution." [*He chuckles.*] After that I asked Brik, "And what did you ask for when they suggested you contact the TsK (ЦК) [Central Committee] about that?"[95] Osip responded, "Well, we said that it would be nice to publish Mayakovsky's works again, write some new critical reviews, print his biography, open a museum, and maybe name a public square after him in Moscow." They responded, "Pick the square!" And Osip, in his own peculiar lilt (I'll try to imitate him now), said, "Give us the Triumfalnaya Square."[96]

I asked Brik, "Why the Triumfalnaya?" He said, "All other good squares are already taken." [*Ardov says this, imitating the voice and intonations of Osip Brik, so it sounds a little funny.*]

At the time I was shocked by his pragmatic attitude to such an unusual issue as renaming a square. But the interesting thing is that people accepted the name change with no problem.

Duvakin: Yes, they accepted it right away.

Ardov: It does not always happen. Take, for example, Zhivoderka Street.[97] When they decided to rename it Vladimirodolgorukovskaya – to honour the Governor-General of Moscow – people refused to use the new name and continued to call it Zhivoderka. Then the street was renamed.

Duvakin: Krasin Street?[98]

Ardov: No, it was Adler Street first, in honour of that Austrian left-wing Social Democrat Friedrich Adler.[99] But no one called the street by that name. And when they named it Krasin Street, the name stuck.

---

95 TsK (ЦК), or the Central Committee of the Communist Party of the Soviet Union, was the executive and highest party organ.

96 Triumfalnaya Square had existed since 1722, when the first triumph arch was built for Peter the Great to celebrate his victory over Sweden. In 1935 it was renamed Mayakovsky Square.

97 This street, located in the centre of Moscow, had many names – Zhivoderka, Vladimirodolgorukovskaya, Adler, and Krasin – but the Moscovites never accepted any of the later names and have continued to call it Zhivoderka.

98 Leonid Krasin (1870–1926) was an engineer by training who worked for the Bolshevik government as a diplomat. In 1924 he became the first Soviet ambassador to France. He left a year later for London, where he died. It was Krasin who proposed to entomb Lenin's corpse in a mausoleum, which he envisioned as a pilgrimage destination similar to that of Jerusalem or Mecca. He also attempted unsuccessfully to cryogenically preserve Lenin's body.

99 Friedrich Adler (1879–1960) was an Austrian ultra-left revolutionary, who is best known as the assassin of Karl von Stürgkh, the minister-president of the Austro-Hungarian Empire (1911–16). For this crime Adler was sentenced to death, but the revolution in Germany freed him. Adler stopped participating in revolutionary activities and in 1940 escaped from the Nazis to the United States. After the Second World War he returned to Switzerland, where he passed away peacefully at the age of eighty.

The same thing happened here: Why did they accept Mayakovsky Square? Because *Triumfalnaya* (*Triumph*) is a word that uneducated Russians couldn't even pronounce correctly; they called the square "Trukhmalnaya." [*He laughs.*]

What I am trying to say here is that after his death Yesenin almost instantly became a legendary poet of great fame, and the "administrative measures" were not able to do anything about it. On the other hand, the excessive official endorsement of Mayakovsky damaged his reputation. That is why many people, even today, view him as a state-owned poet, and that's extremely regrettable.

I'll finish our conversation with one more interesting episode. In 1922–4 in Moscow there was another café, Ne Rydai! [Не рыдай!, Do not cry!]

It was a typical NEP café,[100] which doubled as a small theatre.[101]

---

100 The NEP (New Economic Policy) was introduced by Vladimir Lenin in 1921 when he realized that the country was falling apart, and the economy was about to collapse. It allowed for freedom of trade – essentially, capitalism. Lenin claimed that the NEP was only a temporary measure that was needed to save the republic and that it would be abolished as soon as the Communist revolution had spread around the world. The NEP existed until 1931 and saved the country, but, in spite of the visible economic improvements, it was abolished by Stalin, and any form of free trade was prohibited in the Soviet Union for the next sixty years.

101 Café Ne Rydai! (Не рыдай!) (1922–4) was one of the many cafés opened in Moscow during the NEP period. The special atmosphere in this cabaret, as it was often called, is described in the memoirs of Boris Romashov, *Vmeste s vami* (*Together with You*), (Moscow: Sovetskii pisatel, 1964), 243–4:

Когда вы входили туда, вас окутывали клубы дыма, и вы не сразу могли найти место. В этом кабаре висел плакат с таким гимном:

Если вы в тоске отчаянной,
Сердцу волю дай!
Приходи ты в нашу чайную
Пить почаще чай.
Раз-два-три-четыре –
Сердцу волю дай!
Раз-два-три-четыре –
плюнь и не рыдай!

(When you entered there, you were shrouded in a cloud of smoke, and you could not immediately find a place to sit. In this cabaret hung a poster with the following mantra:

If you're feeling sad and gloomy,
Let your heart rejoice!
Come to our eatery,
Treat yourself to tea.
One, two, three, four, –
Let your heart rejoice!
One, two, three, four, –
Spit and do not cry!)

It's enough to say that Igor Ilyinsky,[102] Rina Zelenaya,[103] and also Mikhail Zharov[104] used to work there. Even your humble servant laboured there for some time as an entertainer. Mayakovsky came to this café (I used to meet him there), as did Yakulov, the actor, and other actors from the MKhAT.[105]

When Vladimir Nikolayevich Davydov,[106] the great Russian actor, happened to be in Moscow, he went there every evening and even sang romances, accompanying himself on a guitar. He was a great performer and an amazing actor.

In his memoirs Davydov wrote about a time when he sang while balancing on a huge ball – he could do that![107] I knew him but not very well. He was a very talented actor, both tragic and comic. But that's not very important.

By 1923, I think the cabaret Ne Rydai! was on Mamonov Lane[108] (this place in now occupied by the Moscow Young Spectator Theatre).[109] We frequented the café, a lot of us, artists, students, musicians, and we all sat at one long table. Normal tables were small, but for us, poor young people, the management specifically set up one big table and served us food at discount prices. In return,

---

102 Igor Ilyinsky (1901–1987) was a celebrated Soviet cinema and stage actor, who dedicated more than sixty years of his life to the theatre. In his youth he was a lead actor of Vsevolod Meyerhold's theatre. One of the most unusual films that Ilyinsky produced was *Eti raznye, raznye, raznye litsa* (*These Different, Different, Different Faces*, 1971), in which he alone played over twenty roles. Ilyinsky died on 13 January 1987 in front of the television, while watching *Karnaval'naya noch'* (The carnival night, 1956), in which he played the lead.

103 Rina Zelyonaya (1901–1991) was a Soviet stage and film actress. During her long life she appeared in fifty-three feature films and provided voice-over for thirty-two animated films. Her voice and her face were recognized all over the Soviet Union, but she only received an official major award just a few days before she died from cancer, at age ninety.

104 Mikhail Zharov (1899–1981) was a Soviet film and theatre actor. Although he never played the lead in any of his numerous films, he was known and loved by millions of people and enjoyed a long, productive, and fairly peaceful life.

105 MKhAT [MXAT in Russian] is the Moscow Art Theatre, founded in 1898 by Konstantin Stanislavsky and Vladimir Nemirovich-Danchenko. This most famous Russian theatre staged plays by Anton Chekhov, Shakespeare, Ibsen, Gorky, and Hauptmann to great acclaim. MKhAT inaugurated Stanislavsky's acting method, which aimed to produce naturalistic plays that differed greatly from the then predominantly melodramatic style of dramatic expression. The theatre proved highly influential in the acting world of Russia and beyond.

106 Vladimir Davydov (b. Ivan Gorelov) (1849–1925) was a legendary Russian performer who worked as a leading actor for the Alexandrinsky Theatre, the oldest Russian theatre, founded by Catherine the Great in 1756.

107 See V. Davydov, *Rasskaz o proshlom* (*A Story about the Past*), (Moscow: Iskusstvo, 1962), 180–1.

108 Mamonov Lane is in the centre of Moscow and was named after one of its famous residents, Count Mamonov, whose ancestors fought with Alexander Nevsky (1242), the great Russian military commander and ruler of Novgorod city.

109 Moscow Young Spectator Theatre (in Russian, МТЮЗ) was founded in 1920 by the order of Anatoly Lunacharsky and became the first Soviet theatre to stage exclusively plays for younger audiences. The very first play presented there was *Mowgli* by Rudyard Kipling (1865–1936).

we entertained the visitors: we would sing, tell stories. People came just to see us as if we were on the program.

One day we were there, having fun as usual, and Yesenin came in. He was not alone; he was with Augusta Miklashevskaya.[110] She is still alive, and her memoirs are very interesting.[111] He wrote a poem for her.

Duvakin: Ah! Remember? "They loved you too much, they made you so dirty … Do you want to be punched in the face?"[112]

Ardov: Yes, this poem. Anyway, they were very open about their affair. She was free; her husband, Lev Lashchilin, had left her a long time before.[113] Then she became Sergei Yesenin's muse, something she discusses very discreetly and tactfully in her memoirs.

Anyway, we were sitting around the table. It was a wonderful, quiet, and joyful evening, and I drew a sketch of Sergei Alexandrovich [Yesenin] (I have to tell you that I am an amateur artist; as a matter of fact, I started as a cartoonist and only later turned to writing) and, you know, it turned out to be a very good drawing.

I was afraid I might lose it, so I gave it to Lev Kolpakchi.[114] He died recently, at the age of eighty. And he lost my drawing! Sergei Alexandrovich had signed it for me. That's one of my biggest regrets.

---

110 Augusta Miklashevskaya (1891–1977) was Yesenin's lover, to whom the poet dedicated seven beautiful poems. Augusta lived a very long life. In 1960s she tried to publish her memoirs about Yesenin, but the manuscript was mercilessly censored and cut. By then, Yesenin had already become an iconic figure, almost like Mayakovsky, and the Communists did not want to know the truth about his life, love life, and death.

111 See Augusta Miklashevskaya, *Vospominaniya o Yesenine* (*Memoirs about Yesenin*), (Moscow: Moskovskii rabochii, 1965). About Miklashevskaya see also Vladimir Likhonosov, *Zapisi pered snom* (*Notes before Sleep*), (Moscow: Sovremennyi pisatel, 1993).

112 Duvakin is quoting from one of Yesenin's poems, written in Berlin in the summer of 1923 when the poet felt seriously depressed and drank a lot. He had not met Augusta Miklashevskaya yet.

> Излюбили тебя, измызгали,
> Невтерпеж!
> Что ж ты смотришь так синими брызгами,
> Иль в морду хошь? ("Сыпь, гармоника. Скука ... Скука ...," 1923)
>
> (They loved you too much, they made you so dirty,
> Couldn't wait!
> Why do you flash your big blue eyes at me,
> Do you want to be punched in the face?)

113 Ardov is mistaken. Lev Lashchilin (1888–1955) had an affair with Augusta Miklashevskaya, but he was married to another woman and never planned to divorce her, even though Augusta became pregnant by him.

114 Lev Kolpakchi (1891–1972) was a Soviet literary critic who wrote about theatre. He worked for a while with Vsevolod Meyerhold and Vera Komissarzhevskaya.

Duvakin: I was waiting to meet with him [Kolpakchi], wanted to record him as well, but I missed him.

Ardov: That's too bad. He knew a lot. Before the revolution he worked for many newspapers and magazines, so he saw a lot and heard a lot. [*Sadly.*] Oh, well, what can we do?

Anyway, this is just about everything that I can tell you about Yesenin.

Duvakin: Maybe you can add something about Mayakovsky? Last time you told me many interesting things about him.

Ardov [*sounding very tired*]: I am sorry, but today I probably won't be able to tell you more about Mayakovsky. I think that's all, I think I told you everything.

[THE RECORDING ENDS.]

DIALOGUE 2
With Viktor Ardov on 19 August 1974*

In this last conversation with Viktor Ardov the main subject is the theatre scene in Moscow during the 1920s–30s. Ardov focuses on Vsevolod Meyerhold, in whose theatre he had worked as an administrator for about five months in 1922. Ardov's observations about the character, the creative method, and the irrepressible energy of the director are subtle and witty. He addresses various rumours about Meyerhold's theatre and presents the famous Russian director, actor, and producer in a new, often surprising light.

Duvakin: Victor Yefimovich, you said that you also knew Vsevolod Meyerhold.[1]

Ardov: Yes.

Duvakin: Maybe we should talk about him today.

Ardov: With pleasure. You know, for the youth of my time Meyerhold was an idol. We literally adored him. The situation with him was very similar to that with Mayakovsky and Yesenin: when he was alive, people were divided into two camps – those who loved him and those who hated him.

I was among those who adored him, admired his various productions, all the original artistic discoveries and new techniques that marked each performance.

---

* Length of interview – 62 minutes

1 Vsevolod Meyerhold (1874–1940) was a renowned theatre director and producer. After starting as an actor on the stage of the Moscow Art Theatre, he soon founded his own theatre, the Meyerhold Theatre. His originality and experimentation exerted great influence on world theatre practices. After the revolution, while on tour in France, he had a chance to defect, but he decided to return to Russia. After the staging of the famous *Dama s kameliiami* (*La dame aux camélias*), which met with Stalin's severe disapproval, his theatre was closed, and soon thereafter Meyerhold was arrested, tortured, and sentenced to death.

2.1. Vsevolod Meyerhold and Zinaida Raikh, Moscow, 1920s. Photographer unknown.

Of course, we should take into account the larger historical context here: after the Soviet revolution, as many historians have already noted, there was a desire for everything to be new. And, of course, the old forms of theatre did not appeal to the tastes of the so-called enlightened youth and Red professors,[2] the students of the Sverdlov Communist University,[3] and others. Therefore, we liked it very much that Meyerhold broke away from all the old theatrical traditions,

2 The Institute of Red Professors was established by order of the Bolshevik government in 1921. This so-called university was supposed to prepare new faculty in three major disciplines – economics, history, and philosophy – and then the faculty members would disseminate their newly acquired knowledge to all institutions of higher education across the country. In 1924, 194 Red professors celebrated their graduation and immediately set out to spread the Bolshevik ideology throughout the country. The consequences of this political move were serious: the study of philosophy was distorted, history was rewritten, and the science of economics was replaced by a set of non-existent politically motivated postulates.

3 Sverdlov Communist University was created in Moscow right after the revolution (1918) to prepare future Bolshevik leaders. The university existed until 1937 when it was closed by order of the Communist Party.

although he himself, before the 1917 revolution, served as director of all imperial theatres in Saint Petersburg![4]

Duvakin [*very surprised*]: Really? Of all theatres or just Alexandrinsky?[5]

Ardov: No, he served as director of the Mariinsky[6] and Mikhailovsky[7] theatres as well. He was in charge of all three of them. He [Meyerhold] staged *Don Juan* at the Alexandrinsky Theatre,[8] where Konstantin Alexandrovich Varlamov,[9] a great comedian, used to perform. His memory was very bad, especially when he acted in dramas or tragedies. He did not memorize the text and improvised a lot instead. Knowing that, Meyerhold prepared a surprise for him: when Varlamov appeared on stage, wherever he moved, every time it was his turn to speak, there was a prompter! In total, there were seven prompters serving this extraordinary comedian! But he played marvellously, and he and Meyerhold understood and accepted each other completely.[10]

---

4 Imperial theatres were supported and financed by the Russian government. They were established throughout the Russian empire in 1756 by the order of Catherine the Great and existed until the October Revolution of 1917. The three major imperial theatres of Saint Petersburg were Mariinsky Theatre, Alexandrinsky Theatre, and Mikhailovsky Theatre.

5 Alexandrinsky Theatre (1756) was the first permanent dramatic theatre in Russia, established by Catherine the Great and headed by the father of Russian theatre, the actor Fyodor Volkov. In 1832 the famous Italian architect Carlo Rossi (1775–1849) built one of the most beautiful buildings in Saint Petersburg, which was given to Alexandrinsky Theatre. The theatre could accommodate more than 1,700 spectators.

6 Mariinsky Theatre (known as the Kirov Theatre in the Soviet era) is the second most important opera and ballet theatre in Russia. It was founded in 1783 by the order of Catherine the Great. In 1860 it received its permanent building, and the season opened with the opera *Zhizn' za Tsaria* (*A Life for the Tsar*) by Mikhail Glinka. Among its most notable twentieth-century ballet dancers were Rudolf Nureyev and Mikhail Baryshnikov.

7 Mikhailovsky Theatre is one of the most significant opera and ballet theatres in Russia. It was founded in 1833 by the order of Emperor Nicholas I, and its stage welcomed many famous performers from around the world, including Fyodor Chaliapin and Sarah Bernhardt. Johann Strauss conducted its orchestra, and Leo Tolstoy and Piotr Tchaikovsky were among its frequent visitors.

8 *Don Juan*, a play by Jean-Baptiste Molière (1622–1673), was written and staged in 1665 in Paris. It was considered to be so scandalous that after a few performances Molière decided to take it down, fearing prosecution from the Inquisition. In Russia the play was first staged in 1816 to great acclaim and has been part of the repertoire of many theatres ever since.

9 Konstantin Varlamov (1848–1915) was an eminent comedian of the Alexandrinsky Theatre. His popularity was so high that at one time the Saint Petersburg tobacco factory sold a brand of cigarettes named after him, Dyadya Kostya (Uncle Kostya). The theatre was invariably full when Varlamov was playing. Even when he became sick and thus incapable of moving freely on the stage, Varlamov continued to play, sitting. He had performed more than a thousand roles by the end of his career.

10 According to Boris Alpers, a reputable Soviet historian of the theatre, Varlamov's original techniques were very close to Meyerhold's. See Boris Alpers, *Teatralnye ocherki* (*Theatre Essays*), 2 vols. (Moscow: Iskusstvo, 1977), 1:140.

However, his close friend and colleague Vladimir Nikolayevich Davydov,[11] himself an important actor and a leader of the Russian theatre during the 1920s, told me something different.

During the period of 1922–3 I was a frequent visitor at the Café Ne Rydai![12] (I already told you about it when we talked about Yesenin.) Anyway, Vladimir Nikolayevich was good friends with the owner of that café, the operetta comedian Koshevsky,[13] so he used to go there every evening. He liked to pamper himself and gave in to every whim he had. He liked to drink, Davydov. There was a certain quirkiness about him: he liked to sing couplets.

Duvakin [*a little impatiently*]: But what did he say about Meyerhold?

Ardov: I will tell you now. I already mentioned that at that time I held an administrative position at his theatre. One day Davydov told me (I will try to imitate his tone now), "I do not like your Merinhold!"[14] Yes, that's exactly what he called him – Merinhold!– and added, "He is a crazy kangaroo who ran away from a circus."

(It is true that, in profile, Meyerhold – with that nose of his, the stoop, and his long dangling arms – looked very much like a kangaroo.)

Davydov continued: "You know that he was appointed director of our theatre! One day I learned that he was going to stage *Krechinsky's Wedding*,[15] and I was to play Rasplyuev.[16]

"I did not go to the first rehearsal. When I entered the theatre hall later, I saw that he [Meyerhold] had gathered all the actors on-stage and was busy telling them exactly what to do. So I turned around and prepared to go home. He saw me and called out to me: 'Vladimir Nikolayevich! Where are you going? We have rehearsal!' And I replied: 'You are the one who has rehearsal, not me. I am not going to do what you want me to. And, by the way, I have played the role of Rasplyuev many times over the years.'[17] Meyerhold responded: 'I will not touch your scenes.' 'Oh,' I said, "that's fine then.'"

11 About Davydov, see note 106 to dialogue 1.

12 About Café Ne Rydai, see note 101 to dialogue 1.

13 Alexander Koshevsky (1873–1931) was often called the Davydov of the operetta. In addition to being a talented comedian, he worked briefly as a stage director and wrote several successful romance novels.

14 In Russian, *merin* means "a gelding" or a castrated horse, which turns *Merinhold* into an insult.

15 *Krechinsky's Wedding* (1852–4) is a play by Alexander Sukhovo-Kobylin (1817–1903). It was a very popular play in Russia, as well liked by theatre-goers around the country as such famous comedies as *Revizor* (*The Government Inspector*) by Nikolay Gogol, and *Gore ot uma* (*Woe from Wit*) by Alexander Griboedov.

16 Rasplyuev is one of the protagonists in the comedy *Krechinsky's Wedding*. He is Krechinsky's neighbour and a real scoundrel.

17 By the time (1917) Meyerhold was staging *Krechinsky's Wedding* at the Alexandrinsky Theatre, Davydov had already played Rasplyuev for many years. (He first performed the role in 1875.) He always believed that it was one of his best roles.

Duvakin: Sorry, did he say, "I will not touch your scenes?"

Ardov: Yes, "your scenes." Meyerhold meant that he'd let all the scenes with Rasplyuev stay as they were and let Davydov play them as he wanted. By the way, Davydov played Rasplyuev while Sukhovo-Kobylin was still alive,[18] and Alexander Vasilyevich [Sukhovo-Kobylin] was not happy at all with his performance. He said: "Your Rasplyuev is a tramp, not a landowner. They would not let such a man into in a decent house. But since the public likes it, then please, do as you like."[19]

Anyway, that's not very important. As I said, there were a lot of people who did not like him [Meyerhold] and his theatre. But we, of course, loved him.

Meyerhold after the Revolution

Ardov [*continues*]: Meyerhold's life after the revolution turned out to be very interesting. Sometime in 1918, or in the beginning of 1919, he staged the *Mystery-Bouffe* by Mayakovsky.[20] [*Here Duvakin tries to interrupt Ardov and*

18 Alexander Sukhovo-Kobylin (1817–1903) was a Russian philosopher, translator, and playwright. His most famous play, *Krechinsky's Wedding*, was written while he was in jail. In his travels abroad, Sukhovo-Kobylin became acquainted with a certain Louise Simone Dimanche, of whose murder he was charged and then acquitted. Unfortunately, almost all the philosophical manuscripts of Sukhovo-Kobylin perished during a fire on his estate, but the house was reconstructed and is now a museum. Near the end of his life he moved to France, where he lived with his only daughter, Louise.

19 It is possible that Ardov here confused Davydov with Prov Sadovsky (1818–1872), a legendary Russian actor who played almost all the major roles in significant Russian plays of the nineteenth century. It was Sadovsky who interpreted Rasplyuev as a "tramp," which Sukhovo-Kobylin did not like at first, but later he changed his mind. A contemporary of Davydov described him in the role of Rasplyuev thus:

> Расплюев-Давыдов появляется на сцена в поломанном цилиндре, в неправильно застегнутом сюртуке, с избитым, опухшим лицом, с трясущимися руками. В каком-то оцепенении он двигался прямо по направлению к рампе, и казалось, что он не остановится и пройдет через весь зал. (Vera Michurina-Samoilova, *Shest'desyat let v iskusstve* [*Sixty Years in the Art*], [Moscow: Iskusstvo, 1948], 52)
>
> (Rasplyuev-Davydov appears on stage in a squashed top hat, in a misbuttoned coat, with a battered, swollen face, and shaking hands. In a kind of stupor, he moved straight towards the ramp, and it seemed that he would not stop and would march on through the theatre hall.)

20 *Misteria-Buff* (*Mystery-Bouffe*, 1918) was the first of Mayakovsky's plays, written to commemorate the first anniversary of the October Revolution. It is notable for its futuristic content and innovative form. Vsevolod Meyerhold directed the play, Kazimir Malevich created the stage design, and Mayakovsky performed a small role.

reminds him that he has already discussed Mayakovsky.] Please don't interrupt me. I have my reasons to talk about it again. It's important.

So, he staged the *Mystery-Bouffe* in its first version in Saint Petersburg and afterwards, because of the horrible famine, moved to the south. He ended up in Novorossiysk.[21] Novorossiysk then was under the Whites. Meyerhold was arrested right away because of his collaboration with the Bolsheviks. He had joined the Bolshevik party.

Duvakin: That happened, if I am not mistaken, only in 1920?

Ardov: Maybe. In any case, he was in jail and most likely would have been sentenced to death. But the most interesting detail is that at that time the prison commandant was Ensign Lavrentiy Beria.[22]

Duvakin [*whistling from surprise*]: You don't say!

Ardov: Yes. An actor who was in Novorossiysk at that time, Shatov,[23] told me that, and I think we should note it here.

Duvakin [*thoughtfully*]: Yes, very interesting.

Ardov: Anyway, then he [Meyerhold] returned to Moscow, and they [the Bolsheviks] gave him the former Zon Theatre,[24] which used to belong to the French entrepreneur Aumont.[25] This Aumont turned the theatre into a proper cabaret, with its famous mirror foyer and everything. After the revolution he [Aumont] escaped to Paris, where he made a fortune off Russian money, and the theatre stayed empty.

---

21 Novorossiysk, founded in 1838, is the largest Russian port on the Black Sea.

22 Lavrentiy Beria (1899–1953) served as chief of the People's Commissariat for Internal Affairs (NKVD, later KGB) from 1938 to 1946. After Stalin's death (6 March 1953), Beria conspired to become the next leader of the USSR and the Communist Party, but he was arrested and then put on trial by Nikita Khrushchev. The trial lasted three months and revealed to the public his numerous atrocities and arrests and executions of many innocent people, party leaders, academicians, artists, and intellectuals. Beria was sentenced to death and executed on 23 December 1953. His demise marked the end of the era of repressions. Beria's presence in Novorossiysk when Meyerhold was jailed there is not confirmed; in 1919 he was in Baku.

23 Aleksandr Shatov (1899–1961) was a film actor, known for his roles in *Velikii Glinka* (*The Great Glinka*, 1946), *Zolotoy eshelon* (*The Golden Echelon*, 1959), and *Bogatyr' idyot v Marto* (*Bogatyr' Goes to Marto*, 1954).

24 The theatre was named after its owner, Ignaty Zon, the Russian entrepreneur, who owned several theatres in Moscow. After the revolution he emigrated to France, and the theatre was nationalized by the Bolsheviks.

25 Charles Aumont was a French entrepreneur who founded the first Russian cabaret, *Grand théâtre concert parisien*. Scared by the first Russian revolution of 1905, Aumont rushed to emigrate, leaving behind his troupe and thousands of dollars of debt.

First, the Bolsheviks gave it to Fyodor Komissarzhevsky,[26] brother of Vera Komissarzhevskaya.[27] He [Komissarzhevsky] managed to put on a few plays. It was during that period that Igor Ilyinsky made his debut.[28] But then Komissarzhevsky fled abroad, and the theatre and almost all of its troupe were given over to Meyerhold. And he decided to stage the *Mystery-Bouffe* for a second time.

Duvakin: Are you saying that Meyerhold inherited the troupe of Komissarzhevsky?

Ardov: Yes. He added some actors, changed a few things, but in general it was still the troupe of Fyodor Komissarzhevsky. There was, for example, Alexander Yakovlevich Zakushnyak.[29] He played Figaro under Komissarzhevsky.[30] And Igor Ilyinsky played the gardener – a small role, but he played it marvellously. He is a splendid actor. He is still alive, and his talent, despite his seventy years of age, is in full bloom. So, Meyerhold was even some kind of a banner for us.

Duvakin: I am sorry, were you working for him [Meyerhold] then?

Ardov: No. I started to work for him in 1922 as an administrator, worked for him for about five months, and then left because I was bored. At that time, I had already begun my work as a journalist and was also attending college. I graduated from the Department of Economics of the Plekhanov

26 Fyodor Komissarzhevsky (1882–1954) was one of the most influential theatre directors of the twentieth century, along with Konstantin Stanislavsky (1863–1938) and Vladimir Nemirovich-Danchenko (1858–1943). After the 1917 revolution he emigrated to London, where he staged all the plays of Anton Chekhov (1860–1904) to great acclaim. He was also known for his new and ground-breaking interpretations of Shakespeare. In 1939 he emigrated to the United States, where he successfully continued his career in theatre.

27 Vera Komissarzhevskaya (1864–1910) was a Russian superstar at the turn of the twentieth century. She performed on stage all the coveted female roles, including Ophelia in *Hamlet*, and Margarita in *Faust*. However, her most famous role will always remain that of Nina Zarechnaya in Chekhov's *Seagull*. Komissarzhevskaya worked with Konstantin Stanislavsky and then with Meyerhold. Eventually, in 1904, she founded her own theatre, the Komissarzhevskaya Theatre, which remains one of the best-known theatres in Saint Petersburg today. It was at her theatre that Meyerhold staged Aleksandr Blok's notorious play *The Puppet Show* in 1906. She died from smallpox, while travelling on tour.

28 About Igor Ilyinsky, see note 102 to dialogue 1.

29 Alexander Zakushnyak (1879–1930) had a long history with Meyerhold, having acted in his Fellowship Society for New Drama and at the Vera Komissarzhevskaya Theatre before the revolution. He became especially known for his readings of short stories by Anton Chekhov, Guy de Maupassant, Mark Twain, and Sholom Aleichem.

30 *The Mad Day, or the Marriage of Figaro* (*La Folle Journée, ou Le Mariage de Figaro*, 1778) is a comedy by Pierre-Augustin Caron de Beaumarchais (1732–1799). The famous opera buffa by Wolfgang Amadeus Mozart, *The Marriage of Figaro* (*Le nozze di Figaro*, 1786), is based on it.

Institute.[31] (It was then called Karl Marx Institute.) But it does not matter now. The important thing is that I did not work for him for long, but due to my later duties I was able to meet Meyerhold quite often.

At that time, he did not have his theatre. Why? Well, because he was not, in general, a man of this world, so to speak. One day he decided to go after Lunacharsky's position and started scheming his way towards a People's Commissar appointment.[32] It was, of course, a senseless undertaking that ended up with Lunacharsky, in revenge, taking his theatre away from him.

During the time I worked with Meyerhold, he was unable to get his theatre back. So, in the building on Novinsky Boulevard[33] (now Tchaikovsky Street), a building that does not exist any more, there were two semi-detached houses that belonged to the lawyer Plevako.[34] This *zlatoust* [Chrysostom][35] had bought a whole block of buildings in Moscow! Meyerhold established the Higher Theatre Workshops in there. Then he added one word to it, *gosudarstvennie* [State] – and got an ugly abbreviation: GVYRM [in Russian, ГВЫРМ, Государственные Высшие режиссерские мастерские], or the State Higher Theatre Workshops.[36]

Precisely at that time I started to work in his [Meyerhold's] theatre. A little later he was given his own theatre, where he staged the famous *Magnificent Cuckold*.[37] I attended the rehearsals since I was already working there.

Duvakin: Oh, how interesting! You say that Meyerhold first had his theatre, then he lost it, and then he got it back?

Ardov: Exactly right.

---

31 Plekhanov University of Economics is the oldest and largest university of economics in Russia. It was founded as a small college by the Moscow Commerce Society in 1897. In 1906 it obtained the status of an institute of higher education and was named the Moscow Institute of Commerce. The Bolsheviks nationalized the university, renamed it Karl Marx Institute, and replaced the old rigorous curriculum with a new one, created and approved by the Communists.

32 About Anatoly Lunacharsky, see note 80 to dialogue 1.

33 About Novinsky Boulevard, see note 50 to dialogue 1.

34 Fyodor Plevako (1842–1909) was a famous Russian lawyer. He defended the accused parties in about two hundred judicial court cases and won all of them. In his court speeches Plevako avoided excesses, sought to raise reasonable doubt, and offered rigorous analyses of the presented evidence. He soon became known as one of the best lawyers in Moscow, often not only helping the poor for free but sometimes even paying for their unforeseen expenses.

35 John Chrysostom (349–407), the Golden-Mouthed (Zlatoust), was an archbishop of Constantinople and was considered the best orator of the Eastern Orthodox faith. By calling Plevako a *zlatoust*, Ardov implies that his oratorical talent was so great that he could win anyone over to his own position.

36 The Bolshevik government used many abbreviations. Some of them survived three generations of Soviet citizens and were known by anyone born during the Soviet era: ГПУ (GPU), ЧК (Cheka), Моссельпром (Mossel'prom), ВХУТЕМАС (VKhUTEMAS), РОСТА (ROSTA), ЦК (TsK), КПСС (KPSS), and many others.

37 About *The Magnificent Cuckold*, see note 68 to dialogue 1.

Duvakin: Do you recall when that happened?

Ardov: No. I am afraid I can't tell you the exact dates.

Duvakin: So, by 1922 he already had it back, yes?

Ardov: The première of *Le Cocu Magnifique* took place in April 1922.

Duvakin: And the première of the *Mystery-Bouffe* was in 1920, in November.

Ardov: Right. Now you can figure out for yourself when they took the theatre from him. I don't remember the exact dates.

Duvakin: But are you really sure that this happened?

Ardov: Of course. I will tell you that I participated in the newspaper campaign that demanded the return of the theatre to Meyerhold because they [the government] wanted to give the entire building to the musical comedy theatre. And right at that moment, *Pravda* published an article that resolved the dispute.[38]

This article was written by some Boris Samsonov,[39] an Old Bolshevik.[40] He worked for *Pravda* for a while, then headed the satirical magazine *Krasniy perets* (*The Red Pepper*).[41] Later he went to work for *Krokodil.*[42] He was a very intelligent, reserved, and talented man. He was older than many of us, so he treated us like a father would. Anyway, he wrote that article in *Pravda*. I do not remember how it was titled. Perhaps, "The Dawns" or "The Poopsik"? *The Dawns*, as you know, that was…

Duvakin: The play by Verhaeren?[43]

---

38 When the Bolsheviks liquidated all non-Communist publications in 1918, *Pravda* (*Truth*) became the main and most influential newspaper for the next seventy years. It was published daily, and, to make sure that the citizens of Moscow and Leningrad received the latest issue at the same time, a special airline between the two cities was established in 1931. It ensured that the newspaper arrived in Leningrad on time regardless of the weather. The best pilots in the country worked for this airline, known as the "postal squad."

39 Boris Samsonov (1888–1933) was a Soviet satirist.

40 The term *Old Bolshevik* was often used to refer to those who became Communists during Lenin's regime; they were seen as the most uncompromising Bolsheviks. Among them were Yakov Sverdlov, Leon Trotsky, and Sergo Ordzhonikidze. Most of them were murdered by Stalin during the Great Purge (1936–8).

41 *Krasniy perets* (*The Red Pepper*) was a Bolshevik-controlled satirical magazine, which was founded in 1923 and closed in 1926.

42 About the Soviet satirical magazine *Krokodil*, see note 8 to dialogue 1.

43 Émile Adolphe Gustave Verhaeren (1855–1916) was a famous Belgian avant-garde poet who wrote exclusively in French. A lawyer by education, he soon left his profession to dedicate his time to poetry. Verhaeren was one of the founders of the school of Symbolism and was nominated six times for the Nobel Prize in Literature. Following the outbreak of the First World War, Verhaeren emigrated to England, where he died under the wheels of a train after accidentally falling off the platform.

Ardov: Yes, and the *Poopsik* was a low-quality German operetta. Anyway, that article solved the problem. *Izvestiya* also helped our cause,[44] not just *Pravda.* There was a man called Khersonsky, who used to be, at some point, a student of Meyerhold's. By the way, Sergei Mikhailovich Eisenstein[45] and Sergei Iosifovich Yutkevich[46] were in that same class!

Duvakin [*surprised*]: They all studied at GVYRM?

Ardov: Yes. There were a lot of talented people there who later became prominent film directors. They ended up in Moscow, or other places. Now I cannot recall all the names. But there was a real old "Meyerhold brotherhood," that exists even today. Oh, yes! Pyryev, Ivan Aleksandrovich, was also there.[47] And someone else ... There were a lot of people. And Raikh was there, Zinaida Mikhailovna, I think.[48]

Duvakin: Zinaida Nikolayevna.

---

44 *Izvestiya* (*The News*) was the longest surviving Soviet official daily newspaper. It started its publication in 1917 and ended in 1991, with the fall of the Communist regime.

45 Sergei Eisenstein (1898–1948) was one of the most influential cinema directors of all times. His *Bronenosets Potemkin* (*Battleship Potemkin*, 1925) was lauded not only in the USSR but also in the West. Eisenstein was invited to work for Paramount Pictures in April 1930, but for various reasons the collaboration did not work out, and the contract between them was declared null and void in October 1930. At the same time, Eisenstein received a personal invitation from Stalin to return to the USSR. Owing to his enormous international prestige, he was able to survive the repressions and make two more landmark films: *Alexander Nevsky* (1938) and *Ivan Grozny* (*Ivan the Terrible*, 1945; unfinished). All his life Eisenstein taught and wrote about film theory. He died from a heart attack at the age of fifty, while working at his desk on an essay titled "The Colour Film."

46 Sergei Yutkevich (1904–1985) was a prominent Soviet film director and a friend and colleague of Sergei Eisenstein and Grigori Kozintsev. One of his most famous films was *Othello* (1955). Along with his successful career as a director, Yutkevich became an eminent professor of cinema studies, a film theorist, and a mentor to many generations of young artists and future film directors. He was also an accomplished painter, although he never publicly exhibited his work.

47 Ivan Pyryev (1901–1968) was an eminent Soviet film director, mostly known for his comedies. As a director for Mosfilm, the largest Soviet film production company, Pyryev had great administrative power, but unfortunately, he too often misused it to destroy the careers of talented people whom he disliked. Also talented as an artist, but very difficult as a person, Pyryev was known among his colleagues by the nickname "Ivan the Terrible."

48 Zinaida Raikh (1894–1939) was Vsevolod Meyerhold's wife and a brilliant theatre actress. A few years after staging the famous *La dame aux camélias,* which met with Stalin's disapproval, the Meyerhold's theatre was closed in 1938. Zinaida wrote a letter to Stalin in which she explicitly told him that he had no taste or understanding of theatre. Twenty-four days after Meyerhold was arrested in 1939, two individuals (possibly NKVD operatives) broke into his apartment and brutally murdered Zinaida Raikh. Meyerhold himself was executed a few months later.

Ardov: Right, Zinaida Nikolayevna. Meyerhold married her soon afterwards. The whole affair unfolded in front of our eyes. She had just divorced Yesenin[49] – she had two children with him– and then she married Meyerhold.

Meyerhold's Character and His Method

Ardov [*continues*]**:** I had a chance to observe Meyerhold very closely and have to say that he suffered from theatrical, shall we say, infantilism. He had an inherent desire to stun and surprise the audience, even if that audience consisted of only one person. For example, many of those who wrote memoirs about him described the same anecdote: They go to see Meyerhold. At his door they ring the bell and wait. Moments later the door *next* to it opens, and Meyerhold suddenly emerges from there, laughing happily that he had been able to surprise his visitors.[50]

This is, of course, just a small example, but it is very characteristic of Meyerhold. He always wanted to do the unexpected, to be different. For example, one day he said to us: "I will be staging *Hamlet*! Zina [Zinaida Raikh] will play Hamlet. The critics will come, Beskin will come,[51] and he will be eager to find out how Meyerhold has staged the famous monologue, 'To be or not to be?' I already have an idea about how to do it!" "How will you do it, Vsevolod Emilievich?" "I will get rid of it!"

This is typical Meyerhold. One day I visited the theatre cabaret One-Eyed Jimmy[52] and saw there a few parodies, written and produced by Aleksey Alekseyev. These parodies presented how the play *Marriage*[53] by Gogol[54] would be

49 About Sergei Yesenin, see note 4 to dialogue 1.

50 This episode may be found in Aleksey Gladkov, *Vospominaniya, zametki i zapisi o Meyerkholde* (*Memoirs, Essays, and Notes about Meyerhold*), (Kaluga, Russia: Kaluzhskoe knizhnoe izdatelstvo, 1961), 299.

51 Ardov refers here to Immanuel Beskin (1877–1940), a notable Soviet historian of the theatre and a literary critic. Immanuel should not be confused with his brother, Osip Beskin (1892–1969), who was also a literary critic.

52 *Odnoglazyi Dzhimmi* (*One-Eyed Jimmy*) was a small theatre cabaret created by a group of artists in 1917. Its name derives from the one-eyed effigy that sat on an oak barrel in the centre of the basement. The shows presented there were distinguished by their subtle humour and superb acting. The civil war scattered the troupe, and by 1921 the cabaret had ceased to exist.

53 *Zhenit'ba* (*Marriage*) is a comedy that was written by Nikolay Gogol between 1833 and 1842.

54 Nikolay Gogol (1809–1852) was a pre-eminent Russian writer, poet, and dramaturge. His works, such as *Nevsky Prospekt*, *Mertvye Dushi* (*Dead Souls*), and the comedy *Revizor* (*The Government Inspector*), inspired many future Russian authors, including the young Dostoevsky, who considered Gogol to be the greatest writer of Russian literature.

performed in several different theatres – Maly Theatre,[55] MKhAT,[56] the Jewish Theatre,[57] the Moscow Young Spectator Theatre,[58] and, of course, the Meyerhold Theatre. For the parody of Meyerhold's style they brought on stage two cages with hens and roosters. These had nothing to do with the play; they just cackled, ran around, and in every way entertained the audience.

The next day, when I saw Vsevolod Emilievich at work, I said, "Yesterday I watched a parody of your production at the *One-Eyed Jimmy*." He asked, "What kind of parody?" I answered, "They put cages with live hens and roosters right on stage and let them cluck to their heart's content." Meyerhold cried, "Damn it! They did it first!" It's hard to imagine a similar response from anyone else, ever![59]

Meyerhold was very unusual in this regard: he created his own style, which was truly unique – think, for instance, about the constructivist style of *Le Cocu Magnifique*.[60] Let me tell you more about this play and its production.

The stage design featured some kind of mechanical construction, empty walls, bare bricks – everything looked shabby, covered with dust. And all the left critics immediately started to praise it in unison: yes, this is the future of Soviet theatre! But Meyerhold continued in this fashion for a little longer and then unexpectedly changed course again – now turning away from the officially approved Soviet directives.

---

55 Maly Theatre in Moscow is the oldest drama theatre in Russia, founded in 1756 by order of Empress Elizabeth, daughter of Peter the Great. It officially opened its doors to audiences in 1824. It was then that the theatre received its nickname "Maly" to distinguish it from the Bolshoy ("Big").

56 About MKhAT, see note 105 to dialogue 1.

57 In 1919 the first Soviet Jewish Theatre (GOSET) was established in Petrograd. The performances, performed in Yiddish, revived the classics of Jewish literature. In 1948 its director, the talented Soviet actor Solomon Mikhoels (1890–1948), was brutally assassinated. In the following year the NKVD closed the theatre because it was deemed not "Soviet friendly."

58 About Moscow Young Spectator Theatre, see note 109 to dialogue 1.

59 Leonid Varpakhovsky (1908–1976), a literary critic, theatrical director, and amateur artist, shared the following story with Victor Duvakin during an interview: "В 1934, когда он планировал ставить сельские эпизоды 'Дамы с камелиями,' он мечтал о том, что в новом театральном здании на сцену будет выведена настоящая корова, Маргарита Готье будет ее доить на сцене и просто пить молоко. Он говорил: 'Эту сцену я посвящу Эйзенштейну.'" (Department of Oral History, Scientific Library of Moscow State University, file 224; In 1934, when he planned to stage the rural episodes of the *La dame aux camélias*, he dreamed that in his new theatre, a real cow would appear on stage, and Marguerite Gautier would milk this cow and drink its milk. He said, "I will dedicate this scene to Eisenstein.") It is possible that Meyerhold wanted to dedicate this cow-milking scene to Eisenstein because Eisenstein's final silent film, *The Old and the New* (also known as *The General Line*), had a lot of bovine imagery and a famous collective-farm, cream-separator sequence.

60 About *The Magnificent Cuckold*, see note 70 to dialogue 1.

Duvakin: Do you mean to say those approved by the Soviet intelligentsia? The authorities at that time were not very … [*Duvakin's comment here is inaudible.*]

Ardov: The authorities, obviously, could not accept such a turn. Regarding *The Magnificent Cuckold,* for example, Lunacharsky[61] (who, despite all the intrigues against him, of course continued to be the minister of education), right after seeing the play, sent a letter to the editor of *Izvestiya*, in which he deemed the performance outrageous from a moral point of view and said that he was greatly disturbed by it, that he felt as if they [the producers] had spat in his soul.[62]

Such a position was, of course, to be expected from the leader of Soviet culture. But for those of us whom Lev Davidovich Trotsky[63] called *levteretsy* [from *levye teatral'nye retsenzenty*], the leftist theatrical critics …

Duvakin: *Levteretsy*?

Ardov: Yes, *levteretsy*. He coined the term in an article somewhere. So, we, the *levteretsy*, were similar to Tarelkin, who, as we all know, liked to give eulogies at his own funerals.[64] According to a popular contemporary saying very worthy of Sukhovo-Kobylin, Tarelkin was, in fact, a New Man, a superior forward thinker, able to grab on to everything new and progressive. When *progress* became the new buzzword, Tarelkin immediately became a "progressivist," so that he actually came first, and progress followed him.[65]

Anyway, that was true of all of us: we were leading the way, and progress followed. I was a part of that group. I praised Meyerhold, too, criticized all

---

61 About Anatoly Lunacharsky, see note 83 to dialogue 1.

62 Anatoly Lunacharsky's exact reaction can be found in "Zametki po povodu 'Rogonostsa'" ("Notes about the 'Rogonosets'"), *Izvestiya*, 14 May 1922, 3: "Уже саму пьесу я считаю издевательством нам мужчиной, женщиной, любовью и ревностью. Издевательством, простите, гнусно подчеркнутым театром. Я ушел со второго акта с тяжелым чувством, словно мне в душу наплевали." (The play itself I consider a mockery of man, woman, love and jealousy. A mockery, which is, forgive my language, vilely promoted by the theatre. I left after the second act with a heavy feeling as if they spat in my soul.)

63 About Leon Trotsky, see note 36 to dialogue 1.

64 Tarelkin is the protagonist of the comedy *Smert' Tarelkina* (*Tarelkin's Death*) by Alexander Sukhovo-Kobylin (1817–1903).

65 In the final scene of the play Tarelkin, who has faked his own death to get rid of his creditors and assumed the personality of a deceased neighbour, says: "Господа, вам не надо управляющего имением? Я вам севообороты заведу, и с каким угодно удобрением. Либихов порошок своими руками сделаю. Одно слово: введу вам прогресс!" (Alexander Sukhovo-Kobylin, *Trilogiya* [*The Trilogy*], [Moscow: Iskusstvo, 1966], 347; Gentlemen, do you need an estate manager? I'll implement crop rotation for you, with any kind of fertilizer. I will make the Liebich's powder with my own hands. In one word: I will bring you real progress!)

academic theatres, and wrote that Meyerhold represented the real, revolutionary, Soviet art. [*He sighs.*] Now, about Meyerhold himself …

Duvakin: Could you say a bit more about *The Magnificent Cuckold*?

Ardov: Ah, yes. It was a translation of a Belgian play by Crommelynck, I think. This was a sophisticated, unusual play. Its content relies upon a psychological improbability: someone, a Belgian village farmer named Bruno, for no apparent reason grows jealous of his wife, Stella, who is faithful to him. In fact, the husband has no real reasons for jealousy. But since he is tormented by the question of whether his wife is cheating on him or not, he makes an absolutely monstrous decision. He pushes her to give herself to almost all the villagers, and only then does he calm down: at least now he knows what really happened.[66]

Meyerhold redesigned this horrific story in three acts in such a way that there was absolutely nothing left of the original plot line. The village was replaced by wooden machinery: there were some wheels spinning, there were stairs, passages. The stage designer was, I think, Popova, but maybe I am mistaken. Lyubov Popova was an artist.[67] And the whole construction set – wooden and misaligned – was creaking and making a lot of noise throughout the performance.

Now, what else? All the actors were dressed in blue linen uniforms, which they also wore while doing their biomechanics training, another one of Meyerhold's inventions.[68] They had to jump and tumble daily, do different exercises. So all the characters wore the same clothes. Igor Ilyinsky starred as Bruno,[69] and the day after the première he woke up as a celebrity, but Meyerhold hated him for this. They quarrelled many times because Meyerhold did not like that Ilyinsky became the audience's favourite.

---

66 Bruno says to Stella: "в моем распоряжении находится лекарство от того сомнения, полное решительное средство, немедленная и универсальная панацея: чтоб мне больше не сомневаться в твоей верности, мне надо быть уверенным в твоей неверности … Я хочу, чтобы ты была нечистой, а я – опозоренным. Никаких компромиссов, сегодня же я буду рогат или умру. Рога или веревка. Выбирай за меня." (Fernand Krommelink, *Velikodushnyi rogonosets. Fars v trekh deistviiakh* [Moscow-Leningrad: Izdatel'stvo khudozhestvennoi literatury, 1926], 73, 75; I have at my disposal a cure for that doubt, a complete and decisive remedy, an immediate and universal panacea: so that I no longer doubt your loyalty, I have to be sure of your infidelity ... I want you to be unclean, and I want to be disgraced. No compromises; today I will either have horns or die. Horns or the rope. Choose for me.)

67 Lyubov Popova (1889–1924) was a Russian avant-garde artist, a Cubist, and later a Suprematist. She belonged to the artistic circle of Kazimir Malevich and for a time worked as a designer for Meyerhold's theatre. She died unexpectedly from scarlet fever, which she had contracted from her young son, in 1924, at the height of her artistic career.

68 A precursor of physical theatre, biomechanics was a method of actor training developed by Meyerhold during the 1920s and 1930s. Its goal was to express through bodily movements the emotional aspects of the play that could not be represented easily through traditional naturalistic acting.

69 See note 102 to dialogue 1.

2.2. Varvara Stepanova and Lyubov Popova, Moscow, 1924. Photographer: Alexander Rodchenko.

The play was very difficult to perform because the setting was unreal, the feelings were absolutely abstract. But to this day I still picture Ilyinsky performing that difficult role. By the way, I have a photo of him, I can show it to you: Igor as Bruno, with his inscription. Clearly, Lunacharsky, as a kind and respectable man, could not accept such a horrifying production. His protest fell on deaf ears, though, and the scandalous play continued its run with great success.[70]

But Meyerhold's next productions did not attract large audiences. After all, what did he do? He changed the essence of the play, its heart. When he staged *The Lake Lyul*, a play by Alexey Fayko, he presented to the author a picture of himself, with the inscription: "To Alexey Fayko, with gratitude for giving me such wonderful dramatic material for my play *The Lake Lyul*."[71]

70 It is interesting to note that Ilyinsky defends Meyerhold in his memoirs and claims that what he did was the only possible and the best interpretation of Crommelynck's play. Igor Ilyinsky, *O samom sebe* (*About Myself*), (Moscow: Iskusstvo, 1976), 176–7.

71 See Alexey Fayko, *Zapiski starogo teatral'shchika* (*Memoirs of an Old Theatre Man*) (Moscow: Iskusstvo, 1978), 194.

In my opinion, the playwright must have found that insulting. Meyerhold ruined Fayko's other play, *Uchitel' Bubus* (*The Teacher Bubus*), because he reworked it completely. Fayko's light comedy could not withstand the additional ballast.[72]

Meyerhold had irrepressible creative energy. He led two theatres at once and could manage five more because his imagination was boundless. He thought, we might say, in world categories. He studied Japanese theatre, Indian drama; he went to Greece; he saw all those ancient Hellenic theatres.

In his performances he made use of all previous dramatic achievements, all techniques, all methods of even non-European theatres. We know from his biography that he founded the Old Intermedia House in Saint Petersburg, and he even tried to lead Vera Feodorovna Komissarzhevskaya[73] towards artistic Formalism.[74] It all ended with her asking him, in the middle of the season, to leave her theatre.[75]

Each play staged by Meyerhold incorporated dozens of creative innovations, which were immediately adopted by many other theatres: by his students and even by directors of other, less experimental, theatres. For instance, we know that using fabric as a theatrical back-drop was first proposed by Meyerhold.[76] This is only one of the many ways he revolutionized the stage. He also had numerous other ideas, which were never realized. Why? First, because many of his actors were quite bad. He did not care whether his actors played well or not, but when Ilyinsky performed well, it upset him.

---

72 Meyerhold took many liberties with the play *The Teacher Bubus*, and the resulting production was quite poor. The play did not have any success. See Aleksey Fayko, *Zapiski starogo teatral'shchika* (Moscow: Iskusstvo, 1978), 210.

73 About Vera Komissarzhevskaya, see note 27 to this dialogue 2.

74 Russian Formalism was a school of literary criticism in existence from the 1910s to the 1930s. Formalists advocated a "scientific" method for studying poetic language, to the exclusion of traditional psychological and cultural, historical approaches. It exerted great influence on such later theoretical schools as structuralism and post-structuralism. Under Stalin *formalism* was used as a pejorative term to designate elitism in art.

75 Vsevolod Meyerhold was working at the Komissarzhevskaya Theatre when, in November 1907, Vera Feodorovna wrote him a letter: "За последние дни, Всеволод Эмильевич, я много думала и пришла к глубокому убеждению, что мы с Вами разно смотрим на театр, и того, что ищете Вы, не ищу я … Я смотрю будущему прямо в глаза и говорю, что по этому пути мы с Вами вместе идти не можем, – путь этот Ваш, но не мой … Поэтому я более не могу считать Вас своим сотрудником." (Yulia Rybakova, *Vera Feodorovna Komissarzhevskaya: Letopis' zhizni i tvorchestva* [*Vera Feodorovna Komissarzhevskaya: A Chronicle of Life and Work*], [Saint Petersburg: Rossiiskii institut istorii iskusstva, 1994], 375; In recent days, Vsevolod Emilievich, after giving this issue a lot of thought, I have come to the conclusion that you and I view theatre very differently, and what you are looking for is not the same as what I'm looking for ... If I have to be completely honest about the future, I have to say that we have to part ways. You are on a very different path ... Therefore, we can no longer work together.)

76 Ardov might be mistaken here: using fabric as a stage back-drop may have been first proposed by Konstantin Stanislavsky (1863–1938) or Gordon Craig (1872–1966), an English Modernist theatre director.

2.3. Maria Babanova, Moscow, 1950s. Photographer: Boris Ignatovich.

Babanova was a very gifted actress who played the role of Stella,[77] but he [Meyerhold] later began to mistreat her just because she was much more talented than Zinaida Raikh was,[78] and she was standing in her way.

Raikh didn't have much finesse as an actress, but she was quite charming as a woman. Meyerhold came up with a number of masterful devices to hide her inability to portray powerful emotions. For example, in *Les* (*The Forest*)[79] he made her perform all monologues and love dialogues while she was setting the table. All her lines were skilfully rearranged, and she was able to manage them all well. Without these "devices" she would not have been able to handle her role adequately.

77 Maria Babanova (1900–1983) was a talented Soviet actress. She played all the leading female roles in Meyerhold's theatre productions. However, as Meyerhold wanted that distinction for his wife, Zinaida Raikh, Babanova had to leave his theatre. She continued to have enormous success on the stage and, despite everything, always praised the genius of her teacher.

78 About Zinaida Raikh, see note 48 to this dialogue 2.

79 *Les* (*The Forest*) is a play by Alexander Ostrovsky (1823–1886). It was first performed at the Alexandrinsky Theatre in 1871, to great acclaim.

Meyerhold normally worked like this: for each production he prepared a few folders, in which he kept all his drawings and other preliminary materials. Then he called in the whole troupe and gave them the "director's explication," as he called it. Vladimir Zakharovich Mass,[80] my old friend, once told me a story …

Duvakin: Is he already back?

Ardov: What?

Duvakin: I know that he was arrested and sent to the East. Did he return already?

Ardov [*with passion*]: That cannot be! He never left Moscow. He was always a very loyal Soviet writer. He is eighty now and lives in the same 1920s apartment – number twenty-six – in the Vakhtangov Theatre house,[81] on Shchukin Street. He has lived there for the last fifty years.

So, Mass was in charge of literary office in the Theatre of Revolution. One day Meyerhold decided to gather their entire troupe and present to them his explication of how he was planning to stage *Woe from Wit*.[82] He ended up producing that play later, at a different theatre, though. (I will tell you more about it later.) Anyway, that day, right before he left his office to talk to the actors, he whispered into Mass's ear, "I am not really going to stage it, but there are certain circumstances that force me to pretend that we *will* stage it."

And then he gave his troupe a brilliant explication of a production that he knew would never happen. His audience members were so impressed by his genius that they burst into spontaneous applause at the end of it. This was the type of man he was!

Duvakin: So the play was never staged?

Ardov: In the Theatre of Revolution, no. But he eventually put on *Woe from Wit* at his own theatre. I will tell you about it now.

At that time we all felt very ashamed to be living in such a backward country, which couldn't boast of any technological advances, urban centres, etc., wasn't highly industrialized. And one day Alexander Tairov,[83] who, by the way, used

80 Vladimir Mass (1896–1979) was a writer and a playwright. In 1933, while working on the Soviet blockbuster film *Vesyolye rebyata* (*Jolly Fellows*, 1934), he was arrested and sentenced to three years of hard labour. It was only in 1943 that he was allowed to return to Moscow and continue his work as a screenplay writer.

81 Vakhtangov Theatre was founded in 1921 by a talented Russian director of Armenian origin, Yevgeny Vakhtangov (1883–1922), who died from stomach cancer one year later.

82 *Gore ot uma* (*Woe from Wit*, 1822) is a comedy by Alexander Griboedov (1795–1829) that offers a daring critique of Russia's nobility. During Griboedov's life the play was heavily censored and published only in a very abridged form.

83 Alexander Tairov (1885–1950) was one of the most important Soviet theatre innovators. In 1914 he founded his own theatre, Kamerny Theatre (Chamber Theatre), which existed until

2.4. *From left to right, sitting*: Dmitry Shostakovich and Vsevolod Meyerhold; *standing*: Vladimir Mayakovsky and Alexander Rodchenko, 1929. Photographer unknown.

to argue with Meyerhold constantly (I should say that Meyerhold was the one who almost always initiated those quarrels), decided to stage Chesterton's *The Man Who Was Thursday.*[84]

Duvakin [*with excitement*]: I remember the playbill, but I did not see the play.

Ardov: It was based on a very weak novel. Chesterton was certainly not a great writer.[85] But the play, when staged, was overloaded with urbanistic stuff – elevators,

1949 when the Bolshevik government decided to prohibit the staging of foreign plays. Tairov's theatre was closed down, and the troupe was dissolved and scattered to many different theatres. Tairov, in recognition of his long service to the country, was given a generous pension and forced to retire. Humiliated and offended, he fell into deep depression and died soon thereafter.

84 *The Man Who Was Thursday* (in Russian, *Chelovek, kotoryi byl Chetvergom*, 1908) is an original philosophical novel by G.K. Chesterton (1874–1936). At the request of Alexander Tairov, in 1923 a stage adaptation of the novel was made by Sigizmund Krzhizhanovsky (1887–1950), which turned Chesterton's biblical allegory into a crude anti-religious farce. Chesterton was scandalized by this "Bolshevization" of his novel.

85 Gilbert Keith Chesterton (1887–1936) was a celebrated and prolific English novelist and Catholic essayist. His collected works total eighty volumes. He was close to the leading intellectuals of his time, polemicizing with Bernard Shaw, H.G. Wells, Bertrand Russell, and many others.

other machinery, many moving parts everywhere. When Meyerhold found out about this, he immediately decided to put on *Ozero Lyul'* (*The Lake Lyul*)[86] in the exact same urbanistic manner and to première it two months earlier than Tairov did.

Tairov was furious. He shouted at Meyerhold, accused him of stealing his ideas. Meyerhold, in return, called him an idiot. Anyway, these disputes were very interesting for us, the young intelligentsia. Even Igor Ilyinsky notes in his memoirs that one day he and Meyerhold were walking in the street when a car tire blew nearby. Meyerhold immediately dived under the arch of the closest gate, called out to Ilyinsky to follow him immediately, and announced: "This is Tairov. He hired Ardov to kill me." You can read about this in his book, if you like. Nikolay Dmitrievich Volkov,[87] a very talented playwright, excellent critic and theatre scholar, wrote a monograph about Meyerhold, but he limited himself …

Duvakin: Was it published recently?

Ardov: No. Volkov died when he was already over seventy. The book came out in the 1920s, and it intentionally focused only on Meyerhold's pre-revolutionary theatrical activity.[88] Nikolay Dmitrievich did not want to write about his activities after the revolution. Meyerhold's position at that time was already such that to do so could be dangerous.

So when I wrote my memoirs about Meyerhold, I asked him [Volkov] to read them. And Nikolay Dmitrievich asked me, "How come you know all this?" I replied, "For a few months I worked in his theatre as an administrator." Then Volkov asked me, "So, when did he declare you an enemy?" "Why do you say that?" "Because he eventually declared everyone who worked with him an enemy," said Volkov.[89]

Indeed, he [Meyerhold] usually grew tired of people he worked with. He started to dislike them, then became rude to them, and began spreading

---

86 *Ozero Lyul'* (*The Lake Lyul*, 1923) is a play by Alexey Fayko. Its plot revolves around a crime mystery that takes place in an imaginary country and contains veiled jabs at the revolutionary leaders. The censorship at that time was not tight yet, so the play was staged without problems and with moderate success.

87 Nikolay Volkov (1894–1965) was a talented playwright. In 1937 he wrote the script for the first and most successful adaptation of Tolstoy's *Anna Karenina*. The play was staged at the MKhAT (Moscow Art Theatre) and directed by Vladimir Nemirovich-Danchenko. In 1929 Volkov wrote the first biography of Vsevolod Meyerhold. For years after the 1940 arrest and execution of Meyerhold, Volkov lived in fear that he, too, would follow his friend's tragic destiny.

88 See Nikolay Volkov, *Meyerhold* (Moscow: Academia, 1929).

89 It is unfortunate but true: both Igor Ilyinsky and Alexey Fayko confirm this assessment. See Igor Ilyinsky, *O samom sebe* (Moscow: Iskusstvo, 1976), 255; and Alexey Fayko, *Zapiski starogo teatral'schika* (*Memoirs of an Old Theatre Man*), (Moscow: Iskusstvo, 1978), 252.

2.5. Dmitry Shostakovich and Vsevolod Meyerhold, 1932. Photographer unknown.

rumours about them, making it very hard for them to stay on. He was unfair to people. And those who naively believed that by working beside a great man they would be guaranteed a job, fame, or simply a piece of bread, all were wrong because he made them all leave. He even got rid of his literary adviser who translated *The Magnificent Cuckold* for him – Ivan Vasilyevich Aksenov.[90]

He had a difficult character, somewhat moody, I would even say not feminine but infantile. He got tired of people, of things, even of ideas. He always wanted everything to be new. Do we still have tape for recording?

Duvakin: Yes, everything is in order. Please continue.

Ardov: Just recently I wrote a review about *Les* (*The Forest*) at the Maly Theatre. It was staged by Igor Ilyinsky. I saw the same play in 1924, by Meyerhold, with Ilyinsky in the role of Arkashka.[91] Now he played the same role in his own production. In the review I noted that, fifty years before, I had seen the eccentric Ilyinsky in Meyerhold's circus-like play. Fifty years later, that's very rare! So I went to see the play with great interest and wrote the review.[92]

90 About Ivan Aksenov, see note 66 to dialogue 1.

91 Arkady Schastlivtsev, one of the protagonists in the play.

92 See "Les-74," *Literaturnaya gazeta* 20 (17 May 1974): 11.

Duvakin [*sounding very interested*]: And how was it?

Ardov: You know, Ilyinsky staged the play well, and he himself played marvellously. He saved everything good that was in Meyerhold's play, but all the eccentricities, all the clown tricks, those were gone. Instead Ilyinsky focused on the details, so to speak, and showed his hero from the inside – as a man accustomed to sorrow – and he did it very skilfully. Not many actors would be able to do that. It was not a paroxysm of grief; it was precisely the experience of continuous grief, adversity, need, hunger. You could see it all on his face. And all his tricks, all his bodily movements came from his [Ilyinsky's] comedic repository.

In Meyerhold's production the stage was dominated by a staircase, maybe about a hundred steps high, and all the scenes in the forest took place around those stairs. The music we heard was a nineteenth-century waltz performed by three accordions. A man called Valentin Kruchinin – a rather unremarkable composer – had adapted this waltz (it was already free of copyright as the composer had died some time in the last century), and a bad poet by the name of Pavel German wrote the horrible lyrics.[93] The song was called "The Bricks" [Kirpichiki, Кирпичики].

It started like this: "На окраине где-то города,/ Я в убогой семье родилась" [On the outskirts of a city, I was born in a poor family].

Duvakin [*very surprised*]: So that's where this song came from, from Meyerhold?

Ardov: It was a vulgar song that fit very well the petit bourgeois love of the young Vosmibratov[94] for – what was her name? Anyway, it doesn't really matter.

Duvakin: Sorry, I did not understand. Were the song's lyrics also part of the play?

Ardov: No, Meyerhold used only the music; there were no words. It was only later that German took this melody and wrote the vulgar lyrics for it.

Duvakin: But how did it happen that the song became so popular? At that time sound films still did not exist.

Ardov: Ah! In fact, a song becomes popular if people happen to like the melody. The composer is the one who makes it happen. When you have a good melody, the words don't really matter.

Duvakin [*humming*]: "I was born in a poor family…" Interesting!

---

93 Pavel German (1894–1952) was indeed a mediocre poet. Sometime before the revolution he wrote one beautiful romance that is still popular – "Tol'ko raz byvaiut v zhizni vstrechi…" (Only once in a lifetime you meet someone who …) – but after 1917 he wrote cheap and mostly propagandistic songs. It is not surprising that Ardov had such a low opinion of him.

94 Another character from the play *Les* (*The Forest*).

2.6. Dmitry Shostakovich and Vsevolod Meyerhold, 1928. Photographer unknown.

Ardov: People sang many songs at that time. There were street songs, and gang songs, prison songs.

Duvakin: I don't remember those accordion songs. Demyan Bedny's songs were very popular,[95] that's for sure. Do you know, by chance, how that song ["Kirpichiki"] became so well liked?

Ardov: I don't think we should continue talking about it. It's quite simple: if people liked the melody, even if it was only played in the restaurants, in the pubs – that's enough. Restaurant music always becomes very popular.

Anyway, I would like to continue about *The Forest*. There were some interesting characters: the guests of that lady, the hostess – what was her name? Ah, Gurmyzhskaya.[96] Those guests all wore clown-like wigs: one was blue, another was green, and another red. Boris Evgenievich Zakhava played the older Vosmibratov very well.[97] He came from the Vakhtangov Theatre.

Duvakin [*surprised*]: And he performed in *The Forest* at the Meyerhold Theatre?

---

95 About Demyan Bedny, see note 55 to dialogue 1.

96 Raisa Gurmyzhskaya is one of the principal characters in Ostrovsky's play *The Forest*.

97 Boris Zakhava (1896–1976) was a notable stage actor, critic, historian, and pedagogue. A student of Yevgeny Vakhtangov, he remained connected to the latter's theatre, where he dedicated himself to teaching a new generation of actors.

Ardov: Yes. He received permission from his theatre to get some practical experience with Meyerhold where he played Vosmibratov.

Duvakin: Oh, yes, I remember that scene.

Ardov: When they took their clothes off and threw them at Gurmyzhskaya, they were trying to prove that they were not swindlers but, instead, were ready for any sacrifice. It was all done according to the principles of biomechanics: in order to take off his shoes, the old man first had to lie on the floor; then he, barefoot, went over to his son, and his son also had to lie on the floor and take off his shoes. It was fun to see but hard to comprehend – why were they doing that?

When Meyerhold decided to stage *Woe from Wit*,[98] he renamed it *Woe to Wit*. He did it after he had consulted Griboedov's first drafts where he called the comedy this way but later changed the title himself. Meyerhold decided to build his new version around the old title. Garin[99] played Chatsky.[100] And Ilyinsky played Famusov![101]

And there was a very interesting twist: when Sofia [Famusov's daughter] appears on stage, Famusov at that very moment tries to rape Liza [a maid] behind the screen covering the sofa.[102] But the apex of the play was a scene, in which all guests – about forty of them – sit in a line, and this live chain starts spreading the rumour that Chatsky is insane. It had tremendous success!

After that he [Meyerhold] staged *The Government Inspector*,[103] also distorted. There were other plays too, but I stopped going there around that time.

Duvakin: You said that you were among those young people who applauded Meyerhold, right?

---

98 About *Woe from Wit*, see note 82 to this dialogue 2.

99 Erast Garin (1902–1980) was a comedic actor in Soviet theatre and cinema. His manners, moves, and especially voice, were very different from those of other actors, and this was why Meyerhold noticed him and invited him to play Chatsky. Garin was the only one who never betrayed his master, Meyerhold, even when his theatre was closed. Meyerhold spent the night before his arrest by the NKVD in 1939 with Garin and his wife, discussing the future production of Nikolay Gogol's play *The Marriage*, which he would never see on stage.

100 Chatsky is the principal character in the comedy *Gore ot uma* (*Woe from Wit*) by Alexander Griboedov.

101 Famusov is another important character in Griboedov's comedy.

102 This scene was very important for Meyerhold whose interpretation of Famusov's character differed significantly from the tradition of presenting him as an old, passive man, a father, who is not interested in anything besides politics, gossip, and money. Meyerhold saw him as a man full of will, passion, and desires.

103 *Revizor* (*The Government Inspector*) is Nikolay Gogol's most famous comedy, written in 1835. Allegedly inspired by an anecdote that Pushkin had shared with Gogol, the play aimed to reveal the all-pervasive greed, stupidity, and corruption in imperial Russia. Vsevolod Meyerhold's 1926 staging of the play emphasized its surrealistic, dreamlike essence, which had been completely lost in the previous century of simplistically reducing it to mere photographic realism.

Ardov: Yes, I was.

Duvakin: I ask because you sound angry when you talk about it.

Ardov: I'll tell you this: fifty years have passed, and I have changed my position, so to speak. I have changed my position. I still believe that he [Meyerhold] had great talent, but it was completely wild, unchecked. And that is why he sometimes ended up producing absolutely ridiculous, incomprehensible plays.

Duvakin: Have you seen *Klop* (*The Bedbug*),[104] or *Bania* (*The Bathhouse*)?[105]

Ardov: Of course.

Duvakin: And you didn't like them either?

Ardov: I did. *The Bedbug* was good. The stage design for the first act (before the fire happens) was by Kukryniksy,[106] and it was really interesting. But the fact is that Mayakovsky couldn't foretell much about the Communist future; all he could envision for it was that hygiene would reign supreme. It was all connected with the trauma of losing his father to sepsis very early on. After that he became obsessed with hygiene, and consequently that's what he had to offer his audiences. And that's really all he had to offer in *The Bedbug*. But Igor Ilyinsky's performance was excellent. The conversation he has in the second act with the bedbug, in which he is happy it has followed him from the old world – that's very interesting.

As for *The Bathhouse*, I think it was a poor play altogether. That's why it failed, and it became one of the causes of Mayakovsky's death.

Duvakin: But now it's very popular in the West.

Ardov: Yes, but still it is not an interesting play at all. And all these attempts to show us the beautiful future are ineffective. I saw both plays. I even heard Mayakovsky reading *The Bathhouse*. But it was all just empty declamation, which left the audiences completely indifferent because it was already impossible to sell to people such cheap propaganda about an unknown future that nobody believed in.

---

104 *Klop* (*The Bedbug*, 1929) was a play by Mayakovsky, first staged at the Meyerhold Theatre. Its success was moderate at first, but following Mayakovsky's suicide in 1930, the official critics amended their assessment and proclaimed it to be a "Soviet *Government Inspector*."

105 *Bania* (*The Bathhouse*, 1929), "a drama with circus and fireworks," was written specifically for the Meyerhold Theatre. Its première met with severe criticism, and the play was swiftly banned. It was restaged to great acclaim and popular success in the 1950s.

106 Kukryniksy was a group of three Soviet artists – Mikhail Kupriyanov, Porfiry Krylov, and Nikolay Sokolov. Their mostly satirical work became especially famous after Hitler's invasion in 1941. They are considered classic representatives of Soviet political satire. For a long time it was rumoured that they were connected to the NKVD, but now historians believe that that was not the case. It is hard, however, to deny the fact that their art often served party purposes.

2.7. *Sitting*: Vissarion Shebalin, Vsevolod Meyerhold. *Standing*: Vladimir Mayakovsky, Pavel Chetnerovich, and an unknown person. At the rehearsal of Mayakovsky's play *Bania*, Moscow, 1930. Photographer: Alexey Temerin.

2.8. Vsevolod Meyerhold shows a mise-en-scène at the rehearsal of Mayakovsky's play *Bania*, Moscow, 1930. Photographer: Alexey Temerin.

Duvakin: I don't completely agree with you here. In fact, both plays are now quite popular. But that's a different matter.

Ardov [*indifferently*]**:** Yes, perhaps.

Duvakin: But I am still very surprised by what you say, that people were left indifferent listening to him [Mayakovsky].

Ardov: Very indifferent. And soon almost everyone left.

But I would like to return to Meyerhold. When he came to the rehearsals, he always already knew what he was going to rehearse, what his demands of each actor would be. He also always tried to help everyone, and, if necessary, he would simply go on the stage and demonstrate what he wanted, act things out himself. He did that very well, like a real actor.

I remember how one day when they were rehearsing *The Magnificent Cuckold*, Ilyinsky, following a rather calm conversation about his wife cheating on him with another character, was supposed to give him a slap in the face because of his presumed lustful expression. Ilyinsky interrupted the scene and said: "Vsevolod Emilievich! I cannot slap him in the face right after such a friendly talk! I have to justify this somehow." Meyerhold responded: "You do not need to justify anything; just slap him in the face, and the spite will follow."

Of course, everything happened as he predicted, but what's interesting is that this is exactly Stanislavsky's system.[107]

I have to tell you that Meyerhold respected Stanislavsky a lot. For example, it's a known fact that he went to see *Goriachee serdtse* (*An Ardent Heart*) a few times,[108] and he advised everyone to watch it. My wife, who at that time worked with Stanislavsky, told me that Meyerhold would always sit in the second row and laugh a few seconds ahead of everyone else because he knew what would happen, while others did not.

Duvakin [*chuckles*]**:** Interesting!

Ardov: Yes. I often saw him in theatres. He went to watch new performances, wanted to see the method used, the stage designs, the actors' performances, but it usually took him about ten minutes to become totally bored. It was not possible for him to leave unnoticed as they always gave him a seat in the first row.

---

107 Konstantin Stanislavsky (1863–1938) was the most famous Russian theatre director, actor, and professor of dramatic art, best known today for his system of actor training, preparation, and rehearsal technique. Together with Nemirovich-Danchenko, he founded the Moscow Art Theatre in 1898. His fame was enormous, and probably the reason he managed to survive Stalin's Great Purge.

108 *Goriachee serdtse* (*An Ardent Heart*, 1858) is a play by Alexander Ostrovsky that was staged by the Moscow Art Theatre in 1926 under the direction of Stanislavsky.

So he would just sit there, greedily soaking in everything new that he saw, then he'd get bored and try to escape after the first act. That's quite understandable: you didn't have to be Meyerhold to get bored in our theatres in those days – and now, too!

Boris Alpers sometime in the 1930s described the situation as the "beneficial levelling of theatres."[109] So awful! It's hard to imagine a more sacrilegious opinion of the art.

When he [Alpers] was young, he wrote poetry and one day showed it to Alexander Blok, who promptly told him, "You will never be a poet." And he decided to become a critic.

Duvakin [*laughs*]**:** That's a funny story!

Ardov: Meyerhold was also a very conceited man. He used to say, "If I open today's newspaper and do not find the name Meyerhold anywhere, that newspaper means nothing to me."

Duvakin [*very surprised*]**:** Really? Did you hear this yourself?

Ardov: Yes, I heard it myself. He said that back stage. I often attended his rehearsals because they interested me. He had to attract as much public attention as possible: there were too many people who hated him, who thought that everything he did was wrong, and he had to fight them constantly. All that ended very tragically. [*Ardov sighs.*]

Duvakin: Yes, that's true.

Ardov: I will share one more episode with you. This story was told to me by a Lubyanka agent.[110] The closure of Meyerhold's theatre was not accidental; it was planned in advance.

Duvakin: In 1938, yes. He was arrested.

---

109 Boris Alpers (1894–1974) was a theatre critic. He served as secretary at Meyerhold's studio, 1913–15; as artistic director of the Ligovsky People's, New Drama, and Proletkul't theatres in Petrograd, 1921–4; as chairman of Repertkom in charge of state theatres, from 1922; and as chief dramaturge at the Moscow Theatre of Revolution, 1924–7. Although always loyal to the Communist Party, he was persecuted in 1937 but managed to avoid being sent to a labour camp. To avoid further complications, Alpers became a theatre professor and theatre historian.

110 The Lubyanka building housed the main headquarters of Cheka, GPU, NKVD, and KGB between 1919 and 1991. Now it belongs to the Federal Security Bureau (FSB). The building is located in Moscow, not far from the Kremlin, on Lubyansky Square. The building also served as a prison for a time. Among some of the most famous prisoners held there were Alexander Solzhenitsyn and Osip Mandelstam. See also note 28 to dialogue 1.

Ardov: No, they closed his theatre first. And this was when almost all his so-called friends turned their backs on him. Prov Sadovsky,[111] for example, published an article in which he stated that it was a good decision to close Meyerhold's theatre.

Then they went to Nemirovich-Danchenko,[112] but he refused to say anything bad about Meyerhold, and Stanislavsky employed him in his musical theatre.[113]

Later, in 1940, the First Conference of Theatre Directors took place.[114] Meyerhold was the biggest celebrity there! He was elected to serve on the board, and after his speech he was applauded for a long time.

[*There is a break in the recording.*]

Duvakin: I am sorry. Please continue.

Ardov: Yes. Every time that someone mentioned his name [Meyerhold's], the audience burst into applause. I think that's why he got arrested. When in 1956 the authorities thought about rehabilitating him, they called Igor Ilyinsky and asked if in his expert opinion it was a good idea to rehabilitate Meyerhold.

Of course, Ilyinsky offered the most glowing review of Meyerhold, but when they told him that Meyerhold was shot by Beria himself, Ilyinsky fainted.[115]

Duvakin [*sounding very surprised*]**:** Oh, so they told him that!

Ardov: Yes, but what is also interesting is that Meyerhold's old enemy, Tairov,[116] faced the same destiny: his theatre was closed, and Alexander Yakovlevich … [*He cannot continue because he begins to cry.*]

---

111 Prov Sadovsky (1874–1947) was the director of the Maly Theatre. In 1936 he met Meyerhold and invited him to stage something interesting at the Maly Theatre, but just two years later, when Meyerhold was arrested, Sadovsky wrote an ugly article about him.

112 Vladimir Nemirovich-Danchenko (1858–1943) and Konstantin Stanislavsky are the two most important and best-known figures of Russian theatre. In 1898 they founded the Moscow Art Theatre (MKhAT), where they worked together for the next thirty years. From 1928 until his death, Nemirovich-Danchenko directed the theatre alone, while Stanislavsky, owing to health problems, focused on creating and writing about his system, which became internationally known as the Stanislavsky method.

113 Stanislavsky indeed offered Meyerhold work when, fearing serious repercussions, almost everyone else had turned their back on this director who had fallen out of favour with Stalin. Stanislavsky bravely invited Meyerhold to direct *Rigoletto* at his Opera Theatre in 1938.

114 The conference took place in June 1939. Not only did Meyerhold deliver a brilliant speech there, but he was also elected to serve on the board of directors. Nevertheless, he was arrested just a few days later.

115 That rumour has no historical justification. It is documented that Meyerhold was executed in Butyrsky Prison (a special NKVD prison in Moscow) on 2 February 1940 by the NKVD agent Alexander Kalinin.

116 About Alexander Tairov, see note 83 to this dialogue 2.

2.9. *Sitting*: Vasily Kamensky, Alisa Koonen, and Alexander Tairov, 1910s. Photographer unknown.

Duvakin [*sadly*]: I understand, it's very emotional. What happened with Tairov?

Ardov: He was not arrested; he died soon after, from grief. And his wife, Koonen,[117] cursed the three men who inherited Tairov's theatre: Vanin, Ganshin (who were actors from his old troupe), and Matusis, the administrator.[118]

117 Alisa Koonen (1889–1974) was a famous actress and Tairov's wife. When Tairov's theatre was closed in 1949, she quit her job. Koonen lived for another twenty-five years after her husband's death. All her life she cherished and tried to preserve his memory for future generations.

118 Vasily Vanin and Vasily Ganshin died a few years after they took over Tairov's theatre. Yakov Matusis's fate is not known.

Duvakin [*enthusiastically*]: Koonen is still alive. I hope to interview her soon.[119] Well, that's all, as far as Meyerhold is concerned. Do you have anything else to add about him? You told me so many interesting things about Yesenin. Do you remember anything else, or should we move to the next topic?

Ardov: Let's move to the next topic.

[THE RECORDING ENDS.]

119 Duvakin tried to make an appointment with Koonen a few times, but something always came up, and the appointments were cancelled. In 1974 she passed away before he had the chance to record her reminiscences. Her memoirs have been published: Alisa Koonen, *Stranitsy zhizni* (*Pages from Life*), 2nd ed. (Moscow: Iskusstvo, 1985).

DIALOGUE 3
With Vladimir and Ariadna Sosinsky on 18 June 1969*

The couple with whom Duvakin conducts this interview lived an extraordinary life. In the 1920s Vladimir Sosinsky left Communist Russia for Berlin and then moved to Paris. His wife, Ariadna, though born abroad, had moved to Russia after the revolution but left in the 1920s with her husband.

This conversation is about the life of the Russian political émigrés in Czechoslovakia and France. The Sosinskys talk about Ivan Bunin, Dmitry Merezhkovsky, Konstantin Balmónt, and Alexander Kerensky. The main focus of this dialogue, however, is Marina Tsvetaeva, whom the Sosinskys knew well.

Duvakin: Vladimir Bronislavovich, first of all, tell us a little about yourself.

Vladimir Sosinsky: I was born in August of 1900, in a family of an engineer. My father was educated in Europe, and because of his job we lived all over Russia. I went to school in Borovichi.[1]

Then I went to study in Saint Petersburg, at the same college that was attended long ago by Nadson[2] and Garshin.[3] I never lived with my family. Perhaps that's what cast such a dark shadow over my childhood and affected my future life.

Duvakin: Why didn't you live with your family?

---

* Length of interview – 62 minutes

1 Borovichi (founded in 1770) is a small town located about 250 miles northeast of Moscow.

2 About Semyon Nadson, see note 86 to dialogue 1.

3 Vsevolod Garshin (1855–1888) was a prominent Russian writer, the creator of the Russian "long short story" or novella. Since childhood Garshin suffered from mental problems that became more pronounced as time went by. Clinically depressed, he committed suicide at the age of thirty-three.

3.1. Marina Tsvetaeva, Prague, 1924. Photographer unknown.

Vladimir Sosinsky: Because the town where they lived never had a good school for me there. [*He laughs sadly.*] Maybe this was my destiny – never to be with my family, to live alone.

Duvakin: But how did you get to Constantinople?

Vladimir Sosinsky: There was a tragic event in my family – my sister died – and I left home. On the way I encountered a military squad that took me in (it happened to be the White Army).[4] I stayed with the Whites until the Perekop.[5]

Duvakin: So were you evacuated from Sevastopol?[6]

Vladimir Sosinsky [*laughs*]: Not evacuated – I fled! My half-brother, with whom I went to school in Borovichi, was a sailor and six months before Wrangel

4 About the White Army, see note 34 to dialogue 1.

5 Perekop Isthmus connects the Crimea peninsula to the mainland. The Siege of Perekop by the Red Army in late 1920 was a major episode in the civil war.

6 Sevastopol, located at the southwestern point of Crimea, is the largest city and port of the peninsula; it currently has a population of more than half a million people.

was defeated,[7] he got me on a ship sailing to Constantinople. From there I went to Bulgaria, then to Berlin, but most of my life in emigration I spent in Paris. That's where I started to publish.

Duvakin: Did you publish any short stories?

Vladimir Sosinsky: Yes. I published some of my works in the magazine *Volya Rossii* (*The Will of Russia*), which also published "Krysolov" ("The Ratcatcher")[8] by Marina Tsvetaeva.[9]

Duvakin: Oh, how interesting!

Vladimir Sosinsky: Yes, it was an amazing time. It deserves its own introduction, we might say. The literary Russian Paris! [*sounding very emotional*]. We were immersed in it for almost twenty years.

In 1929 we lived in Clamart,[10] alongside the likes of Nikolay Berdyaev, Karsavina, the Skryabins. We celebrated our wedding there. Maybe it makes sense to tell you about our literary life there first, before we continue with our biography?

Duvakin: Vladimir Bronislavovich, perhaps now we can turn to Ariadna Viktorovna and ask her to tell us a bit about herself? Where did you come from?

Ariadna Sosinsky: I was born in Paris, but I spent my early years in Italy, among Russian revolutionaries who had escaped from the Russian authorities. We lived in a big country house, by the sea.

---

7 Pyotr Wrangel (1878–1928) was a commander-in-chief of the White Army of southern Russia. In addition to leading the army charged with protecting Crimea, he took care of the local people and tried to improve their economic situation. When the White Army was defeated in 1920, Wrangel organized the massive evacuation of the army and people to Constantinople; he knew that the Bolsheviks would make everyone pay dearly for their different political affiliations. In 1927 Wrangel settled in Brussels and worked as an engineer. He died suddenly, which has prompted some to believe that he was poisoned by one of his servants, who was actually an NKVD agent.

8 "Krysolov" ("The Ratcatcher") was a poem by Marina Tsvetaeva, inspired by the medieval German legend about the Pied Piper of Hamelin. It was published in *Volya Rossii* in 1925, in Prague.

9 Marina Tsvetaeva (1892–1941) is considered to be one of the greatest Russian poets of the twentieth century. She was famous not only for her brilliant and probing poetry but also for her brilliant translations of poetry from French, German, Czech, and Italian – languages that she spoke fluently. In 1922 Tsvetaeva left Communist Russia and spent seventeen years abroad. In 1939 she returned to the USSR. Soon thereafter, her daughter, Ariadna, and her husband, Sergei Efron, were arrested on charges of espionage. Tsvetaeva could not stand it any more and she committed suicide in August 1941. Her husband was executed shortly afterwards.

10 Clamart is a small town located about five miles from Paris. It is famous for its exquisite culinary scene and for a failed attempt to assassinate the French president Charles de Gaulle there in 1962.

Vladimir Sosinsky: Sorry to interrupt: that country house was called Villa Ariadna – after my wife.

Duvakin: What's your maiden name?

Ariadna Sosinsky: Chernova.

Duvakin: And you were born in Paris?

Ariadna Sosinsky: Yes. The place where I lived in Italy was visited by many Russian Socialists, even Gorky![11]

Sosinsky: Right. And Benito Mussolini,[12] when he was still a Socialist.

Ariadna Sosinsky: He came just once. A lot of people visited us, and all of them talked about Russia all the time. Although I grew up in Italy, I always lived with Russia in my heart.

That is why when the revolution started, in 1917, we all immediately fled to Russia. It was very difficult: we had to go through London. The First World War was going on, and we had to leave Italy by ship so that the Germans were less likely to catch us.

Duvakin: Ah! So you got to London by sea?

Ariadna Sosinsky: Yes. From Italy to London, then to Russia through Norway.

Duvakin: So you arrived around the same time as Lenin did? He returned on 3 April 1917.[13]

---

11 Maxim Gorky (b. Aleksey Peshkov) (1868–1936) was a major writer in the Bolshevik era and the leading promoter of socialist realism after 1934. He did much to save the lives of fellow writers. In 1921, horrified by the terror that the Bolsheviks had initiated, Gorky left the USSR and spent several years in Italy. After receiving a personal invitation from Stalin in 1931, he decided to return to the USSR, but his relationship with Stalin soured quickly. In 1934 he was placed under unofficial house arrest in Moscow. In 1936 he was hospitalized for a lingering illness and died shortly thereafter.

12 Benito Mussolini (1883–1945), known as El Duce (leader), was the founder of Italian fascism. In 1922 he became the youngest prime minister in Italian history, until the appointment of Matteo Renzi in February 2014. After removing all political opposition with the help of his secret police, and outlawing labour strikes, Mussolini and his followers consolidated their power through a series of laws that transformed the nation into a one-party dictatorship. Within five years Mussolini had established dictatorial authority by both legal and extraordinary means and aspired to create a totalitarian state. By 1945 he had lost his hold on power, his army was defeated, and, during an attempt to flee to Switzerland, he and his wife were caught and brutally murdered by Italian guerrillas.

13 Vladimir Lenin (b. Ulyanov) (1870–1924) was the leader of the Bolshevik party. In early 1917 he returned to Russia from exile in Switzerland. He took a train from Finland to Saint Petersburg on 3 April and on the very next day published his infamous "April Theses" – the

Ariadna Sosinsky: It's interesting that my first impression of Russia was that it didn't seem foreign to me at all. Just the opposite: I immediately felt at home there. And the experience during the revolution influenced me enormously. It was a life that was very different from anything we had considered normal. I felt that there had been a seismic shift, and life now was moving in a completely different direction – and all this influenced me a great deal.

I had the same feeling later, after I moved to France, when the war started.

Duvakin: Was that in 1940?

Ariadna Sosinsky: Yes. We felt a great solidarity with the French people. My husband signed up as a volunteer in the French army and went to the front, and I felt really close to the French women because we all were sending packages, and we all had the same anxieties. Anyway, at that moment we did not feel like foreigners any more.

Duvakin: How did you end up living abroad? You said you were about nine years old?

Ariadna Sosinsky: Yes.

Duvakin: Did you start your studies abroad?

Ariadna Sosinsky: Yes, I started there but then I came to Moscow. Ekaterina Peshkova organized it all.[14]

Duvakin: Oh, you are talking about the Children Salvation League?[15]

---

ten directives to the Bolshevik party on how to defeat the provisional government. The thesis called for the confiscation of any private property, the nationalization of all banks, the dissolution of the police, and the abolition of all official military forces.

14 Ekaterina Peshkova (b. Volzhina) (1876–1965) was Maxim Gorky's official wife (they never divorced, even after he began living with the Moscow Art Theatre actress Maria Andreyeva, and they maintained a friendly relationship until Gorky's death). She became the first Soviet human rights activist. Through her tireless and fearless efforts the lives of many distinguished writers, artists, and poets were saved during Stalin's purges.

15 Children Salvation League was founded in 1918 by several notable political activists (Ekaterina Peshkova, Ekaterina Kuskova, Vladimir Korolenko, Sergei Prokopovich, and Nikolay Kishkin) to help combat the devastating effects of widespread famine on children. Thousands of children survived thanks to the league's work during the two and a half years of its existence. But the Bolsheviks (especially Vladimir Lenin) grew very suspicious of the league's activities: they terminated the organization, arrested its members, and a few months later sent them into exile to Europe. Both daughters of Marina Tsvetaeva, Ariadna (Alya) and Irina, were temporarily placed in the orphanage run by the league in 1919–20 in Kuntsevo, near Moscow; the two-year-old Irina died there in February 1920. Later in the interview, Duvakin refers to another charity organization that included the same activists, Pomgol (Relief for the Starving), which was also closed by the Bolsheviks in 1921.

Ariadna Sosinsky: Yes. It was a new organization.

Duvakin [*sounding sad*]: Did you know that I also was one of those saved by the league?

Ariadna Sosinsky [*very surprised*]: Really? Then, we could say that we had a similar childhood.

[*There is a break in the recording.*]

Ariadna Sosinsky: At the end of 1921 we went abroad. My sister was already very sick, and, thanks to Maxim Gorky, they allowed us to leave the USSR. So we went first to Berlin, then to Prague, then to Paris.

Duvakin: Was this after the Bolsheviks had already closed down Pomgol [Relief for the Starving]?

Ariadna Sosinsky: Yes. They shut down everything. My father was already there [abroad], so we left, too. When we arrived, we were the first people with Soviet passports. That was very strange. [*She laughs.*]

Duvakin: So they allowed you to leave?

Ariadna Sosinsky: My sister was very sick by then. But later, after us, many people started to arrive from the USSR. Osorgin also came.[16]

Duvakin: There were many who left – all the historians, like Klyuchnikov.[17]

Ariadna Sosinsky: Berdyaev also.[18]

---

16 Mikhail Osorgin (b. Ilyin) (1878–1942) was a prominent Russian writer, essayist, and literary critic, and a connoisseur of Italian Futurism. Although he actively participated in the Children Salvation League, he was arrested by the Bolsheviks three times, exiled to Kazan, and eventually deported to Germany in 1922. From there he moved to France, where he died in the village of Chabris in 1942.

17 Yuri Klyuchnikov (1886–1938) was a distinguished lawyer, specializing in international law. He was personally invited by Lenin to participate in the Genoa Conference (1922) and accomplished his mission well. Nevertheless, he was expelled from Soviet Russia on the so-called philosophers' ship in 1922. He decided to return to the USSR after a couple of years in exile – a decision he was to regret ten years later when, in 1934, he was arrested. The following year he was sentenced to death for "counter-revolutionary activities" and was executed in 1938.

18 Nikolay Berdyaev (1874–1948) was one of the most original and prominent Russian philosophers of the twentieth century. The Bolsheviks arrested him in 1921 and forced him into exile on the famous "philosophers' ship." Berdyaev settled in France near Paris. He had a small house where, every Saturday, he hosted gatherings for members of the Russian intelligentsia living abroad. Berdyaev was nominated for the Nobel Prize seven times but never received it. He died unexpectedly from a heart attack, at his desk, working on a book manuscript.

Duvakin: But he came later.

Ariadna Sosinsky: We were the first to leave the USSR with Soviet passports. Initially we went to Estonia, and from there to Berlin, and then to Prague where we first met Marina Ivanovna Tsvetaeva.

Duvakin [*surprised*]**:** Had she arrived there before you? She was not exiled, was she?

Ariadna Sosinsky: I don't think so. We met her in Prague. We happened to rent rooms in the same building where she and many other Russians lived. We became neighbours.

She lived on the same floor. Quite often we'd see her passing by, with a rather unusual expression on her face: as if she were absorbed in something else, and was not even aware of other people's existence. Everyone who knew her personally remembers her peculiar expression of a complete detachment from the real world.

Duvakin: Are we talking about 1922?

Ariadna Sosinsky: It was already 1923.

Duvakin: Then you were about fourteen years old at the time, correct?

Ariadna Sosinsky: Yes. I lived with my mother. Marina Ivanovna Tsvetaeva lived in the same building, with her husband and daughter.

Duvakin: With Efron?[19] And Alya was there too?[20]

Ariadna Sosinsky: Yes, of course.

Duvakin: At that time she [Tsvetaeva] was probably around thirty.

Ariadna Sosinsky [*passionately*]**:** It was perhaps the happiest time of her life. Although we all wanted to leave Czechoslovakia, we thought that it was boring,

19 Sergei Efron (1893–1941) was the husband of Marina Tsvetaeva and the father of her three children. He met Tsvetaeva in 1911 in Crimea when she was only eighteen, and they married in the following year. Efron volunteered for the Russian army in 1914 but later joined the White Army and left Russia after the civil war. Tsvetaeva emigrated from Russia to join Efron in 1922; they lived in Czechoslovakia and then, for fourteen years, in France. In 1937, after his involvement in the assassination of the Soviet defector Ignaz Reiss, Efron fled to the USSR where he was later arrested, spent two years in prison, was brutally tortured, and finally was shot in 1941.

20 Ariadna Efron (1912–1975), a talented artist and writer, was the oldest daughter of Marina Tsvetaeva and Sergei Efron. Alya, as everyone called her, was the first in the family to return to the USSR, in 1937. In 1939 she was arrested and sent to labour camps for eight years. Only at the end of her life was Ariadna allowed to return to Moscow. She died from a heart attack on 26 July 1975.

that it couldn't compare to life in Paris. Still, she lived very well there. First, she was reunited with her husband. Then, no matter how difficult life would seem, at least she received a government stipend and could live on it fairly well. It was a much easier life than the one later, in Paris, and, of course, during the first years.

Duvakin: Here?

Ariadna Sosinsky: Yes, after the revolution.

Duvakin [*sounding surprised*]: But who paid her the stipend?

Ariadna Sosinsky: The Czechs. If you remember, they took out the Russian gold reserve and, because of that, felt somewhat obliged to support and help Russian émigrés. That is why life in Prague was so different from life in Paris. In Prague people had some money, they did not have to work, and overall they led a much quieter life there than in other places. And Marina Ivanovna was able to write because she had free time and some cash.

Duvakin: What was she working on at that time?

Ariadna Sosinsky: She was writing "Mólodets" [A young fellow], then "Poema kontsa" [A poem of the end], and "Poema gory" [A poem of the mountain].[21] In fact, it was about a romantic relationship that she had lived through recently. She wrote about it after the fact.

Duvakin: That romantic relationship was not with her husband?

Ariadna Sosinsky: No. She had many romantic relationships. In most cases they were purely platonic, but as a poet, as a writer, she needed them. I don't know.

Vladimir Sosinsky: She needed them to help her create an imaginary interlocutor – someone who was her friend but not really grounded in an actual person.

Ariadna Sosinsky: She had to have her imaginary world. She hated practical existence. She always had a hard time living because she simply didn't know how to do things. Simple things, like cooking, were a challenge, and so was –

Vladimir Sosinsky: – starting the fire in the stove.

21 All three poems were written in Prague between 1923 and 1924. The poem "Mólodets" is based on folkloric material; "Poema kontsa" and "Poema gory" form a diptych of poems, in which the divine and the mundane are intertwined.

Ariadna Sosinsky: – starting the fire, using coal, kerosene. She always managed to burn herself on the kerosene stove. But at the same time she never lived a Bohemian life: she had a husband, she had children – one girl, at first, then two children. She had to cook for them, have dinner ready on time (it didn't matter if it was good or bad).

She was a very organized person, who always did everything she was supposed to, whether she liked it or not.

Mornings she always reserved for herself, for writing. She could not let a day go by without writing at her desk. Even if she was not working on anything new, she busied herself with something old, revising, polishing it. She could not imagine doing anything else in the morning.

Duvakin: So you are saying she took her duties very seriously?

Ariadna Sosinsky: Absolutely. But only in relation to her family. She didn't feel the same sense of duty towards her friends. She would start a friendship, sometimes even somewhat romantic – and it did not matter if it was with a man or a woman – she would be so enthusiastic, and then, just like that, it would all end. She simply did not like to have this kind of responsibility, you understand. She did not have a sense of gratitude; she believed that if someone did something for her, he did it for himself first.

Duvakin [*smiling*]**:** That's not necessarily contradictory.

Ariadna Sosinsky: I think it's natural. She also did a lot for others.

Duvakin: That's right, she did. Sometimes she would even thank *you* when it was *she* who did something nice for you.

Ariadna Sosinsky: She did not even think about all that; she simply did it for herself. When she loved someone, she did what she could – for herself! And she thought that others would do the same for her.

Duvakin: And what did you think of all that? You were a girl at that time, weren't you?

Ariadna Sosinsky: We met her by accident. She stopped by to borrow forks and spoons. She had invited some guests and did not have enough silverware. Mother gave her what she needed. We had probably three or four forks and a couple of knives – from Corsica – engraved with the word *Vendetta* on them. Those were crude, primitive knives. Mother had brought them over from Corsica.

For the first time Marina Ivanovna saw us not just as her neighbours but as her kind of people – those, for whom material things, like silverware, did not matter. She especially liked those Corsican knives! [*She chuckles.*] And that's how our friendship began.

My mother had a lot of French books, sent by her sisters, who lived in Paris. At that time everyone was in love with André Gide.[22] His books were published in great numbers.

There was also another writer, Kessel,[23] who everyone thought would become a great writer one day, but that never happened. Marina Ivanovna borrowed all those books to read, and that's how she and my mother became very close friends. I was still a girl then, and Marina Ivanovna loved to give me advice about what I should read. George Sand, for example.[24]

Duvakin: She was suggesting that you read George Sand? Oh, my God!

Ariadna Sosinsky [*smiling*]: Yes. Also, Marie Bashkirtseff,[25] Zola,[26] especially his novel *Le rêve.*[27] She [Tsvetaeva] loved this book. She seemed to be reliving through me her own childhood, her passions, as if she was being transported back in time. Well, I think her life had gone through many different periods. It'd be very interesting for someone someday to do the research and show how her poetry gradually changed, grew – even trace the changes in her literary tastes.

---

22 André Gide (1869–1951) was a prominent French writer, poet, and essayist whose works influenced an entire generation. In 1947 he was awarded the Nobel Prize for his "deep and artistically significant works in which human problems are presented with a fearless love of truth and deep psychological insight" and also received an honorary degree from Oxford. In 1936 he visited the USSR and, upon return, published the book *Retour de l'URSS*, in which he severely criticized the Soviet suppression of freedom of expression. His books were immediately banned from publication in the USSR, and his name there was forgotten.

23 Joseph Kessel (1898–1979) was a French writer, largely remembered today thanks to his novel *Belle de Jour* (1928), which was turned into a film by Luis Buñuel, starring Catherine Deneuve as Severine.

24 George Sand (b. Aurore Dupin) (1804–1876) was a famous French writer and a close friend (or lover) of some of the most interesting people of the time, including Frédéric Chopin, Franz Liszt, Alfred de Musset, Alexandre Dumas son, and Victor Hugo.

25 Marie Bashkirtseff (1858–1884) was a Russian artist and writer. Diagnosed with tuberculosis at an early age, she left Russia in search of better climates and spent most of her life in France. She is best known for her diary, originally written in French, which was later translated into twelve languages, including Russian. It was popular in Russia at the beginning of the twentieth century.

26 Emile Zola (1840–1902) was a famous French writer and a pre-eminent practitioner of naturalism in literature. He was instrumental in the exoneration of the falsely accused Alfred Dreyfus – which ultimately forced him to emigrate to England and may have cost him his life. In 1902 Zola died in his own house from carbon-monoxide poisoning, which supposedly had been the result of a malfunctioning chimney. Many scholars believe that he was actually murdered by one of his many political enemies.

27 *Le rêve* (*The Dream*) is the sixteenth novel in the Rougon-Macquart series by Émile Zola. Set in the years 1860–9, it is about an orphan girl who falls in love with a nobleman.

Yes, she kept changing, but that was the result of a natural growth. We also discussed Dickens quite often.[28] She loved Dickens dearly, she knew all the literary types he had created, and we kept looking for them among our acquaintances. We talked about his characters as if they were close friends.

I have to say that, when reading a book, Marina Ivanovna did not behave as a writer at all; instead she was an attentive reader. She wanted to understand what the writer was trying to say, and she needed to fall in love with the author or his characters. She was a real reader – the kind of reader every writer wants – who keeps searching for the author's intention, falls in love with his heroes.

Vladimir Sosinsky: Can you say something about how she looked at that time?

Duvakin: Yes, that's very interesting.

Ariadna Sosinsky: She always had bangs. She was very slim but not flexible at all. She carried herself very straight, as if she were in a corset, an inner corset supporting her all the time. She smoked a lot, and one could often see her sitting, elbow leaning on her knee, with a cigarette in her mouth.

When she was with other people, she would always choose to focus on one of them and talk to him only, as if there was no one else in the room. Although, of course, she addressed everyone present.

Vladimir Sosinsky: She used a lorgnette.

Ariadna Sosinsky: Yes. She never wore glasses although she was extremely near sighted.

Duvakin [*surprised*]**:** Near sighted? I did not know!

Ariadna Sosinsky: Very near sighted. But she thought that near-sightedness was a blessing because it allowed one to see people's faces as more beautiful than they really were.

She saw the sun as a huge ball, and she was surprised that to those of us with normal vision it seemed small. That is why she did not want to wear glasses and preferred to use the lorgnette instead. At the same time, she never came across someone like Gippius, you know.[29]

Duvakin: A snob.

---

28 Charles Dickens (1812–1870) was an English writer and critic. The author of fifteen novels, five novellas, and countless stories and essays, he generously promoted the careers of other novelists in his weekly journals and concerned himself with social issues. He created some of the world's best-known fictional characters and is regarded by many as the greatest novelist of the Victorian era.

29 Zinaida Gippius (1869–1945) was a brilliant literary critic, poet, writer, and dramaturge. She was a co-founder, with her husband, Dmitry Merezhkovsky, of Russian Symbolism, and a seminal figure in the Russian avant-garde movement.

Ariadna Sosinsky: Yes, a snob. Tsvetaeva was very different: she simply used the lorgnette when she wanted to look at something very carefully, and there was nothing snobbish about that.

Duvakin: Such an interesting observation!

Ariadna Sosinsky: The skin of her face was quite dark, and the large dark circles around her eyes made them – already very bright– look even brighter.

Duvakin: Were they blue?

Ariadna Sosinsky: No, green, but very light green, especially because of those circles. And her hair had started to turn grey.

Duvakin [*sounding very surprised*]: Turning grey? Already? But she was only thirty-three.

Ariadna Sosinsky: Yes, yes. I noticed that her hair grew greyer and greyer with time, but she never dyed it. She always said she did not want to colour it because she didn't want every man she met to think that she did it for him. She had such pride.

Vladimir Sosinsky: Could you tell how she read her poetry?

Ariadna Sosinsky [*passionately*]: She read very well!

Duvakin: Did you hear her read? Her "Poem of the End," for example?

Ariadna Sosinsky: Yes, I did, and then ... She really loved "Pereulochki" ("The Lanes")[30] back then. At that stage of her life she used to say that if you didn't like her "Pereulochki," you didn't like her! [*She chuckles.*]

Maybe later she changed her mind, but at that time "Pereulochki" was particularly close to her heart. The poem was dedicated to Chabrov, who had a tremendous influence on her life.[31]

Duvakin: Chabrov? Who is that? I don't know him.

Ariadna Sosinsky: He lived in Moscow all his life. They took walks around the city together, and he showed her where the Khlysts used to live.[32] "Pereulochki" was inspired by all those places.

Duvakin: I don't understand a lot in that poem.

---

30 The long poem "Pereulochki" ("The Lanes") was written by Marina Tsvetaeva in Moscow in 1922, before she emigrated from the USSR, and was published in 1923 in the collection *Remeslo.*

31 Alexander Chabrov (1888–1935) was a Russian musician and actor and a close friend of Alexander Scriabin (1871–1915). In the 1920s Chabrov emigrated to France, hoping to establish his own theatre there. Instead he converted to Catholicism and became a priest.

32 See note 39 to dialogue 1.

Ariadna Sosinsky: I loved to read that poem. Sometimes I would read it out loud, and Marina Ivanovna would listen.

Vladimir Sosinsky: Ariadna read her poems very well, it's true. Especially "Mólodets." Later, already in Paris, I remember Tsvetaeva saying that no one read "Mólodets" better than Ariadna did.

Duvakin [*thoughtfully*]: You were immersed in that epoch. Here, at that time life was also saturated with poetry. And you shared a roof with a great poet. I also used to remember many poems back then; they were inscribed in my memory. Could you please recite something from what you heard then?

Ariadna Sosinsky: Well, maybe this one:

> Молодой колоколенкой
> Ты любуешься - в воздухе.
> Голосок у ней тоненький,
> В ясном куполе - звездочки.
>
> Куполок твой золотенький,
> Ясны звезды - под лобиком.
> Голосочек твой тоненький,
> Ты сама колоколенка.
>
> [A young thin belfry
> You admire in the air.
> Its voice is high pitched,
> Stars dot its bright dome.
>
> Your little dome is golden,
> Bright stars peek under your forehead.
> Your little voice is high-pitched,
> You yourself are a belfry.][33]

Duvakin: Oh, I see that you're trying to imitate Tsvetaeva's intonation!

Ariadna Sosinsky: A little.

Duvakin: Her voice was quite low, wasn't it?

Ariadna Sosinsky: Yes, her voice was lower than mine, and she read poetry as if she were singing. I will try to read another one, "Mólodets."

Duvakin: Now that I have a chance to look at your book *Remeslo* (*The Craft*), I see the dedication says, "To my half-daughter and half-sister." What does that mean? Is it dedicated to you and your mother?

---

33 "Молодой колоколенкой" is a short poem that was written by Marina Tsvetaeva in 1918.

Vladimir Sosinsky: No, this is for her [Ariadna].

Ariadna Sosinsky: Yes, it was for me, but at that time I was too young to … [*She pauses.*]

Duvakin: … to be a sister, and too old to be a daughter!

Vladimir Sosinsky: The full dedication was: "To Ariadna Chernova – half-daughter, half-sister."

Duvakin: Please, read another poem.

Ariadna Sosinsky:

> Синь да сгинь – край села,
> Рухнул дуб, трость цела.
> У вдовы у той у трудной
> Дочь Маруся весела.
>
> Как пойдёт с коромыслом –
> Церкви в звон, парни в спор.
> Дочь Маруся румяниста –
> Самой Троице раздор!
>
> [Bluish and expired: on the edge of the village,
> An oak has collapsed, but the cane is intact.
> The gloomy, difficult widow has a daughter,
> Marusya, who is always cheerful.
>
> Every time she goes to fetch water –
> Church bells toll, guys brawl.
> The beautiful Marusya
> Could rupture the Holy Trinity itself!][34]

We spent the summer of 1924 with Marina Ivanovna in the countryside, in a village called Jíloviště. We lived in different houses, but we met every day. In the morning Marina Ivanovna worked, and after lunch she went for a walk with my mother and me. She loved long walks, and she always took a walking stick with her. She liked canes that were thin, long, and beautiful. She could walk for hours and always very fast. And while walking, she would talk about herself and books. It was her favourite time of day – except for the time she was writing, of course, when she …

---

34 This excerpt is from the poem "Mólodets," written in 1922 in Moscow and dedicated to Boris Pasternak.

Duvakin: After lunch, you say?

Ariadna Sosinsky: Yes, after lunch, when she could escape from the house routine, from all errands, when she could walk and talk. I think she never felt comfortable inside – she always wanted to get out, to be free. At the same time she loved to have company while she walked.

She even had designated special people for that; they were not close friends, but she could walk with them and talk. There was a young man, Prince Obolensky – he did not like to talk. So she used to say, "He is like a good dog. I love to walk with him."

Marina Ivanovna told me a lot about her childhood, but you can find those stories in her prose, so there is no need to repeat them here. Like the time when she met Voloshin.[35] She wrote about everything: her childhood, Tarusa, everything.[36]

Duvakin: There is almost nothing written about Sergei Yakovlevich [Efron]. I wanted to ask you, where was he at this time? Why was she alone?

Ariadna Sosinsky: She was not alone. When she lived in Prague, he was also there. We met him very often, and we liked him very much. He was a charming man.

Duvakin: Please tell me about him.

Ariadna Sosinsky: He was absolutely charming, yes, very special, and they complemented each other really well. She was a little impatient, and he was just the opposite, but in a good way. They complemented each other. But in one way they were similar, unfortunately: both were very impractical as far as life and money were concerned.

Sergei Yakovlevich always worked, was always busy, but this work did not bring him any money. If he was the editor of a certain journal, that journal did not pay its employees. He was often called upon to serve as the arbiter in a conflict because everyone liked him a lot. But in terms of money, he was not able to help Marina Ivanovna.

---

35 Maximilian Voloshin (1877–1932) was a Russian Symbolist poet, translator, literary critic, and artist. His translations of French poetry remain unsurpassed to this day. After the revolution Voloshin settled in his family house in Crimea, but times were such that he had to be flexible: to save his private property, which would have been seized and nationalized by the Bolsheviks, Voloshin converted his house into a free bed and breakfast for Soviet writers. Thanks to this move, he was able to continue living and working in his own house until he passed away from a stroke in 1932.

36 Tarusa, or the "Russian Barbizon," as it was called by Russian artists because of its natural beauty and tranquillity, is a small town near Moscow, on the banks of the Oka River. In the 1960s Tarusa became a favourite place for many Russian dissidents, like Joseph Brodsky and Alexander Solzhenitsyn. Svyatoslav Richter, the pianist, built a summer house there. As a child, Marina Tsvetaeva spent her summers in Tarusa.

Duvakin: Where did they meet?

Ariadna Sosinsky: They met in Moscow and got married when both were very young.[37] Sergei Yakovlevich was already sick – he had bad lungs. He liked to tell her stories. There was one, very funny, about how he tried to pass an exam on religion. He didn't know anything but did his best to answer the questions – and passed. Marina Ivanovna loved to listen to his stories.

Even though she was very self-centred, constantly preoccupied with her own thoughts, she knew how to listen to people and always tried to find what was interesting in everybody. In this way, she could create her own unique image of the person that she would always remember. She also enjoyed discussions, especially when there were many people, and they were trying to answer a certain question. She preferred this type of conversations where more than two people were involved.

Duvakin: When people think together.

Ariadna Sosinsky: Yes, think and talk together. And what she especially liked, maybe even too much, were witticisms and smart retorts. She found them exciting.

[*There is a break in the recording.*]

Ariadna Sosinsky: In 1923 my mother and I moved to Paris.

Duvakin: So you moved there before Tsvetaeva did?

Ariadna Sosinsky: Before. And we corresponded with her for a long time. We managed to preserve all her letters to my mother, and we passed them on to TsGALI.[38]

We were afraid to keep them at home: who knows what could happen. We wanted to make sure all the letters – in which she wrote about herself in detail – survived. At that time [when she wrote the letters] her son, "Mur" (Georgy), was born.[39] Life became more difficult for her – another child, you understand, and, of course, there was not enough money.

---

37 Ariadna Sosinsky is misremembering when Tsvetaeva and Efron met: they met in the Crimea at Koktebel on 5 May 1911.

38 TsGALI, now RGALI (Russian State Archive of Literature and Art) is the largest Russian state archive dedicated to literature, art, music, cinema, theatre, and architecture. It was founded in 1941 and has since passed through many difficult times, but its dedicated employees managed to accomplish the impossible: they preserved hundreds of thousands of invaluable documents for future generations of scholars, and they did it in spite of wars, hunger, Stalin's repressions, and Communist dictatorship.

39 Georgy Efron (1925–1944), or "Mur," as Tsvetaeva affectionately called her son, was a talented boy whose life would have been very different had his mother not decided to move to the USSR in 1939. The next five years turned out to be horrific. First, his older sister, Ariadna, and his father were arrested on espionage charges. Then, at the beginning of the war in 1941,

Duvakin: It was her third child, correct?

Ariadna Sosinsky: Yes, but one daughter had died. Her younger daughter died while they were still in Russia. People were starving there then.

Duvakin: And Alya was the oldest?

Ariadna Sosinsky: Alya, Ariadna.

Duvakin: Is she the one who returned to Russia?

Ariadna Sosinsky: Yes. Her name was Ariadna, same as mine. So we moved away and began writing letters to each other. She [Tsvetaeva] described her life in Prague. She said she felt like a convict because she was chained to the stroller, and she had to stop going on her favourite walks because it was impossible to do that with a stroller. Her friends, and also some Czechs, helped her with money for the stroller and some things for the baby, which she would not have been able to buy otherwise.

She was dreaming of coming to Paris. My mother tried to help her. There were many rich people in Paris who sometimes gave money or stipends to writers, but she was not able to find anyone. Nonetheless, Marina Ivanovna finally came, and she stayed in our apartment for some time.

In Paris, Sergei Yakovlevich [Efron] became close to the circle of *yevraziystvo* [Eurasianism].[40] There was such a movement back then. Among them were Pyotr Suvchinsky,[41] and Svyatopolk-Mirsky[42] who later left London to return to the USSR.

Georgy moved with Tsvetaeva to the small town of Elabuga. Soon afterwards, his mentally and physically exhausted mother committed suicide. Georgy volunteered to join the army and was sent to the Eastern Front, where he perished in battle in 1944. He was only nineteen.

40 Eurasianism was a political movement, especially popular in the Russian émigré community during the 1920s. It claimed that Russian civilization should be viewed as belonging not in the "European" or "Asian" categories but instead to the geopolitical concept of "Eurasia." The Bolsheviks embraced this idea, and during the Soviet era history books promoted the notion that Russian people were different from the rest of the world.

41 Pyotr Suvchinsky (1892–1985) was a Russian musician, philosopher, and essayist, who was close friends with such contemporary cultural stars as Igor Stravinsky, Vsevolod Meyerhold, Alexander Blok, and Sergei Prokofiev. Suvchinsky emigrated from Soviet Russia in 1918 and lived a long and fulfilling life in France. In 1937, as a French citizen, he managed to visit the USSR and came back very disappointed by the clear suppression of artistic expression. Among other important documents of the times, his archives hold his correspondence with such significant Soviet writers and musicians as Maxim Gorky, Boris Pasternak, Marina Tsvetaeva, and Marina Yudina.

42 Dimitry Petrovich Svyatopolk-Mirsky (1890–1939) was a prince by birth and a brilliant literary critic. After the revolution he emigrated to England, where he published his famous *History of Russian Literature* (1927). In 1932 he decided to return to Russia, but a few years later he, like many others, was arrested and sent to a labour camp, where he perished.

Duvakin [*excitedly*]**:** I met him! He became close friends with Gorky later.

Ariadna Sosinsky: Yes. He was a very interesting man. Anyway, Marina Ivanovna came to Paris and stayed with us for a while. But her life there was much more difficult. We helped her to organize a reading. Russian writers liked to arrange and attend such events. A lot of tickets were sold, and all the money collected went to her. Tsvetaeva's evening was a huge success. A lot of people came.

Although I have to say that the Russian émigrés' attitude towards Tsvetaeva and Remizov was bad.[43] There were two very different factions: the right-wing one, represented by Bunin[44] and Zaytsev[45] – those who did not accept the USSR altogether – and the group to which Marina Ivanovna and Remizov belonged, who used to read all books coming out of Soviet Russia, by all writers. But for Bunin, for example, those authors simply did not exist. It was enough for him that they were using the new Russian orthography,[46] which all Russian émigrés refused to accept for a very long time.

Duvakin: So you put Bunin in a group together with Merezhkovsky, right?[47]

---

43 Alexey Remizov (1877–1957) was one of the most original Russian writers and painters. His paintings were admired by Pablo Picasso, Marc Chagall, and Wassily Kandinsky. Remizov left Bolshevik Russia in 1922, and he never returned. His life in France was quiet and productive: he was able to write what he believed in and to paint what he wanted. After his death his priceless archive was purchased by the Russian government (2013) and now belongs to the State Museum of Literature in Moscow.

44 Ivan Bunin (1870–1953) was the first Russian writer to receive the Nobel Prize for literature, in 1933. Bunin's articles and diaries of 1917–20 are an important record of Russian life during the years of terror. In May 1918 he moved to Odessa (now in Ukraine) and, two years later, decided to emigrate first to Turkey and then to France, where he lived for the rest of his life. There he became one of the most famous Russian émigré writers. His stories, the novella *Mitina lyubov* (*Mitya's Love*), and the autobiographical novel *Zhizn' Arsenyeva* (*The Life of Arsenyev*) – which he began writing in the 1920s but did not publish until much later – were celebrated by critics and Russian readers abroad as examples of the value of Russian émigré culture. His works, full of nostalgia about the "good, old" pre-revolutionary Russia, are viewed as Russian literary classics.

45 Boris Zaytsev (1881–1972) was one of the last representatives of the silver age of Russian literature. Uncompromising in his attitude towards the Bolsheviks, he emigrated to France where he lived for the rest of his life. A close friend of Anton Chekhov, Ivan Bunin, Vladimir Korolenko, and Leonid Andreyev, Zaytsev was one of the few who, while in emigration, managed not only to preserve his own literary talent but also to develop it to the fullest.

46 The Bolsheviks introduced significant changes to Russian orthography in 1918: they reduced the number of letters in the alphabet and simplified the rules of orthographic writing. The Russian émigré community in Europe refused to recognize the new "Bolshevik" alphabet, and their publications continued to use the former orthography until the 1970s.

47 Dmitry Merezhkovsky (1866–1941) was a prominent novelist, poet, religious thinker, and literary critic in the silver age of Russian literature. One of the founders of Russian Symbolism, he also inaugurated the tradition of the Russian historical, philosophical novel. Merezhkovsky was nominated ten times for the Nobel Prize but never received it.

Ariadna Sosinsky: Yes. Bunin was in that group.

Duvakin: I am sorry to interrupt you. I just wanted to clarify: would it be correct to say that this group shared the monarchist or Kadet political views propagandized by Milyukov's *Poslednie novosti* (*Latest News*)?[48]

Ariadna Sosinsky: Yes, I think so.

Duvakin: Did you meet any of the émigré writers? Bunin, for example?

Ariadna Sosinsky: I met Bunin and Zaytsev. He is a very nice man, but as a writer I do not like him at all.

Duvakin: I read one of his books.

Ariadna Sosinsky: They are too saccharine. But as a person he is very, very nice. His wife, Vera Alekseyevna, was an interesting woman. He was soft and sweet, like a watercolour painting, while she was sharp, direct, and even inappropriate at times. [*She chuckles.*] We met them often. Unfortunately we did not visit Merezhkovsky's place. They were too right wing for us.

Konstantin Balmónt

Duvakin: Where was Balmónt at that time?[49] In Paris?

Ariadna Sosinsky: Yes, in Paris. When we moved to Paris, Marina Ivanovna told us, "You absolutely have to meet Balmónt!"

Duvakin [*surprised*]: Balmónt? That's how she pronounced it?

Ariadna Sosinsky: Yes. This is how he called himself: Balmónt.

---

48 Pavel Milyukov (1859–1943) was a Russian politician and historian, the most prominent member of the Constitutional Democratic Party (known as the Kadets). In 1916, while serving as a member of the state duma, Milyukov accused the Romanov family of treason in favour of Germany, and his scandalous speech was banned from publication. Following the abdication of Nicholas II, Milyukov actively participated in the provisional government. After the Bolshevik coup, he left the country. For almost twenty years he was editor-in-chief of *Poslednie novosti* (*Latest News*), the most popular and influential émigré newspaper, whose last issue, number 7015, came out in 1940, three days before Paris was captured by the Nazis.

49 Konstantin Balmónt (1867–1942) was a prominent Russian Symbolist poet. Being able to speak fluently all major European languages, he worked as a translator and later became a visiting professor at Oxford. After the revolution he emigrated to France, where he lived until his death. Unfortunately, his last years were darkened by a deepening depression and a very difficult financial situation. He died of pneumonia in 1942.

Duvakin [*with excitement*]: Do you know that I managed to record Nina Konstantinovna?[50]

Ariadna Sosinsky: Yes. His daughter was about the same age as me, and we became friends.

Duvakin: With Nina Konstantinovna?

Ariadna Sosinsky: No, with Mirra.[51] Her father [Balmónt] was already old and felt very lonely. No one was interested in his poetry, no one admired him any more, and he, especially during his last years, looked like King Lear. But even though he was already quite old, he was still very interested in women of all ages – from sixteen to sixty. [*She chuckles.*] He kept falling in love, whispered sweet nothings into their ears. He was poor, and his wife was taking good care of him despite his alcoholism. He drank a lot, unfortunately.

He and Tsvetaeva were on informal terms. He called her Marina. Now everyone calls her Marina, but she never liked it. She used to say, "Why do they call me just Marina? Why not use my patronymic?" So even those of us who were her friends always called her Marina Ivanovna.

Duvakin: Perhaps it was just a feature of the Bohemian lifestyle.

Ariadna Sosinsky: I agree. But she did not like it.

Duvakin: Yet Balmónt did it.

Ariadna Sosinsky: He did. He knew her for a long time. He was older, much older. He could be her father. [*She chuckles.*] He dedicated his last years to his poetry, but his later works were very weak. Occasionally he was able to write something interesting, but, in general, his poems were … somewhat old-fashioned, and very few people in the émigré circles cared for them. The new generation of Russian émigrés did not pay much attention to Balmónt.

Tsvetaeva in Paris, and about Mayakovsky

Ariadna Sosinsky: We also met Remizov quite often. His destiny in emigration was very similar to Tsvetaeva's in terms of the kinds of things they wrote, the fact that they both were not understood, and both of them experienced financial difficulties and needed support. Especially Tsvetaeva – she was not understood at all!

---

50 Nina Konstantinovna Balmónt-Bruni (1900–1989) was Konstantin Balmónt's daughter from his second marriage, to Yekaterina Alekseyevna Andreyeva (1867–1952). Although the family was separated later, she always cherished her memories of her beloved father.

51 Mirra (1907–1970) was Balmónt's daughter with his common-law wife, Yelena Konstantinovna Tsvetkovskaya (1880–1943).

Milyukov published her poetry, but mainly because he wanted to help her. But her poetry was not appreciated. Now it is difficult to understand why, but that's how it was.

Duvakin: That happens quite often. I am sorry to interrupt again, Ariadna Viktorovna, but I wanted to ask: are you talking about 1928? Were you in contact with Marina Ivanovna then?

Ariadna Sosinsky: Yes, we were. She lived in Paris, and we did not share living quarters any more, but we met often.

Duvakin: Did she tell you anything about her letter to Mayakovsky?[52]

Ariadna Sosinsky: Yes. She was very upset about what happened afterwards.

Duvakin: I know this letter from 1930. It was shown at Mayakovsky's exhibition. I copied and published it.

Ariadna Sosinsky: This letter cost her the support of many émigrés. They thought that she was corresponding with him, that she was trying to defend him. For many of them everything coming out of the Soviet Union was automatically awful. At least, that was the case for a certain portion of Russian émigrés.

Duvakin: And you, did you hear anything from her directly about Mayakovsky?

Ariadna Sosinsky: Specifically, about Mayakovsky, no, but she read his poetry and liked it a lot.

Duvakin: And you, were you interested in Mayakovsky then?

Ariadna Sosinsky: Very much! Of course. How could it be different? We all saw him and heard him reading when he was in Paris. There were many people there.

Duvakin: Did you go with your mother?

Ariadna Sosinsky [*thoughtfully*]**:** I don't think so. I was already with Vladimir Bronislavovich [Sosinsky] by then.

Duvakin: What year was that? 1929? His most important readings took place in 1925.

Ariadna Sosinsky: I don't know which year it was. Maybe it was 1925.

Duvakin [*excited*]**:** And what do you remember of his performance?

---

52 In 1928 Tsvetaeva wrote an open letter to Vladimir Mayakovsky in which she highly praised his talent and writing. Her fellow émigrés thought that she was insufficiently anti-Soviet, and, following the publication of the letter, she was heavily criticized and unable to print much of her work in the available émigré literary journals.

Ariadna Sosinsky: I remember his unusual voice, his charismatic presence, his remarks to the audience, the elated feeling of something momentous taking place, the power of his voice.

Duvakin: Were you already familiar with his poetry?

Ariadna Sosinsky: Of course.

Duvakin: What had you read, exactly?

Ariadna Sosinsky: Mainly "The Backbone Flute."[53]

Duvakin: Oh, you had read that one? Did you bring it from Russia?

Ariadna Sosinsky: I don't think so. I think we bought it here. It was published by Grzhebin or the Gelikon.[54]

Duvakin: Do you remember anything by heart, by any chance?

Ariadna Sosinsky: I remember "Paris."[55] I think I even had to recite this poem at some event or other. [*She starts reciting, and Duvakin joins her.*]

Билет –
щелк.
Щека –
чмок.
Свисток –
и рванулись туда мы,
куда,
как сельди
в сети чулок,
плывут
кругосветные дамы.
Я хотел бы
жить
и умереть в Париже,
если б не было
такой земли
– *Москва.*

---

53 The long poem "Fleita pozvonochnik" ("The Backbone Flute") was written by Vladimir Mayakovsky in 1915 and dedicated to his lover Lilya Brik. Initially the poem had a different title: "Verses for her." The handwritten edition of this poem (1919) was illustrated by Mayakovsky himself.

54 Zinovii Grzhebin (1877–1929) was a Russian publisher. In 1921 he founded his own publishing house in Berlin. During the few years of its existence Grzhebin managed to publish more than 20 per cent of all the literary works by Russian émigré writers.

55 In fact, this short poem is called "Farewell" and was written by Mayakovsky in 1925, in Paris, where he spent some of the happiest months of his life with Lilya Brik.

[Ticket –
snap.
Cheek –
kiss.
Whistle –
and we rush after
the ladies
who swim
around the world
as herrings
in nets of stockings.
<...>
I would want to live
and die in Paris,
if there were not
such a place as
Moscow.]

Duvakin: That's the poem you recited?

Ariadna Sosinsky: Yes. Although the other émigrés did not like it very much. You know that he [Mayakovsky] wrote many poems in which he made fun of émigrés and the cafés where they used to gather. Do you remember?

Duvakin [*sighs*]**:** Yes, yes.

Ariadna Sosinsky: We had a little group that we called Kochevie [The Nomads]. There were Ladinsky,[56] [Vladimir] Sosinsky, Andreev, Poplavsky – all those young people who did not belong to the circle of Merezhkovsky.

Duvakin: The generation that had grown up in France.

Ariadna Sosinsky: But who promoted Soviet writers. For example, they introduced Babel to the West;[57] they read Leonov.[58]

---

56 Antonin Ladinsky (1895–1961) began writing poetry after he had emigrated to France in 1924. In 1940 he received Soviet citizenship, which later caused him to be deported from France to East Germany. At the end of his life Ladinsky returned to the USSR and published a series of excellent historical novels about Ancient Rome, the Byzantine Empire, and Kievan Rus'.

57 Isaak Babel (1894–1940) was a Russian/Soviet writer, playwright, and translator. He is best known as the author of *Red Cavalry* and *The Odessa Tales* – stories about the life of Jewish gangsters from Odessa. For many years, as Gorky's protégé, he was able to avoid severe punishment for his nonconformist literary practices, but after Gorky's death, Babel was arrested in 1939 on fabricated charges of terrorism and espionage and was executed on 27 January 1940. He was officially rehabilitated in 1954.

58 Leonid Leonov (1899–1994) was a Soviet novelist and playwright whose psychologically complex writing is often compared to that of Dostoevsky. He helped Maxim Gorky found

Duvakin [*sounding surprised*]: Leonov? Really? Did you read *Barsuki* (*The Badgers*)?[59]

Ariadna Sosinsky: Yes, *Barsuki*. It was an excellent novel.

Duvakin: What about Aldanov?[60]

Ariadna Sosinsky: Aldanov never took part in any groups. He was very independent. At the time he was already a renowned writer, and although he was not old at all, we saw him as quite old. We did not run into him often, though. There was another writer – now he is very famous! – Nabokov; he was known as Sirin then,[61] but he didn't belong to our circle.

Duvakin: Nabokov is an émigré writer. I think that now he even writes exclusively in English.

Ariadna Sosinsky: Yes, in English. Anyway, there was a big scandal in the circle we belonged to at that time. But my husband will tell you more about it. This is a story about how he challenged to a duel a writer who had insulted Tsvetaeva and Remizov in one of his articles. He can tell you all about it. [*She turns to Vladimir Sosinsky.*] Would you do it, please?

Meeting Vladimir Sosinsky, and about Relatives

Duvakin: We will certainly ask him about this. But first, when did you two meet?

---

the Union of Soviet Writers in 1934. Leonov managed to maintain the integrity of his talent without "selling" it to the Bolsheviks. His most ambitious novel, *The Pyramid,* a dark nationalistic, religious epic to which he dedicated the last forty years of his life, was published posthumously in 1994.

59 *Barsuki* (*The Badgers*) was Leonid Leonov's first novel, written in 1925. It deals with the impact of the revolution on the Russian village and peasantry.

60 Mark Aldanov (Mark Alexandrovich Landau) (1886–1957) was a Russian émigré writer, essayist, critic, and chemist. His historical novels (about Michelangelo, Byron, Mikhail Lomonosov, Ludwig van Beethoven, and others) have been translated into more than twenty-five languages. He was nominated for the Nobel Prize in Literature multiple times. In 1919 he emigrated to France. Between 1922 and 1924 he lived in Berlin and, between 1941 and 1946, in the United States. After the fall of Communism, Aldanov's works became very popular in Russia.

61 Vladimir Nabokov (1899–1977) was a Russian and American writer who left Russia with his family in 1919 and then lived for a while in Germany and France. After moving to the United States in 1940, Nabokov wrote exclusively in English. For many years he had to make his modest living teaching part-time, first at Wellesley College and then at Cornell University. It was only after the publication of his novel *Lolita* in 1955 that he was able to achieve financial security.

Ariadna Sosinsky: We met in 1925, at Zaytsev's place. I was sixteen at that time, and we were engaged for four or five years before we married.

Duvakin [*laughing*]: That's why you have lived together for forty years!

Ariadna Sosinsky [*laughing too*]: Yes. When we first met, we talked about Tsvetaeva, as a matter of fact.

Duvakin: So, you used to visit Zaytsev?

Ariadna Sosinsky: Often. I knew his wife; she was a very nice woman. Her family was from Moscow, and they knew Remizov from when he was still a child. I think she also knew Pasternak.[62]

Duvakin: She was from a merchant family, wasn't she?

Ariadna Sosinsky: I don't know. But her Russian was incredible – with an excellent Moscow accent. So we were talking about Tsvetaeva. And my mother –

Duvakin: What was your mother's name?

Ariadna Sosinsky: Olga Eliseevna. Her father was Elisey Kolbasin.[63] You know, there is a poem, "My Young Friend, Elisey Kolbasin," by Turgenev. He was a friend of Turgenev,[64] although much younger.

Duvakin [*sounding very surprised*]: Elisey Kolbasin was her father?

Ariadna Sosinsky: Yes. And her uncle, Dmitry, is described in *Fathers and Sons* as Kirsanov.

Duvakin: Pavel Petrovich Kirsanov?[65]

Ariadna Sosinsky: Yes. We all knew that Turgenev based the character of Kirsanov on my uncle: his pink palms, small hands.

Duvakin [*excited*]: And the ring with the sphinx?

Ariadna Sosinsky: And the ring too. Then a mysterious *amazonka* [an Amazon woman] one day just appeared in his life – that really happened! And he lost all his fortune because of her.

---

62 About Boris Pasternak, see note 38 to dialogue 1.

63 Elisey Kolbasin (1831–1885) was a Russian writer and literary critic.

64 Ivan Turgenev (1818–1883) was a Russian novelist, short-story writer, poet, playwright, translator, and popularizer of Russian literature in the West. His short-story collection entitled *Rasskazy okhotnika* (*A Sportsman's Sketches*, 1852) was a milestone in Russian realism, and his novels *Rudin* (1856), *Dvoryanskoe gnezdo* (*Home of the Gentry*, 1859), *Nakanune* (*On the Eve*, 1860), and *Ottsy i deti* (*Fathers and Children*, 1962) are considered to be major works of nineteenth-century Russian fiction.

65 Pavel Petrovich Kirsanov is a protagonist in Ivan Turgenev's novel *Fathers and Sons*.

Duvakin: Did they come from the merchant class?

Ariadna Sosinsky: No. She came from nobility, and her last name, Kolbasin, comes not from "sausage" [Russian, *kolbasa*] but from the Ukrainian Kolba. [*She laughs.*] It has nothing to do with sausage.

Duvakin: Aha! I understand now: she was the daughter of Elisey Kolbasin, a friend of Turgenev, and she married Viktor Chernov.[66] By the way, was he Jewish?

Ariadna Sosinsky: Oh, no! He was from Volga.[67] He was one of the founders of the Socialist Revolutionary Party. Later, after we had already moved back to Russia, my parents separated, and I lived with my mother.

Duvakin: Oh, I see. So you weren't living with your father then?

Ariadna Sosinsky: No. He had left my mother. When we arrived, he already had another wife.

Duvakin: So he did not participate in all the literary discussions?

Ariadna Sosinsky: No. He didn't study literature, but he understood Tsvetaeva deeply and was always surprised by the fact that they [the émigrés] could not understand her. He used to say that every real Russian person who could sing Russian songs (and he himself sang beautifully, he had a wonderful voice) should be able to understand her. Her poetry is made the same way Russian songs are. That's why I also can't understand how other people don't appreciate her poetry.

Duvakin: That's great! I didn't know that Viktor Chernov was such a great admirer of Tsvetaeva's work. It's nice to know that.

Ariadna Sosinsky: Oh, yes. He loved poetry and even translated Verhaeren.[68] He had a particular taste in poetry, a specific taste, maybe slightly political. [*She laughs.*] That is why he loved Nekrasov,[69] Verhaeren.

---

66 Viktor Chernov (1873–1952) was a writer, a revolutionary, and the father of Ariadna Sosinsky, his daughter by his second wife, Olga Kolbasina (1886–1964). Chernov, originally a staunch defender of the revolution, was terribly disappointed when the political power in Russia ended up in the hands of the Bolsheviks. He was forced to leave the Soviet Union forever and, after moving from country to country, finally settled in New York.

67 Volga River is the longest river (2,200 miles) in Europe and one of the five great rivers of Russia. The name Volga first appears in the works of Herodotus. The river flows through central Russia and into the Caspian Sea and is widely regarded as the national river of Russia. Eleven of the twenty largest cities in Russia, including the capital, Moscow, are located in the Volga's watershed.

68 About Émile Adolphe Gustave Verhaeren, see note 43 to dialogue 2.

69 Nikolay Nekrasov (1821–1878) was a pre-eminent Russian poet and publisher whose influential journal *Sovremennik* (*The Contemporary*) was the first to publish the works of such prominent Russian writers as Leo Tolstoy, Fyodor Dostoevsky, and Ivan Turgenev. He died

Duvakin: Yes, their poetry had certain folkloric elements.

Ariadna Sosinsky: Yes, folkloric elements. Maybe for that reason he understood Tsvetaeva so well. But I am afraid we lost track of what we were talking about.

Life in Emigration

Duvakin: This is all very interesting indeed. What really fascinates me is that the émigrés of my generation – those born in the 1910s – still felt connected to Russia as adults.

Ariadna Sosinsky: Yes, they felt connected.

Duvakin: And this generation that was not born in emigration and grew up there, they didn't feel themselves entirely foreign, so to speak.

Ariadna Sosinsky: At least, I have never felt like a foreigner. My sister, for example, even managed to save her Soviet passport.

Duvakin: Is she here?

Ariadna Sosinsky: No, she stayed in France. But she and I, we never felt ourselves close to those émigré circles ... [*She sighs.*] But we've never felt ourselves entirely French either. The French, they always keep to themselves. Sometimes they even say about themselves, "We are the Chinese of Europe; we live surrounded by the Great Wall of China."

Marina Ivanovna, who knew French perfectly and had longed to live in France, never did manage to fit in there at all.

Duvakin [*surprised*]**:** Is that true?

Ariadna Sosinsky: It is. French writers, in general, live like the Olympic gods – even if the writer does not happen to be a very significant one, like Maurois.[70]

Duvakin: Were you in contact with them?

Ariadna Sosinsky: We were not. Marina Ivanovna, in fact, had some connections, more than anyone, because she liked to know people. But she didn't fit in

---

from cancer at the age of fifty-six. In his eulogy, Dostoevsky called Nekrasov the third greatest Russian poet after Alexander Pushkin and Mikhail Lermontov.

70 André Maurois (born Émile Salomon Wilhelm Herzog) (1885–1967) was a French writer who specialized in the genre of the "novelized" biography. He wrote novels about many important figures like Alexandre Dumas, Victor Hugo, Byron, Ivan Turgenev, and Honoré de Balzac. While living in the United States during the Second World War, Maurois taught at the University of Kansas and wrote a series of excellent novelized biographies of Frédéric Chopin, Dwight Eisenhower, Benjamin Franklin, and George Washington.

with the French lifestyle at all: her "immensity in their measured world" – it was absolutely foreign to the French, who love balance.

Duvakin: Harmony?

Ariadna Sosinsky: And harmony too. If she talked about anything, she talked about it with passion, very intensely, very powerfully – which would never happen in a French salon, where you are expected to chat light-heartedly about this and that. She loved the "Old France," the Vendée,[71] the memoirs about Napoleon. She had a few friends among those old French ladies who, like her, loved the Old France. But she did not fit in in the modern France – with its snobbery and everything. She could not. And even her French (she knew the language perfectly!) was a little archaic.

Duvakin: From the nineteenth century.

Ariadna Sosinsky: Now the language has changed a lot.

Duvakin: Changed?

Ariadna Sosinsky: Very much so. And during the last years, even more. Now there is a big American influence, and the language keeps changing.

Duvakin: I can see now that she [Tsvetaeva] must have been very lonely there. It seems that there were both political and cultural reasons for that. Would you agree?

Ariadna Sosinsky: Her character also played an important role in that.

Duvakin: Did she have a difficult character?

Ariadna Sosinsky: Very difficult.

Duvakin: And Efron? Was he in Paris with her?

Ariadna Sosinsky: He was, but they were – he loved her a lot, admired her, never got angry with her even when she did not treat people properly. He always tried to explain that Marina Ivanovna was an unusual woman, that she was a genius, and because of that, we all had to forgive her. For some reason he liked to say, "She is like Beethoven." I don't know why he compared her to Beethoven.

Duvakin: He used to be an army officer. What did he do before that?

Ariadna Sosinsky: He tried theatre acting for a while. He was from a fairly wealthy family and was just a very nice, very kind man.

---

71 Vendée is a department (county) in western France, bordering the Atlantic Ocean. The region takes its name from the Vendée River. It was one of the first counties formed after the French Revolution in 1790, and within three years it had become a centre of opposition to the corrupt revolutionary government.

I do not know much about his family, but he always tried to do good – for the community, for the people. Then he became a Communist.

Duvakin [*very surprised*]: Did he? When?

Ariadna Sosinsky: At first he embraced Eurasianism.[72]

Duvakin: So he forgave her everything – even being unfaithful?

Ariadna Sosinsky: Yes. He understood that she was a poet, and this inner poet had different demands. Do you understand?

But in the last years she stopped having affairs and tried to find outlets for her passions in her personal correspondence. Her addressees were the product of her imagination, and she wrote them magnificent letters, even dedicated poetry to them. And when she'd meet them in person, she'd discover, sadly, that they were nothing like how she had imagined them.

Duvakin: Did you ever see her together with Bely?[73]

Ariadna Sosinsky: My father did, but I did not. My father had some of his books, with personal inscriptions.

Duvakin: She [Tsvetaeva] wrote a brilliant essay about Bely.

Ariadna Sosinsky: Someone who can tell you a lot about Bely is Vadim Leonidovich Andreyev. He met him many times.

Duvakin [*laughs*]: How can I talk to him?

Ariadna Sosinsky: He is going to come to Moscow soon.

Duvakin [*sounding very excited*]: Oh, please introduce me to him!

Ariadna Sosinsky: I certainly will. He comes to Moscow every year or two.

The Duel in Defence of Marina Tsvetaeva

Duvakin: Let Vladimir Bronislavovich tell about the duel in Tsvetaeva's defence.

Ariadna Sosinsky: Such things happened a lot in literary circles at the time.

---

72 See note 40 to this dialogue.

73 Andrey Bely (b. Boris Nikolaevich Bugaev) (1880–1934) was a Russian writer, literary critic, poet, and one of the leaders of Russian Symbolism and Modernism. He was a close friend of Alexander Blok, Valery Bryusov, and Osip Mandelstam. He died in 1934 from a heart attack, which he had predicted twenty-five years earlier in his work *Pepel* (*The Ashes*). His unique ornamental prose exercised an enormous influence on an entire generation of Russian writers. Nabokov considered Bely's *Petersburg* (1913, 1922) to be one of the four greatest novels of the twentieth century.

Vladimir Sosinsky: After many years of continuous efforts, my mother-in-law, Olga Eliseevna Chernova-Kolbasina [Ariadna's mother], managed to bring Marina Ivanovna to Paris. It was difficult, especially financially.

Duvakin: So you met Marina in 1924?

Vladimir Sosinsky: Yes.

Duvakin: And you were engaged for four or five years before getting married? And Vadim Leonidovich Andreyev introduced you to each other?[74]

Vladimir Sosinsky: Correct. So, Olga Eliseevna managed to bring Marina Tsvetaeva to Paris. One of her distant relatives worked for the French government as a minister of health; he probably helped.

So, when the Efron-Tsvetaeva family arrived, they occupied one of the rooms in the house of my fiancée, Ariadna. And Vadim Andreyev and I went to visit them frequently.

Duvakin: So you met Marina Ivanovna in the house of your fiancée, correct?

Vladimir Sosinsky: Yes. Marina Ivanovna made a big impact on all of us, as a poet and as a person.

Duvakin: You can tell us anything you want. I would like to finish our conversation about Tsvetaeva today.

Vladimir Sosinsky: It'd be easier if I just told you what happened about three years after I met Tsvetaeva.

There was a journal, *Novyi dom* (*New Home*), that was published monthly under the editorship of Merezhkovsky, Gippius, Khodasevich,[75] and Berberova.[76] This journal offended Marina Ivanovna gravely.

---

74 Vadim Andreyev (1902–1976) was the son of Leonid Andreyev (1871–1919), the first Expressionist in Russian prose. Andreyev spent most of his life abroad, mainly in France and the United States. During Khrushchev's "thaw" he started his frequent visits to the USSR and in 1964 managed to smuggle out the first two volumes (as microfilms) of *The Gulag Archipelago* by Alexander Solzhenitsyn to the West – a very dangerous task.

75 Vladislav Khodasevich (1886–1939) was a highly influential Russian poet and literary critic. He emigrated to Berlin in 1922, where he published penetrating analyses of contemporary Soviet literature and helped propel Vladimir Nabokov's literary career. Khodasevich's book *Necropolis* (1939) is invaluable for its portrayals of many prominent Soviet poets and writers, including Maxim Gorky and Alexander Blok.

76 Nina Berberova (1901–1993) was a Russian writer and the common-law wife of Vladislav Khodasevich. She chronicled the lives of Russian exiles in Paris in her short stories and novels and corresponded with many of the leading literary figures of the period. In 1958 Berberova took a position teaching Russian literature at Yale University; later she moved to Princeton, where she stayed until her retirement in 1971. Much of Berberova's early literary

Duvakin: How did they offend her?

Vladimir Sosinsky: Well, she was nearly called a prostitute in an article published there.

Duvakin [*surprised*]**:** Was it a special article written about her?

Vladimir Sosinsky: Yes. It was a review of her book *Remeslo* (*Craft*).[77] The author, paraphrasing, compared one of her poems to a brothel. In the same article he heavily criticized Remizov as well.

Duvakin: Sorry to interrupt you again, but I want to make it clear for myself: what was the essence of those charges? Was it immorality or political prostitution?

Vladimir Sosinsky: It was not political. They meant in a sense that she portrays herself as a woman obsessed with erotic love. You remember her "Poema gory" and "Poema kontsa"?[78] They said, "Look at this love-struck poetess, who dares to write such things!" Then they took some lines out of context – and there it was: immorality. That was, in essence, the idea of that article.

Duvakin [*sounding angry*]**:** What they did was obscene!

Vladimir Sosinsky: I agree, their tone was obscene.

Duvakin [*sounding very satisfied*]**:** I've never heard about this episode.

Vladimir Sosinsky: In another article in the same issue they attacked Alexey Remizov as a poet. He was accused of plagiarizing from dead authors, of being a robber and a scoundrel. They said he stole from the protopope [archpriest] Avvakum,[79] that he plagiarized Russian fairy tales, Afanasyev,[80] and so on. At

---

archive (1922–50) is held at Stanford University. Her later literary archive (after 1950) is at Yale University.

77 The book *Remeslo* (1923) was published in Berlin by the Gelikon publishing house. It was heavily criticized by the Russian expatriates.

78 See note 21 to this dialogue.

79 Avvakum Petrov (1620–1682) was a Russian archpriest (a protopope was a priest of high rank in the Orthodox Church), a leader of the Old Believers, and a conservative clergyman who incurred a serious crisis in the history of the Russian church by separating from the Russian Orthodox Church. Notorious for his constant polemics with Patriarch Nikon, and even the Russian tsar, Avvakum spent many years in exile and in prison. Eventually he was burnt at the stake – a rare sentence in Russia. Avvakum was also a prolific and skilful writer. He left about forty brilliantly written theological works that are now viewed as examples of early Russian literature.

80 Alexander Afanasyev (1821–1876) was a Russian ethnographer who collected and published more than six hundred Russian fairy and folk tales, one of the largest collections of such

one literary evening I considered it my duty to defend Marina Ivanovna. There was this young poets' union –

Duvakin: Kochevie?

Vladimir Sosinsky: No, Kochevie [The Nomads] was another organization that we founded together with Mark Slonim and Vadim Andreyev.[81] We wanted it to serve as a counterweight to Zelyonaya lampa [The Green Lamp],[82] which was led by Gippius and Merezhkovsky. The Union of Young Poets was another special group that organized performances once every two weeks. It was a professional organization whose aim was to help poets.

Duvakin: And what kind of performances were those?

Vladimir Sosinsky: Literary ones, of course.

Duvakin: And those evenings, were they open to anyone?

Vladimir Sosinsky: Absolutely open!

Duvakin: Did they sell tickets?

Vladimir Sosinsky: No tickets. They followed the French style: people would go to a café, find a table, and pay only for beer or wine.

Duvakin [*surprised*]: And that was all?

Vladimir Sosinsky: That was all.

Duvakin [*puzzled*]: Then I don't understand. How was it a professional organization?

Vladimir Sosinsky: The Union of Young Poets was professional in the sense that if one of its young members got into a difficult financial situation, others would help him.

---

texts in the world. Some of his tales were interpreted as "unorthodox" by the Most Holy Synod, while others were viewed as obscene; as a result they were banned in his homeland and had to be published in Switzerland. The largest collection of folk-tales, comparable only to that of the Brothers Grimm, had to wait for almost 150 years before it was allowed to be published in full in Russia.

81 Mark Slonim (1894–1976) was a Russian-American writer, literary critic, and translator. After the revolution he emigrated to Europe, where he productively participated in the cultural life of the Russian expatriate intelligentsia. In 1941 he moved to the United States, where he taught Russian literature at Sarah Lawrence College in New York for almost twenty years and continued to write books.

82 Zelyonaya lampa (The Green Lamp) (1927–39) society was founded in Paris by Zinaida Gippius and Dmitry Merezhkovsky. The society met on Sundays, and only carefully selected guests were invited to attend. All visitors had to pay a small entrance fee. Ivan Bunin, Boris Zaytsev, Mark Aldanov, and Alexey Remizov frequently attended those gatherings.

Duvakin: But how?

Vladimir Sosinsky: They would visit the wealthiest members of the Russian community and ask them for money.

Duvakin: I see. At first I thought that those evenings were meant to generate some revenue.

Vladimir Sosinsky: At one of these gatherings I announced that I wanted to slap the editors of *Novyi dom* (*New Home*) in the face. Antonin Ladinsky, who was presiding that evening, turned off the lights. It was a big scandal.

Duvakin [*laughing*]: I bet they wanted to rough you up!

Vladimir Sosinsky: I am sure of that. [*He chuckles.*] Anyway, the next time I went there, the youngest member of the editorial board, Yuri Terapiano[83] (who, by the way, later became a well-known literary critic), came up to me and slapped me in the face. Naturally, we had a fight.

Duvakin: A fight?

Vladimir Sosinsky: Yes, a fight. Anyway, I challenged him to the duel. We all still lived by the traditions of the nineteenth century.

Duvakin: And all of you there were former officers, correct?

Vladimir Sosinsky: I was a former junior officer.

Duvakin: And you were also a nobleman, correct?

Vladimir Sosinsky: A baron, but that doesn't matter. The interesting part is what happened next. I was unexpectedly summoned to the police department. There the commissar, grinning, shows me a petition signed by Merezhkovsky, Gippius, Khodasevich, Berberova, and some other people requesting that I be expelled from France because of my improper behaviour – because I had challenged someone to a duel, an activity that had been banned in France for a long time.

Duvakin: Banned? I didn't know.

Vladimir Sosinsky: Anyway, the police commissar smiled at me and said, "Did you read it?" I read it, signed a form, and the matter was over. But I didn't let

83 Yuri Terapiano (1892–1980) was a Russian literary critic and poet. In 1920, when the Bolsheviks murdered his family, Terapiano joined the White Army and later emigrated to France. He lived a long life, having interesting encounters with many significant cultural figures of the century. He wrote a book about his experiences abroad, which constitutes his major contribution to literature, *Vstrechi* (*The Encounters*, 1953).

Yuri Terapiano off the hook so easily: for a whole year afterwards, every time we met, I slapped him in the face! When Marina Ivanovna found out about this, she sent me, as a present, her silver ring with the Vendée's coat of arms. The Vendée was our symbol of honour and nobility.

Duvakin [*surprised*]: Oh! You were clearly on the side of the royalist Vendée then, as far as the French Revolution is concerned. Correct?

Vladimir Sosinsky: Yes.

Duvakin: That is all history, of course.

The Relationship between Tsvetaeva and Sosinsky

Vladimir Sosinsky: In one of the letters that Marina Ivanovna wrote to me, she said: "When I am no longer on this earth, you will judge me not by my deeds but by my intent. The deeds will be forgotten, and only the intent will be remembered. I will then radiate more light than I do now, because there will be no more notebooks. There will be no more notebooks staring at me with their empty pages and demanding food! There – I will be free from those pages. And then you will understand that I was much better than you can imagine."

We all loved Marina Ivanovna. But we (she and I) never had a romantic relationship; we were not even close friends. Because, no matter how much we all admired her poetry, we were always disappointed in our personal interactions. Why? She was harsh and sardonic, and sometimes her actions were … unseemly.

I understand that she wanted us not to judge her by her actions, but still … She was kind to Daniil Reznikov;[84] she may have been in love with him, even. But she loved many men, sent them letters in which she professed her love. They were figments of her imagination, created according to her needs.

She was, figuratively speaking, thirsty for people, especially for men who were younger, and this was noticeable in her behaviour, and we didn't like it.

There is an anthology of Soviet poetry, recently published in New York, edited by Olga Carlisle.[85] If you get a chance to look at it … that book was disparaged in *Literaturnaya gazeta* not too long ago.[86] [*He sighs.*]

---

84 Daniil Reznikov (1904–1970) was a Russian literary critic and poet. He arrived in France with the first wave of emigration and never returned to Russia. He wrote a book about his meetings with Marina Tsvetaeva: *Vecher Mariny Tsvetaevoy: Biografiya odnogo litsa* (*An Evening of Marina Tsvetaeva: Biography of One Person*), (Moscow: Agraf, 2003).

85 Olga Carlisle, *Poets on Street Corners: Portraits of Fifteen Russian Poets*. New York: Random House, 1968.

86 *Literaturnaya gazeta* (*The Literary Gazette*) was a popular weekly newspaper published in the Soviet Union starting in 1929. It came out every Wednesday, and the intelligentsia of

Duvakin: Was it Pertsov?[87]

Vladimir Sosinsky: Yes, Pertsov, of course, in *Literaturnaya gazeta* on 28 May. The essay about Tsvetaeva in that anthology ends like this: "We were so close with Tsvetaeva that my uncle even challenged to a duel a critic who had dared to offend her."

Duvakin [*surprised*]: Are you that uncle?

Vladimir Sosinsky: Yes, that's me. Olga Carlisle is my niece – Vadim Andreyev's daughter.

Duvakin [*very surprised*]: Oh, how interesting!

Vladimir Sosinsky: I'll tell you another interesting episode that I have never told anyone. It'll show you another side of Marina Ivanovna, a side that is still unknown, perhaps. One day Marina Ivanovna asked me to introduce her to Alexander Fedorovich Kerensky.[88] He was the editor of the newspaper *Dni* (*The Days*) back then,[89] and I was the secretary of *Volya Rossii*, which also was an SR publication. I went to him, and we agreed that he'd come to Chernov's to meet Marina Ivanovna. This Alexander Fedorovich Kerensky was … [*he chuckles*] a very peculiar character.

Duvakin: Is he still alive?

Vladimir Sosinsky: He is. That day we took the subway to Chernov's place. Marina Ivanovna met him at the door, together with Olga Eliseevna [mother of Ariadna Sosinsky], as the two hostesses. They brought him inside, seated him at a table with wine, etc. They started talking. I have to tell you that the

---

the entire country eagerly awaited each issue. Despite the difficult political climate, *Literaturnaya gazeta* dared to tackle the most burning political, cultural, and literary questions. Today it remains among the most popular newspapers in Russia.

87 Viktor Pertsov (1898–1980) was a Soviet literary critic who became famous for writing the "canonical" biography of Vladimir Mayakovsky, in which many facts of his life were distorted or erased in order to please the Communist regime. Pertsov was also one of the most vicious critics of Boris Pasternak's *Doctor Zhivago*.

88 Alexander Fedorovich Kerensky (1881–1970) served as head of the provisional government between the 1917 February and October revolutions. A lawyer by training, he knew how to speak well but did not know how to govern. Although he was warned many times about the coup being prepared by the Bolsheviks against the newly born Russian democracy, he failed to prevent it. When the Bolsheviks surrounded the Winter Palace, Kerensky escaped in the American ambassador's car. He fled to Finland, then to France, and then, in 1940, to the United States, where he taught for some time at Stanford University. He died at the age of eighty-nine in New York City.

89 *Dni* (*The Days*) was a weekly newspaper published by the Russian émigrés first in Berlin, and then in Paris from 1928 to 1933.

conversation was most unusual: Alexander Fedorovich was spewing some nonsense, and Marina Ivanovna immediately took that nonsense, converted it into another nonsense, and returned that nonsense back to him! Two seemingly intelligent people were talking *Bog znaet o chem* [only God knows what about]![90]

They started to talk about Bunin. Suddenly my friend Selivanov, a cab driver, said: "Bunin? What is Bunin? Give me a bottle of red wine, and I'll write you a short story that'll be better than the one he recently published in the *Poslednie novosti*!"[91]

Of course, such a statement had no value at all, but Marina Ivanovna decided to treat this seriously: "Alexander Fedorovich! Just think of what he is saying: with a bottle of red wine he could write better than Bunin! Isn't it amazing?" And Alexander Fedorovich readily responded, "Yes! Let's give him a bottle!"

Anyway, some real nonsense was discussed at length as if it were wisdom, and with serious faces.

Duvakin: I think it was symptomatic of that literary environment.

Vladimir Sosinsky [*sounding annoyed*]**:** Anyway, then Alexander Fedorovich drank a little more and started to tell us what he thought of the new generation of Russian émigrés: "*Chert znaet chto* [Devil knows what it is]! Just a little while ago I met one idiot who told me that now there are many talented writers and poets in the Soviet Union, and we have to change our attitude to the USSR, and so on and so on." That is, he repeated what I had said to him just three hours before while we were travelling on the subway.

Duvakin [*laughing*]**:** That is, the idiot was you!

Vladimir Sosinsky: Right. That idiot was now sitting next to him at the table. This illustrates the kind of behaviour Marina Ivanovna and Alexander Fedorovich were capable of.

The next day there was another visitor: Prince Svyatopolk-Mirsky,[92] the brilliant literary critic and historian who made his reputation at Oxford, and then his fame spread around the world.

---

90 Here and later in the text, to capture the flavour of the original conversations, we will preserve some Russian idiomatic expressions and will provide their closest translation.

91 *Posliednie novosti* (*Latest News*) was the most influential Russian émigré newspaper published in Paris from 1920 to 1940. Pavel Milyukov served as chief editor of the newspaper for almost twenty years. Many works by Ivan Bunin, Vladimir Nabokov, Mark Aldanov, Dmitry Merezhkovsky, Boris Zaytsev, and other Russian authors were published in the literature section of the Thursday issues.

92 About Dimitry Petrovich Svyatopolk-Mirsky, see note 42 to this dialogue.

Duvakin: Didn't he become a Marxist later?

Vladimir Sosinsky: Yes, he became a Marxist and returned to the USSR. So, when he came, Olga Eliseevna opened the door and showed him Marina Ivanovna's quarters. He enters into Tsvetaeva's room, and Olga Eliseevna, who happened to be near the door, hears the following exchange. The Prince asked, "Who is that nice woman who opened the door for me?" And Tsvetaeva answered, "Oh, do not pay her attention. That's my landlady."

Duvakin [*surprised*]: She said this about …

Vladimir Sosinsky: Marina Ivanovna said this about Olga Eliseevna – the woman who helped her come to France, allowed her to live in her own apartment, did not charge her a penny for living in her house. Such an attitude towards her best friend! Well, those things bothered us a lot.

Duvakin: It was a sickness, as we now know. It's very good that you told me about it.

Vladimir Sosinsky: I told you because it would never be possible to say it in public. Let it be, and maybe someday, in the future …

Duvakin: It's very good that you told me about it. It is a sickness, what you just told me – not an expression of a person's moral quality but a borderline psychiatric condition and has to be treated as such. Marina Tsvetaeva will always be a great poet, and this will not blemish her art. What stories one could tell about Dostoevsky!

Vladimir Sosinsky: I agree with you. Absolutely.

Duvakin: I could tell you similar stories about Mayakovsky – to whom I dedicated much of my life. In his personal life he was always very, even extremely polite, but on stage, well, that was different. Just recently I recorded reminiscences about several strange, unprovoked things that he did.

Tsvetaeva and Her Children

Duvakin: Do you have anything else to say about Tsvetaeva?

Vladimir Sosinsky: Marina Ivanovna was in a permanent trouble, but she behaved in a way that made those around her feel they had an obligation to help. And she accepted that help without showing any signs of sincere gratitude.

Duvakin: She took it for granted.

Vladimir Sosinsky: Yes, for granted. In this regard, the life of her daughter [Ariadna Efron] was … [*with passion:*] Marina Ivanovna simply exploited her!

Duvakin [*sadly*]: I didn't know that.

Vladimir Sosinsky: She thought that Alya [Ariadna] had to take care of Mur [Georgy Efron, Tsvetaeva's son] because Marina Ivanovna needed to write.

Duvakin: I understand.

Vladimir Sosinsky: So the girl of ten, twelve, fourteen years, who was growing up in front of our eyes, was abused by her own mother. Not only did she have to be a babysitter for her younger brother, but she also had to do all the housekeeping. But that was simply too much for her. And because of it, she was not able to go to school.

She was a very talented girl who wrote poetry from the time she was seven, and drew beautifully. She had the right to have an education but did not get any because her mother knew only one thing: she had to write. Because of that, she could not take care of Mur; so Mur became Alya's responsibility.

Duvakin: But, nonetheless, Alya became a very educated person.

Vladimir Sosinsky: Yes, but it happened later. She was a very gentle, very kind child who liked to play. When she grew up, she also became quite a difficult character; she most certainly inherited that from Tsvetaeva.

And if we think for a minute about what kind of a person Mur was … He didn't even come to the funeral of his mother.

But Tsvetaeva, if she ever loved anyone, she loved Mur, and only him. Not Sergei Yakovlevich [Efron], not Alya – but Mur, who never showed her any gratitude.

Mur was unfair to her to the end. We saw this happening even when they both were still in Paris. We tried to help her, but it was difficult: she always suffered quietly. On the other hand, she managed to ostracize so many people in her interactions with publishing houses and wealthy donors who wanted to help her …

Duvakin: Everything that you say is very important because it has not been recorded anywhere. And Tsvetaeva's biography hasn't been written yet.

Vladimir Sosinsky: Not yet.

Duvakin: But some day it'll be written.

Vladimir Sosinsky: Someday, of course. I remember another thing: for a while she lived near the sea, in her favourite Vendée. She sent me letters from there – magnificent letters! She described the sea amazingly, in prose and in poetry. She even dedicated one of the poems about the sea to me. I still have it.

Then she started writing about her landlords, who were in love with her. But what was interesting is that just a few weeks later those "wonderful people" melted into nothing, turned into a witch and a sorcerer, the most despicable people in the world, and she, following a public scandal, left their house. I have kept all those letters.

Duvakin: I assume they were simple people?

Vladimir Sosinsky: Yes, very simple people who got fed up with her for being so disorganized, for not knowing how to cook a simple meal, for not keeping her room tidy. In short, for not knowing how to handle daily life – which was very characteristic of Marina Ivanovna.

Duvakin: But Alya, despite everything, still loved her, would you agree?

Vladimir Sosinsky: Alya? At that time, it was hard to say if she loved her, but now she adores her. She adores her so much that she doesn't allow anyone to get close to her memory. She cannot share her mother's love with anyone. Recently, a young man arrived from Ural with a beautiful stone, which he wanted to place in the graveyard of Tarusa,[93] where Marina Ivanovna always wanted to be buried. Alya didn't even want to talk to him. She seems to hate all people who love Tsvetaeva.

Where is it all coming from? From the same source: her mother. She doesn't allow others to love her [Tsvetaeva]; she wants that love all for herself. That is why she presents Sergei Yakovlevich as the perfect father, and her family as the perfect family: husband, wife, two children – and no one else. But there always was someone else!

Duvakin: What about Sergei Yakovlevich? Did he have someone else?

Vladimir Sosinsky: Possibly. I don't know for sure, but the family was far from perfect in this regard. She is determined to clean up the family history, so that the hero of "Poema gory" and "Poema kontsa" would just be a fantasy. So I am afraid, I want this record to stay with you.

Duvakin: It's not going anywhere.

Vladimir Sosinsky: From Paris I brought a stack of letters – maybe fifty wonderful letters, among the best prose Marina Ivanovna has ever produced – her letters to Konstantin Rodzevich,[94] the hero of the "Poema

93 See note 36 to this dialogue.

94 Konstantin Rodzevich (1895–1988) was a friend of Sergei Efron and a lover of his wife, Marina Tsvetaeva, when they all lived in Prague in 1921–3 and later when they lived in Paris. A poet, sculptor, and translator, he was fluent in multiple European languages, which helped to save his life while he was imprisoned in the Sachsenhausen concentration camp. Some scholars believe that Rodzevich was Mur's father.

kontsa" and "Poema gory." When he found out that I was going to the Soviet Union [in 1960], he came to Paris (he lives somewhere in the countryside) and gave me all these letters to give to Alya Tsvetaeva. He gave them to me to preserve as an archive, and I read them all. The letters were fascinating documents, pure literature, absolutely unique and more interesting than "Poema kontsa" or "Poema gory." Much more powerful, I can tell you that for sure.

It was with a heavy heart that I passed these letters to Alya Tsvetaeva. I knew she would burn them.

Duvakin [*surprised*]: And you didn't make copies?

Vladimir Sosinsky: No, I didn't have the right to do that.

Duvakin: But did you at least give her letters to you to TsGALI?[95]

Vladimir Sosinsky: Yes. The letters that she wrote to me – there are about thirty of them – I wanted them to be freely accessible to anyone. But the letters that Tsvetaeva wrote to Olga Eliseevna or Ariadna Sosinsky, Alya Tsvetaeva put a hold on them for twenty-five years.[96]

Duvakin: Well, she had the right to do that, as a daughter.

Vladimir Sosinsky: These letters will have tremendous value for all future Tsvetaeva scholars. She has never been totally open with anyone. She loved to slander sometimes – that was a bad habit of hers. These letters will reveal a lot about her inner world. But I still love her dearly. I am devoted to her muse. I love her poetry more than anyone else's. For me, in all Russian poetry there are only a few real poets, and Tsvetaeva is certainly one of them.

Duvakin [*emotionally*]: This is such an important material for history. Thank you.

How Tsvetaeva Read Poetry, and about Her Appearance

Duvakin: Now, I will ask you a different question: did she ever recite poetry in front of you?

Vladimir Sosinsky: Very often. Once she wrote something new, she would immediately read it out loud. When she was reading, she used to chant, and pause

95 See note 38 to this dialogue.

96 The conversation took place in 1969, and Ariadna Efron had put a twenty-five-year hold on these letters in 1962. The letters are now published.

after each stanza, closing her eyes. Most of the time she recited from memory and kept swaying slightly as she did that.

She would sit in a chair, with her elbow on her knee. A painter would have found her pose very interesting: her lines were sharp, angular. There was not a single soft line in her entire appearance; even her nose was pointed, her cheekbones were pronounced, and her neck had a visible Adam's apple. Everything was sharp. You got the impression that she was not at peace with this world.

Was she beautiful? In her youth perhaps she was, but she was losing that beauty very fast. By thirty-five she already looked older than she was.

Duvakin [*with a sigh*]**:** She had a difficult life.

Vladimir Sosinsky: That's true. She certainly did not have the charm of the thirty-year-old woman that Balzac so admired.

And we all didn't feel comfortable with all those sharp edges, spiky hair, and her sarcastic tongue – she made fun of everything.

Duvakin: When you say "we," do you mean "we the younger generation"?

Vladimir Sosinsky: Yes. Going back to Kerensky: the very next day she (you remember that they were joking around together the whole evening) said: "And such a man could rule Russia? *Da eto kuram na smekh* [Even chickens would laugh at the idea!]"

Duvakin [*chuckles approvingly*]**:** But it's true.

Vladimir Sosinsky: Yes, it's true.

Duvakin: Well, chickens did laugh later as well.

Vladimir Sosinsky: Yes, they did.

Duvakin: Did you have the chance to observe her around other people? The episode with Kerensky that you described is very interesting.

Vladimir Sosinsky: I agree, it was a funny episode. You know, I still feel proud that I helped her publish *Krysolov* (*The Ratcatcher*)[97] in *Volya Rossii*. Mark Slonim was afraid to publish it, and so were other editors. But at *Volya Rossii* there were interesting individuals, like Vasily Sukhomlin,[98] who recently passed away in Moscow, and Mark Slonim, an absolutely brilliant speaker who gave

---

97 See note 8 to this dialogue.

98 Vasily Sukhomlin (1885–1963) was a Russian French literary critic and translator. His French translations of works by Leo Tolstoy, Maxim Gorky, and Mikhail Sholokhov played a crucial role in the dissemination of Russian literature in the West. After the revolution, Sukhomlin lived in many countries, including the United States, but after Stalin's death he chose to return to the USSR, where he died peacefully at the age of seventy-eight.

lectures till the day he died. He could lecture in any language – French, Italian, English, Russian, German. A truly brilliant man! Although he and I always argued about Marina Tsvetaeva and Remizov. But at the same time, I was able to get him to like Boris Pasternak[99] and Osip Mandelstam.[100] He confessed that he had not appreciated them before.

Marina Ivanovna liked me a lot; we had a very good relationship. In one letter she wrote to me: "Volodya! We are not together because neither you nor I have time; but love, love demands a lot of time and a lot of effort, and we are not making this effort." Something along those lines.

Anyway, she was grateful to me for my support. I remember that she wanted to have a good picture of Mur. But to produce a really good portrait, you need a professional photographer. I had a friend, Piotr Shumov,[101] the photographer, and he took dozens of pictures of Mur. Marina Ivanovna was extremely happy – that's how much she liked those pictures. By the way, he also took a great picture of Marina Tsvetaeva. I brought it to Moscow, and it was published in the program for the evening dedicated to Tsvetaeva. It's the best portrait of her we have.

Tsvetaeva and Efron Leaving France

Duvakin: Now please tell me, did you have a chance to see her right before she left?

Vladimir Sosinsky: They came to say goodbye at Andreyev's place. Olga Eliseevna also came. I was not in Paris at that time, so I did not have a chance to see her off. But I know she had bad premonitions about the future and was leaving France with the feeling that life had nothing more to offer any more. Sergei Yakovlevich [Efron] had already left.

Duvakin: He was the first to go?

Vladimir Sosinsky: He fled from France.

Duvakin: He fled? Why?

---

99 About Boris Pasternak, see note 38 to dialogue 1.

100 About Osip Mandelstam, see note 72 to dialogue 1.

101 Piotr Shumov (1872–1936) was one of the best-known photographers in Paris. A close friend of Auguste Rodin (1840–1917), he left a large collection of photographs (149) of all the artistic works of the great sculptor, and fifty-eight photographs of Rodin himself. In addition, Piotr Shumov photographed some of the most important artists of the twentieth century, including Igor Stravinsky, Sergei Prokofiev, almost all the ballerinas of the Russian ballet in Paris, Marc Chagall, Isadora Duncan, Claude Monet, and Albert Einstein.

Vladimir Sosinsky: Because the French police was after him. He was recruiting people for the Spanish Civil War. He worked for Soviet Intelligence.

Duvakin: Was he recruiting French citizens?

Vladimir Sosinsky: Yes. And Russian émigrés as well. Alexey Eisner,[102] for example, was recruited by Sergei Yakovlevich.

Duvakin [*thoughtfully*]: Eisner. I don't recall this name. When did he become known?

Vladimir Sosinsky: Alexey Eisner recently published in *Novy mir* [The new world] his extensive diary about the war in Spain.[103]

Duvakin: Ah, I read it! I simply didn't pay attention to the name.

Vladimir Sosinsky: He was an adjutant to the famous General Lucas.[104]

Duvakin: Well then, Sergei Yakovlevich recruited him?

Vladimir Sosinsky: Yes. When he joined the French Communist Party, he was contacted by Soviet Intelligence, and he recruited for them. He helped them in the kidnapping of Kutepov.[105]

All these and other things made him flee from France. Unfortunately he did not fit in back in the USSR either.

Duvakin: I don't understand how he started working for Soviet Intelligence. Was he such an adventurist?

---

102 Alexey Eisner (1905–1984) was a poet, translator, and literary critic. Although he grew up in France, he longed to return to the USSR. It was probably for that reason that Eisner participated in the Spanish Civil War and worked for Soviet Intelligence. In 1940 he finally returned to his country, where he was promptly arrested and sent to concentration camps, followed by a lengthy exile. During Khrushchev's era, Eisner returned to Moscow and wrote several interesting memoirs about Máté Zalka, Ilya Ehrenburg, and Ernest Hemingway.

103 *Novy mir* (*The New World*) is the oldest monthly literary journal in Russia. Established in 1925, the journal has had its best and worst times: the best times were in the 1960s when it was led by Alexander Tvardovsky and the journal became a liberal "trumpet of the epoch"; the worst times came when Tvardovsky was fired from his post. In the 1990s the journal reached 2.7 million issues per month (when it published *The Gulag Archipelago* by Alexander Solzhenitsyn and *Doctor Zhivago* by Boris Pasternak), but in the last twenty years it has experienced a constant decline – barely reaching 2,200 issues monthly.

104 About "General Lucas" (Máté Zalka), see note 73 to dialogue 1.

105 Alexander Kutepov (1882–1930) was a Russian army general, a hero who fought in the Russian-Japanese war (1904–5) and the First World War. He hated the Bolsheviks with all his heart and, even in emigration, never stopped fighting them by organizing terrorist attacks against Communist leaders. On 26 January 1930 he was kidnapped in Paris by three GPU agents and disappeared. According to the Soviet spymaster Pavel Sudoplatov, "Kutepov died from a heart attack and was buried near Paris"; his body was never found.

Vladimir Sosinsky: He even approached me about this. You know, he was such a man – how can I put it? With two faces, so to speak.

Duvakin [*puzzled*]**:** Ariadna Viktorovna described him as a very charming man.

Vladimir Sosinsky: And he was. That's true.

Duvakin: So, in addition to all that, he had something else in common with Marina – those sharp angles.

Vladimir Sosinsky: Do you remember when Ariadna Viktorovna mentioned Eurasianism?[106]

Duvakin: Of course.

Vladimir Sosinsky: That's what made Sergei Yakovlevich come alive. It was his idea.

Duvakin: What was behind that theory?

Vladimir Sosinsky: The idea was that Russia is historically connected to both Europe and Asia, and in the end it will unite and rule both continents. They had their own journal, *Eurasia,* in which they published articles along those lines.

Duvakin: So Sergei Yakovlevich fled from France straight to the USSR?

Vladimir Sosinsky: Yes. He had to save his life, so he left.

Duvakin: But she [Tsvetaeva] did not know anything about that?

Vladimir Sosinsky: She didn't know what was going on. The only thing she knew was that his job was very dangerous and that one day it could all turn out very badly. She knew that, and the thought tormented her continuously.

Duvakin: She was tormented?

Vladimir Sosinsky: Yes, tormented. She knew that Sergei Yakovlevich had chosen a very dangerous way to return to his country.

Duvakin: Do you know what she thought of the Spanish war?

Vladimir Sosinsky: She shared the same attitude we all had towards Czechoslovakia when Hitler first invaded it.[107]

Duvakin: So you all were anti-Hitler?

---

106 About Eurasianism, see note 40 to this dialogue.

107 In October of 1938, long before the beginning of the Second World War, Hitler annexed the Sudeten region of Czechoslovakia. In March of 1939 he entered Prague, and Czechoslovakia became a protectorate of Nazi Germany.

Vladimir Sosinsky: Absolutely! But the Russian émigré turned patriotic only after Hitler invaded the Soviet Union.

Duvakin: But not all of you. Merezhkovsky …

Vladimir Sosinsky: Yes, Merezhkovsky went to visit Mussolini, then Piłsudski.[108]

Duvakin: Even Mussolini!

Vladimir Sosinsky: Yes.

Duvakin: That's interesting, because during the war, we heard rumours that Merezhkovsky and Gippius had begun to support the Soviet Union.

Vladimir Sosinsky: That's not true. Milyukov, yes, he supported the USSR.

Duvakin [*sounding upset*]**:** Oh, how unfortunate! In my lecture (I used to give lectures on Symbolism) I said that they became anti-Hitler. But that's not true. We didn't know.

Vladimir Sosinsky: I'll even tell you this: Vasily Sukhomlin confirmed it. When they were in Marseille, getting ready to leave for the United States, he talked with Bunin.

Duvakin: Did Bunin also want to return?

Vladimir Sosinsky: Never! Bunin never even considered it. Remizov wanted to return; he even had a Soviet passport.

Duvakin: I knew about Remizov. But Bunin was also in correspondence with Paustovsky.[109] I know that he planned to return, but then Zhdanov made that speech, and everything changed.[110]

---

108 Józef Piłsudski (1867–1935) was a prominent Polish statesman. He served as Poland's chief of state (1918–22) and is considered to be the founder of the Polish army, of which he became the first marshal in 1920. In the USSR, Piłsudski was a persona non grata, and one could be punished for even mentioning his name. Today Piłsudski is hailed as the father of the Polish nation, and his memory is cherished in his homeland.

109 Konstantin Paustovsky (1892–1968) was a Soviet writer, nominated for a Nobel Prize in 1965. A man of great honesty and integrity, Paustovsky always tried to protect persecuted Soviet writers, such as Andrei Sinyavsky and Alexander Solzhenitsyn, by writing letters to Leonid Brezhnev, the head of the Communist Party during that period.

110 In 1946 Andrey Zhdanov, the head of the Communist Party of Leningrad Province, delivered a speech in which he severely reprimanded literary journals that published such "traitors" as Anna Akhmatova and Mikhail Zoshchenko. As a result of his speech, the journals were closed, and the era of oppressive censorship returned. The new wave of Stalin's repressions (1946–9) was already looming; the Iron Curtain separated the world again.

Vladimir Sosinsky: Possibly, although I personally think it can't be true. Well, if he was thinking about returning, why did he not get a Soviet passport?

Duvakin: Was it possible, even if you were living in another country?

Vladimir Sosinsky: Of course. According to the decree of 14 July 1946,[111] we all were given the chance to become Soviet citizens. So Vadim Andreyev and I, and Remizov, we all received Soviet passports. Why did Bunin never request a passport? He simply never went to the embassy like so many of us émigrés did, to talk to the ambassador.

Duvakin: When was that?

Vladimir Sosinsky: 1946 or 1947.

Duvakin: Was Molotov there too?[112]

Vladimir Sosinsky: Yes, he was. At the meeting he sat in the centre, and Remizov sat to his right. Molotov asked, "Well, how's life, Alexey Mikhailovich? I read your work when I was young." Remizov responded, "Very bad, Vyacheslav Mikhailovich." "Why bad?" "Because of a mouse." "What mouse?" "A little mouse comes to me every day from my neighbours."

Duvakin [*laughing*]: What a nice story!

Vladimir Sosinsky [*laughing too*]: Molotov turned to the others and asked, "Is he out of his mind, or what?" He could not comprehend that Alexey Mikhailovich simply wanted to share what was bothering him at that very moment. He was bothered by that little mouse and did not care who happened to be in front of him – the French president or the Soviet bureaucrat Molotov.

Duvakin: We have to talk about Remizov in another session. This is very interesting.

---

111 The Soviet government's decree of 1946 promised all Russian émigrés a safe haven if they chose to return to the Soviet Union. Unfortunately, as had happened many times previously, the Bolsheviks betrayed their own citizens: as soon as people arrived, they were searched and interrogated; many were arrested. Only a few were able to return to Europe in the mid-1970s, that is, thirty years later.

112 Vyacheslav Molotov (b. Skryabin) (1890–1986) was the longest-living member of the Soviet government. Close to Lenin at first, he eagerly supported Stalin against Trotsky and quickly obtained some of the highest posts in the Soviet government, where he managed to survive from 1921 until he was forced to retire by Nikita Khrushchev in 1957. Molotov will always be remembered for his infamous Molotov-Ribbentrop Pact (1939), which was supposed to guarantee that Hitler would not invade the Soviet Union. Although Molotov fell out of favour with Stalin sometime around 1949, he continued to support his policies, even after Stalin's death, and vehemently and openly opposed Krushchev's de-Stalinization efforts.

Vladimir Sosinsky: We can certainly do that. We can talk about Remizov, about Babel, and others.

Duvakin: Coming back to Marina Tsvetaeva, I sense there is something else you want to tell me. Is that right?

[*There is a break in the recording.*]

Tsvetaeva's Death

Duvakin: I ask these questions again and again because that's something that really concerns me: Mayakovsky's death and Tsvetaeva's death. You knew her very closely. How do you explain her tragic death?

Vladimir Sosinsky: I have never, ever had the slightest impression that she could commit suicide. She did not seem to be the type of person who would choose such a fate for herself. I was shaken by her death. But I can see that in the end, after all that pain and suffering (though some of it she made up and created by herself), she came to a point when she had nothing left.

But during the times I knew her, she never reached such a point. I think that her death was caused by her reaching her limit, not only because she was so desperately poor and hopeless, no; it was because no one offered to help. Aseev,[113] Ehrenburg,[114] Pasternak, they all turned away from her! [*He sounds angry.*] They didn't do anything for her. Nothing! They didn't even give her any translation work – so she fell into such despair. It was that despair and Mur's terrible behaviour that brought her to the brink of insanity – and that was when she did it [committed suicide].

Duvakin: What can you tell us about Mur at that time?

---

113 Nikolay Aseev (1889–1963) was a Russian poet, born in the city of Lvov. His poetry was mostly written in the Futurist style. Aseev was awarded a government honour for his poem "Zor" in 1941. He died in Moscow.

114 Ilya Ehrenburg (1891–1967) was a Russian poet, prose writer, critic, and translator who lived in France as an émigré from tsarist Russia in his youth. After the 1917 revolution, Ehrenburg returned to the USSR, but he was still allowed to visit the West. During Second World War, Ehrenburg became so successful at creating anti-Nazi propaganda that Hitler declared him his personal enemy (calling him "Stalin's domesticated Jew") and ordered his murder at any cost. Ehrenburg's multivolume memoirs *Lyudi, gody, zhizn'* (*People, Years, Life*) became tremendously popular during the 1960s and reintroduced Soviet readers to many forgotten or previously banned authors; for example, Tsvetaeva, Mandelstam, and Babel. Ehrenburg was also the author of the 1954 novel *The Thaw,* from which the Khrushchev Thaw got its name.

Vladimir Sosinsky [*angrily*]**:** He was one of the worst little boys I have encountered in my life. So arrogant, the God's little darling, demanding everything for himself, but giving nothing to others. He was a terrible egoist. His behaviour, in addition to her endless love for him, created such drama. And he didn't even come to her funeral.

Duvakin [*sadly*]**:** Yes, I know.

Vladimir Sosinsky: I have to say that for me her death was the most terrible surprise.

Duvakin: Did she want to return to the Soviet Union?

Vladimir Sosinsky: Yes. But we were all afraid that she wouldn't fit in there. I remember her saying once, "I will return to my country not as an antiquated Russian but as a much anticipated guest." That's what she was saying right before she left. And what really happened? [*He sighs.*]

Duvakin: Is this from one of her letters?

[*There is a break in the recording.*]

Vladimir Sosinsky: … as she put it: one's homeland is not a geographical place but a memory stored in the blood. To be away from Russia, to forget it – that could only happen to people who didn't carry Russia within. But those who have it in their blood would only lose it in death. [*He sighs.*]

That's what she thought, what she imagined. Then there was the reality of her return. Back home everything was more difficult. Because in France, if life is difficult, it's understandable; it's not your country. But here, here was Russia, her motherland, and she was a poet of this land. And, on top of all that, the Germans invaded the Soviet Union – the Germans whom she had always hated.

Duvakin: She hated the Germans?

Vladimir Sosinsky: Yes. But fear was also part of it; fear of what was coming. You asked me if I could imagine or suspect such an end for her? No, never. For Mayakovsky, yes, although nobody expected it. For Yesenin, yes. Yesenin could do anything.

Ariadna Viktorovna also could not imagine that. She [Tsvetaeva] loved poetry, loved art so much, she could not part with it all so easily. She loved Mur too much to leave him.

Duvakin: Did you ever feel that she was somewhat decadent? Like Leonid Andreyev.[115]

---

115 Leonid Andreyev (1871–1919) was a Russian writer, considered to be one of the first Expressionists in Russian prose. After the revolution he emigrated to Finland, where he soon died from heart failure.

Vladimir Sosinsky: You mean, somewhat eschatological?[116]

Duvakin: No, eschatology is about the end of the world, the Apocalypse. No, something that's closer to Sologub.[117] Do you remember? "Мой старый друг, мой верный Дьявол ..." [My old friend, my faithful Devil ...][118] Do you understand what I mean?

Vladimir Sosinsky: No.

Duvakin: Flirting with evil, or with death. Or was there still something strong in her, something healthy?

Vladimir Sosinsky: Strong and healthy, yes. There was something purely Russian, deeply connected to Moscow. And that was always in her.

Duvakin: How interesting!

Vladimir Sosinsky: Decadent life was not for her. She was a Bohemian at heart, though: she couldn't think about the future at all.

Duvakin [*puzzled*]: Ariadna Viktorovna told me that she didn't live a Bohemian life, she stayed away from it. She had a husband and children. She had to put dinner on the table, and the room had to be cleaned.

Vladimir Sosinsky: Then I probably will agree with Ariadna Viktorovna. Maybe I am being unfair. I simply never liked her attitude towards life. It was too carefree, so to speak.

Duvakin: Just think how she didn't want to educate her daughter!

Vladimir Sosinsky: Yes. But I don't believe she ever realized that. You asked me if she had a sense of duty. As far as other people were concerned, she did not have it; to her family, yes, towards Mur, yes.

Duvakin: Towards Sergei Yakovlevich?

---

116 Eschatology is a part of theology concerned mainly with the end of the world, the end of times.

117 Fyodor Sologub (1863–1927) was a Russian Symbolist poet, novelist, playwright, and essayist. His writing introduced European fin de siècle themes and language into Russian literature. In the aftermath of the revolution, which he did not accept, he sought to emigrate, but his plans were derailed when his wife, Anastasia Chebotarevskaya, committed suicide. This tragic event prevented Sologub from leaving the country; he stayed in the USSR for another six years, filling his time with literary activities. His most famous novel, *Melkii bes* (*The Petty Demon*, 1907), offers a Symbolist (or decadent, according to some critics) study of the Russian concept of *poshlost* (a word that encompasses "vulgarity," "banality," "lack of spirituality," and "promiscuity") through its main character, Peredonov.

118 This is an excerpt from a short poem of the same title, "My Old Friend, My Faithful Devil..." (1906), by Nikolay Gumilev.

Vladimir Sosinsky: Towards him, no.

Duvakin: But she felt duty to her art, yes?

Vladimir Sosinsky: Absolutely! Everyone had to kneel down before the altar of her art. That's why Alya was deprived of a chance to become an artist. Maybe she could have even become a poet or a writer, but she [Tsvetaeva] deprived her of proper education. And Alya learned French by herself and learned it beautifully.

Duvakin: Didn't she come back when she was twenty-two?

Vladimir Sosinsky: I think so. And here [in the Soviet Union] she became a wonderful translator. Not many of us could boast of such a great command of French. And she learned it on her own.

Duvakin: Let's go back to Tsvetaeva. So you think she didn't like the life of the drinking French Bohemia?

Vladimir Sosinsky: Not at all.

Duvakin: Out of all the Modernist poets I feel her to be the closest to Mayakovsky.

Vladimir Sosinsky: I agree. It is not by chance that she treated him as an equal.

Duvakin: Well, Vladimir Bronislavovich, now I think we can finish our conversation.

Vladimir Sosinsky: We can stop now. But I hope we can talk another time about Alexey Remizov.

[THE RECORDING ENDS.]

DIALOGUE 4 With Roman Jakobson on 21 August 1967*

Victor Duvakin: Roman Osipovich,[1] could you please tell me everything you remember about your acquaintance with Mayakovsky in as much detail as possible. You should rest assured that whatever you choose to share will not be published. I am not planning to write a biography; I don't have time for that right now, though, I must confess, I would love to do it.

I am working for the twenty-first century, and precisely for that reason I value my work so much. Because I can finally do something that I have dreamed of doing for a long time now.

Once I read somewhere how someone in 1900 had come across a peasant woman who had personally met Pushkin,[2] and I thought then: the last witnesses are leaving us.

Your visit here [to Moscow] and our meeting today, that's such a gift, arranged by Vyacheslav Ivanov.[3]

I will not be conducting the usual kind of interview. You will not be tied down by anything, and I will not bombard you with questions. Just tell me

---

* Length of interview – 62 minutes

1 Roman Jakobson (1896–1982) was a Russian American linguist and literary critic of international fame. Together with Shklovsky, he was a founder of the school of Russian Formalism. Jakobson lived and worked in many countries, including Russia, Czechoslovakia, Denmark, Norway, Sweden, and the United States, where he was a professor at Harvard University and the Massachusetts Institute of Technology. During Khrushchev's era (1950s–1960s), Jakobson made seven trips to the Soviet Union, where he met with many progressive people, attended an international symposium, and gave numerous lectures.

2 About Alexander Pushkin, see note 40 to dialogue 1.

3 Vyacheslav Vsevolodovich Ivanov (1929–2017), the son of the Soviet writer Vsevolod Ivanov, was a prominent Soviet linguist. He moved to the United States in 1989 and worked as a professor first at Stanford University, then at the University of California–Los Angeles. He passed away in Los Angeles in 2017 at the age of eighty-eight.

4.1. Roman Jakobson in Mayakovsky Museum, Moscow, 1956. Photographer: Lev Shilov.

everything you remember about my main interest here [Mayakovsky], and if there is something that I will need to clarify, I'll ask you, if you don't mind. I have plenty of tape. [*He chuckles.*]

Roman Jakobson: You will have to confirm the dates, though. But I think that once you know the event, you will be able to figure out also the year and the month.

My First Meetings with Mayakovsky

I first met Mayakovsky at Serov's funeral.[4] At that time I was a Lazarev Institute student.[5] I was very interested in painting and had seen Serov's *Abduction of*

4 Valentin Serov (1865–1911) was a famous Russian artist, especially known for his portraits (the most famous being those of Tsar Alexander III and Tsar Nicholas II), and a member of the Russian Academy of the Arts. Originally impressionistic in nature, his art later became much more modernist in style. Serov's democratic sympathies were clearly obvious in his art following the 1905 revolution. In his last years he turned to mythology and Russian

4.2. Vladimir Mayakovsky, Moscow, 1929. Photographer unknown.

Europe not long before his passing.[6] Serov's death made a huge impact on me and my friends – and my friends were mostly young artists. We all went to his funeral. We walked there, down the Myasnitskaya Street and further.[7]

When we arrived, we stood near the open grave. A young man was talking – very young and very handsome. He had a very pleasant voice and gave a speech, free of any fake pathos, on behalf of Serov's students, who he said would always

---

history for thematic inspiration. He died unexpectedly at the age of forty-six from acute angina pectoris.

5 At that time (December 1911), Jakobson was fifteen and a student in a high school (*gimnazia*), which was part of the Lazarev Institute of Oriental Languages. (Since 1927, the latter has been part of the Moscow Institute of Oriental Languages.) Jakobson graduated in 1914. The institute was founded with money donated by a rich Armenian family, the Lazarevs, who had lived in Moscow for many generations. The institute's initial goal was to allow poor Armenian children to have access to good education. Although the students were taught all subjects, the focus was on the study of Armenian, Turkish, Iranian, and Arabic languages.

6 *The Abduction of Europe* (1910) was one of the last, and most famous, paintings by Valentin Serov. His approach to the well-known mythological subject (first tackled by Titian in 1560, and then by Rembrandt in 1632) was revolutionary.

7 Myasnitskaya Street (*The Butcher Street*) is a well-known and very old street in the centre of Moscow. Its name comes from the sixteenth century when it was lined by many butcher shops. After the revolution the Bolsheviks renamed the street several times. In 1990 it went back to being called Myasnitskaya.

remember their teacher, his guidance, and would continue their march forward. I didn't know who that man was. I was told he was one of Serov's art school students.

Later, on two or three different occasions, mostly at art exhibits, I saw Mayakovsky again. I seem to remember specifically running into him at an exhibit of the Bubnovy valet [Jack of Diamonds] society.[8] He was wearing a very shabby velvet jacket and looked very poor and a bit dishevelled. But his unusual face expression, his overall appearance, were quite striking and immediately drew attention to him. I remember that's when I first noticed him and asked who he was. I wanted to know. There was this young artist in the Jack of Diamonds society – he died very young. Milman was his name.[9]

Duvakin: Milman?

Jakobson: Yes, Milman. You can find his work in the catalogues of the Jack of Diamonds society, in their monographs, too. He was a close friend of Mashkov[10] and Konchalovsky.[11]

So I asked Milman about him [Mayakovsky]. Then I witnessed how the organizers of the exhibit pushed Mayakovsky out of there – I have no idea why. Maybe he insulted them somehow or did something else they didn't like, but there was a brawl. And I became even more curious about him.

Then there was also another strange story. I'll tell you about an episode that became famous later, and I was there to witness the events myself.

At that time I had tickets to a Koussevitzky's concert.[12] I was there with two friends from school. We were listening to Rachmaninov's music – you

8 Bubnovy valet (Jack of Diamonds) was the largest early Russian avant-garde art society. It was formed in 1911, but disappeared after the victory of the revolution of 1917. The members of the society rejected any connections to classicism and nineteenth-century realism. Kazimir Malevich was a member at first but soon left it to pursue his own ideas about art.

9 Adolf Milman (1886–1930) was a Russian painter. From 1911 he was a member of the review board of the Jack of Diamonds art society. His works were displayed at its group expositions in 1912–14. After the revolution he joined the World of Art association and took part in organizing the Fine Arts Department of Narkompros (the People's Commissariat for Education). The last ten years of his life he lived in Paris, but he was not able to paint any more because of health problems; however, he still taught one last student, the Canadian artist Edwin Holgate (1892–1977).

10 Ilya Mashkov (1881–1944) was a Russian/Soviet artist, one of the most important painters of the Jack of Diamonds circle. His style was originally influenced by Paul Cézanne and Henri Matisse. In addition to still lifes, he produced many striking, shocking portraits. After the revolution he offered his talent to the Bolshevik government in exchange for their favours, embraced socialist realism, and never produced anything significant again.

11 Piotr Konchalovsky (1875–1956) was a Soviet painter. Although not very talented, he was prolific, producing more than two thousand paintings.

12 Sergei Koussevitzky (1874–1951) was a prominent Russian conductor. A close friend of Rachmaninov, Prokofiev, Stravinsky, and Ravel, he left Russia shortly after the revolution for the United States, where for many years he led the Boston Symphony Orchestra. He was the

4.3. Ilya Mashkov, 1910. Photographer unknown.

probably already know the story. Mayakovsky and Burliuk didn't have assigned seats,[13] so they were standing next to the wall. Mayakovsky seemed to be very bored, then they both left abruptly. That was the story Mayakovsky told. It was strange to read about it later, since I had been there myself.

Then I heard that Mayakovsky also wrote poetry. So yes, I was still not officially acquainted with him. I saw him at the debate organized by, if I am not mistaken, that same Jack of Diamonds society, at the Polytechnic Museum.[14] They didn't let him talk then. He wanted to participate in the debate. But the members of the society couldn't stand him. They were trying to silence him, but he did not pay attention to them and kept talking.

---

first in the United States to conduct the famous Seventh Symphony by Dmitry Shostakovich. In 1946, after the Second World War, Koussevitzky tried to arrange a series of concerts for the Boston orchestra in the USSR, but his visa application was denied.

13 David Burliuk (1882–1967) is often called the father of Russian Futurism. He was primarily an artist but also a good poet. After the revolution he emigrated to Japan in 1920, and then to the United States, where he lived and worked until his death.

14 About the Polytechnic Museum, see note 5 to dialogue 1.

4.4. David Burliuk, in the United States, 1920s–30s. Photographer unknown.

Still, he was not allowed to continue and was almost forced out – actually no, not almost. He was pushed off the stage with the help of a policeman. Then suddenly Mayakovsky appeared in the gallery of the Polytechnic Museum and started to yell from there with that incredibly powerful voice of his that could drown out everyone else's. He accused the members of the Jack of Diamonds society of being "gendarmes of the new art," et cetera.

Duvakin: He was in Larionov's camp at the time.[15]

Jakobson: Yes, absolutely, he was connected with Oslinyi khvost [Donkey's Tail] at the time.[16]

---

15 Mikhail Larionov (1881–1964) was an artist, a theorist of art, and one of the most prominent founders of the Russian avant-garde movement. During the First World War he settled in Paris, where he became closely associated with Diaghilev and helped him popularize Russian ballet. He never returned to Russia after the revolution.

16 Oslinyi khvost (Donkey's Tail) was an artistic group founded in 1912 by Mikhail Larionov and his wife, Natalia Goncharova. The name of the group comes from the legend that one of the paintings at the 1910 exhibition in Paris was done by a donkey's tail. The group organized a few exhibitions in Saint Petersburg, featuring works by Larionov, Goncharova, Malevich, Chagall, and others.

I remember a lot from the debates. For example, the one following Balashov's slashing of Repin's painting *Ivan the Terrible Murders His Son* [*sic*].[17] Then I heard the joke that it was really a painting of Ivan the Terrible giving first aid to his son. [*He laughs.*] Anyway, the Jack of Diamonds society had invited Maximilian Voloshin to give a talk about that notorious incident at their meeting.[18] He spoke about this story in vivid and courteous language. He didn't accuse anybody in particular, just discussed the cultural context that had led to the event, the crisis of art in general, the current attitudes towards realism, et cetera.

Then there was a discussion, in which various members of the Jack of Diamonds took part. Mayakovsky spoke against them. He started by reciting Prutkov's poetry[19] – he recited beautifully! He said, "Here is what I can tell you about the relationship between the Jack of Diamonds and Maximilian Voloshin as a representative of Symbolism: 'If a worm crawls down your neck, you must squash it yourself, instead of asking a servant!'" And then – well, this may not be that important as far as Mayakovsky is concerned, but the episode did provoke a great reaction in the audience: there was clapping, whistling. People kept asking for the floor. They were given the opportunity to talk. This one old man got up and asked to speak. He said, "Please, can I have the floor, I want to speak."

Duvakin: Who was that?

Jakobson: Repin.[20] He behaved very honourably. I don't remember exactly what he said, but in general he defended artistic independence. That was his position on the matter.

I don't remember if it happened at the same meeting or not, but I also recall speeches given by Burliuk and Larionov. Their main thesis was the following: Jack of Diamonds was reactionary, and Mashkov and Konchalovsky were academicians.

17 Abram Balashov (1885–?) cut the famous Repin painting with a knife, crying "Enough blood, enough death!" Following this event, he was taken to a mental institution and then disappeared from history without a trace. The painting, *Ivan the Terrible and His Son Ivan* (1883), is considered to be one of Ilya Repin's masterpieces.

18 About Maximilian Voloshin, see note 35 to dialogue 3.

19 "Kozma Prutkov" was a literary pen name used by a collective of four writers, Alexey K. Tolstoy and the Zhemchuzhnikov brothers. The group were active in the 1850s–1870s and fell apart after the death of its most talented member, Alexey Tolstoy, in 1875. Mayakovsky was quoting Prutkov's parodic fable "Cherviak i popad'ia" ("A Worm and a Priest's Wife," 1853).

20 Ilya Repin (1844–1930) was one of Russia's greatest realist painters of the Peredvizhniki (Itinerants) school, whose work brought Russian art into the mainstream of European culture. He was living in his house in Kuokkala, Finland, when Russia was torn apart by the Bolshevik Revolution. The territory in which his house was located became a part of Finland, and Repin became an emigrant. In 1924 Stalin sent a special delegation of artists and Repin's close friends to convince him to move back to the USSR, but he refused. Some new documents discovered later reveal that a few of those people who came to convince Repin to return had, in fact, secretly advised him not to do that under any circumstances.

"Here is the New Art!" they claimed, while projecting images of paintings on a screen. That was the first time I saw paintings by Picasso, his early work.

Duvakin: Very interesting. So he was still not known at the time?

Jakobson: Completely unknown. From one side of the room came laughter, hissing, cries of "Pure quackery!," et cetera. The other side was in awe. I was one of those who deeply admired this new work. It impressed me greatly. After that I got really curious: what are those new Frenchmen doing? Shortly afterwards, thanks to Milman again, I was able to get into the Shchukin museum, his house museum.[21]

Duvakin: Roman Osipovich, excuse me, if we can try to establish a time frame here. Are you talking about the winter of 1912–13?

Jakobson: Yes, of course. I could check in Katanian's book,[22] if you happen to have it.

Duvakin: That's not necessary.

Jakobson: You can find the dates for the debates there. It happened at one of those debates. I think it was 1912. I believe it was before *Poshchiochina obshchestvennomu vkusu* (*A Slap in the Face of Public Taste*).[23]

Duvakin: *A Slap in the Face of Public Taste* – that was December of 1912.

Jakobson: Yes, before then.

Duvakin: That's important for me. He was still not known as a poet at the time.

Jakobson: He was not known, not at all. Completely unknown. And now I have to talk about myself a little here.

---

21 Sergei Shchukin (1854–1936) was a Russian merchant, millionaire, patron of the arts and collector of modern French art (Gauguin, Monet, Matisse, Picasso, Cézanne). After the revolution, in 1918, he left Russia. His collection was nationalized and became a foundation of modern art museum collections in Moscow and Saint Petersburg. His own house finally became a museum and was opened to the public in 2009.

22 Jakobson refers here to Vasily Katanian (1902–1980), the last husband of Lilya Brik, who was one of the most prominent Mayakovsky scholars during the Soviet period. He prepared and published the complete works of Mayakovsky and also wrote the poet's most complete biography to date.

23 *Poshchiochina obshchestvennomu vkusu* (*A Slap in the Face of Public Taste*) was a collection of poetry by Cubo-Futurists published in 1912. It included the earliest works of Vladimir Mayakovsky, Benedikt Livshits, Velimir Khlebnikov, David Burliuk, and Aleksey Kruchenykh. Two pieces by Vladimir Mayakovsky ("Morning" and "Night") became emblematic of the Futuristic poetry of the 1910s. Their Futurist Manifesto, published together with their poetry, produced much discussion, and even scandal, in the artistic world. In it, the Futurists suggested that a range of nineteenth-century Russian writers should be "tossed from the ship of modernity."

A Slap in the Face of Public Taste

Jakobson: I bought at the time (I even remember where I bought it) in a bookstore called Education a brochure that really struck me. It was a first edition of *Igra v adu* (*A Game in Hell*) by Khlebnikov[24] and Kruchenykh.[25] The names didn't mean anything to me, but I found the poem striking. At the time I was studying Pushkin, so I noticed something that I don't think anyone else has ever noticed since: the influence of Pushkin's "Adskaia poema" ("Poem of Hell").[26]

You know, in Pushkin there is the line about the "game that is not played for money but for eternity." I was very intrigued; it was all so unexpected. When *A Slap in the Face of Public Taste* came out, I ran to get it, and to this day I am so moved every time I see the cover; I have the same reaction today, as visceral as a memory from one's childhood. In that publication of *A Slap in the Face of Public Taste* there were two poems by Mayakovsky: "Iz ulitsy v ulitsu" ("From Street to Street") and "Noch" ("Night").

Duvakin: "Utro" ("Morning") and "Night," yes. But "From Street to Street" – it wasn't there.

Jakobson: Ah, "Night," yes! "The sullen rain cast a glance. Beyond a clear grille …"[27] Yes. So exciting! The book was very popular. I have to say I was not very impressed by Mayakovsky's poetry. It was Khlebnikov who shook me. His "И и Э" ("I and E"), then "Chased by someone …," everything in "Kon' Przheval'skogo" ("Przhevalsky's Horse").[28]

---

24 Velimir Khlebnikov (1885–1922) was a central figure in the Russian Futurist movement, who was often regarded as a poetic genius. He coined a great number of neologisms and explored the etymological roots of Russian words, seeking to find significance in the sounds of certain Cyrillic letters. Through his verbal experimentation he created "zaum'" a "trans-logical language," whose goal was to make poetic expression new and invigorating. Beloved by fellow and future poets, his work was deemed too difficult by general readers and fell into obscurity after the revolution.

25 Aleksey Kruchenykh (1886–1968) was a Russian poet, perhaps the most radical of all the Futurists. Together with Khlebnikov, he invented "zaum'" the language of extreme artistic experimentation. Kruchenykh wrote the libretto for the Futurist opera *Victory over the Sun*, with sets designed by Kazimir Malevich. His most famous work, *Universal War*, was published in 1916. Kruchenykh was the last survivor who personally knew Vladimir Mayakovsky. After Mayakovsky's death and the massive repressions, Kruchenykh maintained a low profile and stopped writing poetry. Later, after Stalin's death, he conducted valuable research on Yesenin, whom he knew personally as well.

26 Jakobson refers here to an unfinished poem that Alexander Pushkin wrote while still at the Lyceum.

27 This is the beginning of "Morning." "From Street to Street" was published two or three months later.

28 Both poems by Khlebnikov were published in *A Slap in the Face of Public Taste* in 1912.

4.5. Velimir Khlebnikov, Moscow (?), 1910s. Photographer unknown.

Duvakin: "Golden lettered wings . . ." (Russian, "Крылышкуя золотописьмом...")

Jakobson: Yes, yes. It left a great impression on me. Mayakovsky said [*incomprehensible words*]. But I remember that my comrade from the Lazarev Institute,[29] who later became an architect, learned that poem, "The sullen rain cast a glance . . .," by heart and used it to seduce a girl, telling her it was his own poetry. I think he had great success. Anyway, that was a momentous event, the publication of *A Slap in the Face of Public Taste*. Everybody was talking about it. It was sad when ... Do you remember the story, I believe now largely forgotten, about Kandinsky's protests about the way he was . . .[30] Do you know this already?

Duvakin: I don't think so.

---

29 On Lazarev Institute, see note 5 to this dialogue.

30 Wassily Kandinsky (1866–1944) was a Russian artist, a theoretician of art, and one of the most renowned Abstractionists. After the revolution he tried to work with the Bolshevik government but soon understood that was not only impossible but also dangerous. He emigrated to Germany and then, when Hitler came to power, moved to France. In 2017, at the Sotheby's auction in London, his *Painting with White Lines* (1913) was sold for US$42 million.

Jakobson: Kandinsky complained about having his work published in the collection because, as he said, although he supported the left art, he was against hooliganism, and that was hooliganism.

Duvakin: Later Mayakovsky, in his *LEF* article,[31] urged readers to "overthrow Kandinsky's aestheticism."

Jakobson: Then the books started to come out one after the other. I attended various events at which Mayakovsky read his poetry, but I still considered Khlebnikov to be the better of the two. It's interesting what happened with the Futurist artists at the time. They were split into two groups.

There was the camp that supported Mayakovsky, but even more people belonged to the other wing, which claimed that "Mayakovsky is an impressionist, a decadent writer" and that "the present belongs to Khlebnikov." To be more specific, among the latter were Malevich,[32] Filonov,[33] and the late husband of Elena Guro,[34] the composer.

---

31 *LEF* (ЛЕФ) was the journal of the Left Front of the Arts (Левый фронт искусств), an association of a wide range of avant-garde writers, photographers, critics, and designers in the Soviet Union. The journal had two runs, one from 1923 to 1925 as *LEF*, and later from 1927 to 1929 as *Novy LEF* (*New LEF*). Osip Brik and Vladimir Mayakovsky served as the chief editors of the original publication, which promoted mostly the interests of the productivist left wing of the then very popular constructivism. The members of *LEF* rejected their connection with the classical forms of art. The extreme "Left" even declared that Pushkin, Gogol, Tolstoy, and Dostoevsky no longer had artistic value. Some of the most notable people associated with the movement were Boris Pasternak, Isaak Babel, Aleksey Kruchenykh, Sergei Eisenstein, Lyubov Popova, Viktor Shklovsky, and Dziga Vertov.

32 Kazimir Malevich (1879–1935) was a Russian/Soviet avant-garde artist and art theorist. He was the founder of Suprematism, one of the earliest forms of modern abstract art. His artwork and theoretical writing influenced the development of non-objective art in the West as well. Born to an ethnically Polish family in Kiev, he later moved to Moscow. After the revolution Malevich held several prominent teaching positions and had a solo show at the sixteenth State Exhibition in Moscow in 1919. He then moved to Vitebsk, where he became the director of the new Vitebsk Art School. Some of the famous artists associated with the work of the school were El Lissitzky, Lazar Khidekel, Nikolai Suetin, Ilia Chashnik, Vera Ermolaeva, and Anna Kagan. Their goal was to promote Suprematist aesthetics by incorporating it into society in general. By 1922 the core of this society, also known as УНОВИС (UNOVIS), had broken up, and it ceased to exist. After Malevich's death in Leningrad in 1935, his body was cremated and his ashes buried under his favourite oak tree near the village of Nemchinovka (near Moscow), where he used to spend summers and work.

33 Pavel Filonov (1883–1941) was a Russian/Soviet artist, one of the leaders of the Russian avant-garde. After the revolution he was not allowed to exhibit or sell his work. He survived the Great Purge but died from famine during the siege of Leningrad (1941–4). Almost all his paintings, which until his last day decorated the walls of his tiny apartment, were given to the State Russian Museum.

34 Elena Guro (1877–1913) was a Russian poet, writer, and artist. She died young, at the age of thirty-six, from leukaemia. Her work, a beautiful combination of poetry, prose, and impressionistic painting, secured her a lasting place in the history of Russian arts.

Duvakin: Matyushin.[35]

Jakobson: Matyushin. They were against Mayakovsky, and for Khlebnikov and his *zaum'* group.[36] I heard many conversations about that. I remember when the two plays came out, Kruchenykh's play *Victory over the Sun* with Khlebnikov's prologue, and Mayakovsky's *I*,[37] we thought that, after all, the present and future of art belonged to Khlebnikov and Kruchenykh, not Mayakovsky. There was too much leftover symbolism in Mayakovsky, which we couldn't stand any more.

Duvakin: Symbolism or the nineteenth century?

Jakobson: No, Symbolism, Impressionism, and so on. I personally remember changing my mind about him only after I read his "Oblako v shtanakh" ("A Cloud in Trousers"),[38] which greatly impressed me with its poetry.

Duvakin: Were Khlebnikov and Kruchenykh grouped together?

Jakobson: Yes, they were grouped together.

Duvakin: Yet there's a big difference between them.

Jakobson: Right. But there was a lot about Kruchenykh that was absolutely amazing, striking: a new path forward, a new understanding. It was all there. I remember very well the time Burliuk was about to deliver a public lecture. There were posters advertising the event all over the Polytechnic Museum and all around it. The title was "Pushkin and Khlebnikov." I had a major fight about it with my father, who said, "What garbage!" and I said, "Not garbage at all." [*Both men laugh.*]

Duvakin: Did your father belong to the intelligentsia of the Chekhov generation?

---

35 Mikhail Matyushin (1861–1934) was a Russian artist, composer, and one of the leaders of the Russian avant-garde movement. In 1913 he wrote the Futuristic opera *Pobeda nad solntsem* (*Victory over the Sun*), which was staged in Saint Petersburg and made Kazimir Malevich famous. Matyushin's house in Saint Petersburg, where he lived with his wife, Elena Guro, became the headquarters for the Russian avant-garde artists. Mayakovsky, Malevich, Kruchenykh, Khlebnikov, Filonov, and even Maxim Gorky were among his many famous visitors.

36 *Zaum* ("beyond sense" or "transrational") can be defined as an experimental poetic language characterized by indeterminacy in meaning, used by poets like Velimir Khlebnikov and Aleksey Kruchenykh.

37 *I* (Russian, "Я") was the first poetry collection, published in 1913, by Vladimir Mayakovsky. The book consisted of only four poems and was written by hand; only about three hundred copies were printed by lithography.

38 "Oblako v shtanakh" ("A Cloud in Trousers") was a long poem by Vladimir Mayakovsky written in 1914 and first published by Osip Brik in 1915. The poem was dedicated to Lilya Brik, who was Mayakovsky's muse for many years.

4.6. *From left*: Mikhail Matyushin, Alexey Kruchenykh, and Kazimir Malevich, Saint Petersburg, 11 December 1913. Photographer: Karl Bulla.

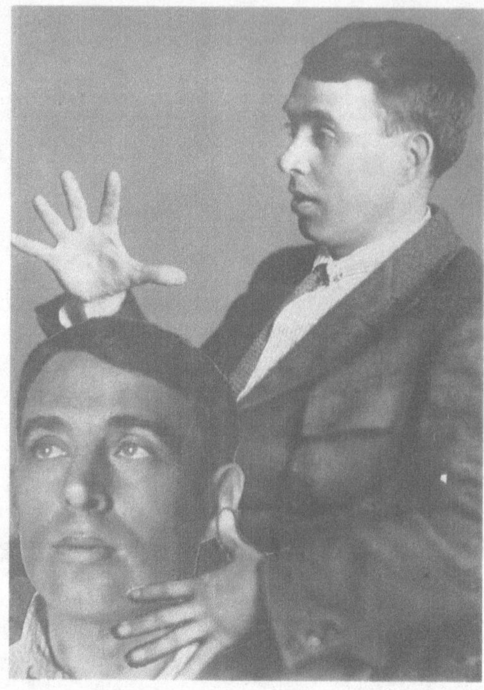

4.7. Photomontage of Alexey Kruchenykh reading his poetry, Moscow, 1927. Photographer: Gustav Klutsis.

Jakobson: Yes, yes. He read the very first edition of *The Brothers Karamazov* when it first came out.[39] By the way, I myself just delivered a lecture: "Pushkin and Khlebnikov."

Jakobson's Personal Acquaintance with Mayakovsky

Jakobson: Mayakovsky and I were not personally acquainted at that time. Here is how the two of us actually met. If memory serves me right, in February of 1914 Marinetti arrived in Moscow.[40] As you know, the [Russian] Futurists

39 *Bratya Karamazovy* (*The Brothers Karamazov*, 1880) was Fyodor Dostoevsky's last novel and his final philosophical and narrative masterpiece.

40 Filippo Marinetti (1876–1944) was an Italian poet and the founder of the Futurism movement in Italy. In 1914 he was invited by the Russian Futurists to visit Russia, but when he arrived, he caused much animosity with his behaviour. In Italy Marinetti became a supporter of Fascism and a close friend of Benito Mussolini. During the Second World War he fought

were very hostile towards him. They were planning to throw rotten eggs at him. That they didn't do, but he still got a very hostile reception. Then there was a partial and somewhat convivial reconciliation. Specifically, Marinetti and Larionov became friends.[41] Mind you, Marinetti didn't speak a word of Russian, while Larionov knew only Russian. But they drank together, and Larionov showed him his paintings. Somehow they were able to understand each other very well.

I remember this clearly: there was a discussion with Marinetti at a meeting of the literary and art circles, at the Society of Free Aesthetics.[42] It was conducted partially in Italian and partially in Russian. By the way, one of the participants in this discussion later died. You might have come across his name in historical works; he was a lawyer, Vilenkin.[43]

Duvakin: Vilenkin?

Jakobson: I think so, if memory serves me right.

Duvakin: I think there was a Vilenkin who was an SR [Socialist Revolutionary].[44]

Jakobson: He took part in the murder of ...

Duvakin: Mirbach?[45]

Jakobson: Uritsky, I believe.[46]

---

against the Soviet Union. He died in 1944 while working on a collection of poems praising the war-time achievements of the Decima Flottiglia MAS (an Italian flotilla created during the Fascist regime).

41 About Larionov, see note 15 to this dialogue.

42 The Society of Free Aesthetics was founded in 1907 by a group of notable art collectors (such as Sergei Koussevitzky, Vladimir Girshman, and Ivan Troyanovsky) whose self-proclaimed goal was "to contribute to the success and development of arts and literature and to facilitate the communication between artists." By 1914 the society had 165 active members, but unfortunately after the revolution many emigrated to Europe or the United States.

43 Alexander Vilenkin (1883–1918) was an officer in the Russian army and a well-known lawyer. Very intelligent and well read, he spoke fluently in English, French, German, and Italian. After the revolution he immediately started participating in the anti-Bolshevik movement, and in 1918 he was arrested. After a series of brutal interrogations Vilenkin was shot by NKVD.

44 About Socialist Revolutionaries (SRs), see note 26 to dialogue 1.

45 About Mirbach, see note 32 to dialogue 1.

46 Moisey Uritsky (1873–1918) was the head of the Petrograd (Saint Petersburg) NKVD. He and Felix Dzerzhinsky were solely responsible for the death of hundreds of people who were arrested and then murdered without any proper investigation. In 1918 he was shot by Leonid Kannegisser, but this act of revenge only triggered the so-called Red Terror: over the next two days the Bolsheviks executed 512 people and, over the next two months, more than 800, and arrested about 7,000.

Duvakin: Right, he was an SR. Vilenkin was a well-known Left SR. So, he participated in debates with Marinetti?

Jakobson: That's correct.

Duvakin: Did he have any connections to the arts?

Jakobson: Yes, to literature. I think he even wrote poetry. Anyway, the conversation with Marinetti lasted very long. And Larionov, who didn't understand a word, was bored out of his mind. So he told Marinetti, "Let's go drink." Marinetti didn't understand. And then Larionov – I included that anecdote in my article for the collection of essays to be published in honour of Kuznetsov.[47]

Larionov then had an idea: he went up to Marinetti and started tapping his fingers on his throat, making a clicking sound. Marinetti looked at him in amazement.

Duvakin: He didn't understand what it meant?

Jakobson: He did not. [*He laughs.*] And I remember, Larionov then said, "What an idiot! He doesn't understand even that!" [*They laugh.*] I don't recall the exact order of events, but Mayakovsky also spoke that night. I don't remember what he talked about, but he was dressed in a red tail-coat. He was in his red tail-coat period at the time.

Duvakin: And that was in February 1914?

Jakobson: Yes. And then Larionov jumped up – that is, he half ran, half threw himself on the stage – and yelled, "The fool in a red tail-coat is talking, and the fools in black are listening!" Following that event we all found ourselves in the Alpenrose café.[48]

Anyway, there were a lot of people there, including Larionov and Goncharova. Larionov and I were remembering that evening, three or four years ago, in Paris. Marinetti was there. We were very indignant that the owner of that place was a German and that he served vodka in decanters marked in centimetres like measuring cups, so it was clear how much we drank. There were many people there; I cannot remember everyone right now. And then Mayakovsky came to join us.

---

47 Piotr Kuznetsov (1899–1968) was a prominent Soviet linguist and one of the founders of the Moscow School of Phonology.

48 The Alpenrose (Alpine Rose) restaurant was opened in the 1870s and was one of the most exquisite restaurants in Moscow where they served European (mainly German) food. The restaurant existed until 1935 when the Bolsheviks closed it and gave the entire building to the Teachers' Association.

Duvakin: Were you already acquainted?

Jakobson: No. He sat at the table next to ours, and he somehow all of a sudden called me to his side. Something must have happened to occasion that, but I don't recall what. Or maybe he didn't call me to his table at all. I somehow managed to knock down his box of Iu-Iu cigarettes,[49] and the cigarettes scattered all across the floor.

I was very embarrassed and started to collect them right away, but Mayakovsky said [*He imitates Mayakovsky*]: "Don't worry, kid. Leave them alone. I'll buy another box." That was our first conversation. Then he joined us, and we chatted for a while. He asked me – I was dressed in the uniform of the Lazarev Institute – "Do you attend the Stroganov Academy?"[50] Their uniforms were very similar to ours.

So that was our first conversation. I don't remember what else we talked about. I do remember how, because nobody else knew French, I had to talk to Marinetti. Marinetti spoke about things that were later published in different articles: that there was no Futurism in Russia, that it was all decadence.

I talked to him about Khlebnikov. He responded, "Well, from what you are telling me about Khlebnikov, he is an archaist, who describes the stone age and invents unnecessary language." It was all kind of – but he did write down my name and later sent me one of his poetry collections with a personal inscription.

That was my only meeting with Mayakovsky at the time. I already knew Khlebnikov then, and we were already quite close; I was close to Kruchenykh, too. I first met Khlebnikov on 30 December 1913.

As for Kruchenykh – as it happens, yesterday I was shown a letter from me to Kruchenykh, which had somehow survived, a very long letter that I don't remember writing at all, and it was dated either February or March of that year, shortly after the conversation with Marinetti – so it must have been March 1914. Anyhow, I am not here to talk about Khlebnikov or Kruchenykh.

Duvakin: That's also interesting!

---

49 The Iu-Iu (Ю-Ю) cigarettes were one of the many brands of the largest Saint Petersburg tobacco company, Shaposhnikov and Co., founded in 1873. The company existed until 1918 when it was nationalized by the Bolsheviks and renamed the Trotsky Tobacco Factory.

50 Stroganov Academy (now the Moscow State Stroganov Academy of Design and Applied Arts) was founded in 1825 by Count Sergei Stroganov, a member of a noble Russian family, who wanted to invest in the development of national art and industry. Since then the Stroganov Academy has produced many talented artists and designers who are famous worldwide.

4.8. Elsa Triolet, Moscow, 1924. Photographer: Alexander Rodchenko.

Jakobson: Yes, but let's stick with Mayakovsky for now. I met him again later, during the war, towards the end of 1916, at Elsa's.[51]

Going back, I am remembering the summer of 1914. [*incomprehensible*] … a young student. I think her brother was to become a rather famous biologist. Her last name was Roginskaya. We were in a boat when we started talking about Mayakovsky. She said, "How can you talk about Mayakovsky seriously? Do you know how he began writing poetry? Burliuk taught him how to write rhymes and then incorporate those into poems." There were such rumours

51 Elsa Triolet (b. Kagan) (1896–1970) was the younger sister of Lilya Brik. For about a year and a half Elsa and Mayakovsky had an affair, but in 1915 Elsa introduced Mayakovsky to Lilya, and their romantic relations ended. Elsa emigrated from the USSR to France, where she married Luis Aragon and became a prominent writer. She and her husband visited the USSR many times, and Elsa even managed to print her books there. Later, in the 1960s, Elsa published some compromising memoirs about Lilya and Mayakovsky. This angered the Communist government tremendously, and her visa to the USSR was permanently revoked.

about Mayakovsky going around, that Burliuk taught him how to write poetry. But I have to say, it was all pure drivel. Still, I heard such things myself on several occasions.

Duvakin: And how do you explain that?

Jakobson: You mean how the rumour started? There was some truth to it, as it was really Burliuk who convinced him to try writing poetry. Another thing is that Mayakovsky often started with jotting down some rhymes. So that rumour appeared somehow.

Duvakin: Chekrygin[52] said that Shekhtel[53] made Mayakovsky write poetry on their school's staircase. At any rate, that's not true, that Burliuk taught him how to write poetry.

Jakobson: Right, but it's true that Burliuk convinced him to become a poet – Mayakovsky himself said it.

Duvakin: That was already known back then?

Jakobson: Yes, it was. I think Mayakovsky himself told that story, about how he transitioned from being an artist to becoming a poet. Around that time, before the war, he was expelled from the School of Painting, Sculpture, and Architecture.[54] Burliuk was also expelled. I remember I met him – I was already acquainted with Burliuk then. So Burliuk told me (he had a slight, soft Ukrainian accent), "I should kill myself, but I am actually full of life and joy!"

When I saw Burliuk in New York many years later, he asked me to write something in his guest album (he had such a thing). I wrote that I "often remembered the incredible words, which you shared with me after your (and Volodya's) expulsion from the School of Painting: 'I am full of life and joy!' I recall them often, and they always invigorate me." That was what I wrote.

---

52 Vasily Chekrygin (1897–1922) was a Russian avant-garde artist. Very talented, at the age of thirteen he was admitted to the Moscow School of Painting, Sculpture, and Architecture. He died very young (at the age of twenty-five) in a train accident.

53 Lev Shekhtel (in 1915 he took the name Lev Zhegin) (1892–1969) was Mayakovsky's friend and schoolmate at the School of Painting. His sister, Vera Shekhtel (1896–1958), had a love affair with Mayakovsky for some time. Both Lev and Vera were children of a talented Russian architect, Fyodor Shekhtel (1859–1926).

54 The School of Painting, Sculpture, and Architecture, founded in 1865, was one of the largest and most prestigious educational institutions in Russia. The course of study was extremely long and difficult: to receive their diploma, the artists had to study for eight years. The course of study for architects lasted ten years, after which they had to work for another five years as an apprentice in order to receive their full licence. The school was much more liberal, however, than the Imperial Academy of Arts in Saint Petersburg, and many young artists preferred to study there.

4.9. Vasily Chekrygin, Moscow, 1913–15. Photographer unknown.

Once Burliuk read it, he ran up to me and said: "What did you do? My wife did not know I was expelled. What am I to do now?" We had to tear out that page, and then I wrote something else, a bit more academically minded.

Duvakin: How odd.

Jakobson: By the way, it was kind of amusing that I kept telling Burliuk all these stories: "Do you remember how we met? Remember this, remember that …" And he couldn't even remember *me*. And then I was with him; I used to live nearby, on Long Island, next to New York. I was staying at a hotel there.

One night, we were sitting quite solemnly at a table in the restaurant there, having dinner, when suddenly a car drove up, and Burliuk was in it, with a bunch of people, all drunk. And then he yelled at me: "I remember now! You are Romochka, but you were very different back then, so young. You used to sit on Osya's lap, and when we argued, you took Osya's side."[55] Suddenly he

55 About Osip (informal, Osya) Brik, see note 90 to dialogue 1.

remembered. And after that he began writing to me and sent me some of his pictures. There you have it.

So, in the beginning of the fall of 1916, I happened to be visiting with Elsa, later Elsa Triolet. We decided to go out some place – the theatre or somewhere else, I don't recall now. She went to change, and I stayed by myself in the living room. I saw two books lying around there, and they impressed me greatly. She took a long time to change, so I was able to look at them properly.

The first one was very thin. It was "A Cloud in Trousers." Oh, no, it was "The Backbone Flute."[56] And there were many lines in it, added by hand, those that had been left blank by a censor. Mayakovsky himself had added them. This book really shook me; it impressed me so much. I also recall later talking with her [Elsa] about it, telling her how interested I was, but also wondering how one could compare him with Khlebnikov. We had a whole argument about that.

The other thing, the other book, let me mention it in passing, was the first edition of essays on the theory of poetic language, edited by Osip Brik. And I told her, "You should be ashamed of yourself. Why didn't you tell me?" And she said, "I didn't know you were interested in such things." Then I picked up that book and finally understood the kind of work they were engaged in.

Antonina Gumilina

Jakobson: I met Mayakovsky at Elsa's a little later. Once, he was there (but I don't want to talk about it, though it was an important moment in Mayakovsky's biography), and, to his great annoyance, another artist was there, too, Gumilina,[57] in whose life he played a big role. Later she killed herself, and Mayakovsky could not get her suicide out of his head to the end, till the day he took his own life.

Duvakin: This is extremely important. When did this story come out? Half a century has passed already. I heard about it but without the name.

---

56 "Fleita-pozvonochnik" ("The Backbone Flute") was a long poem written by Vladimir Mayakovsky in 1915 and dedicated to his lover, Lilya Brik. Initially it had a different title, *Verses for Her*. Mayakovsky illustrated the handwritten, 1919 edition of the poem.

57 Antonina Gumilina (1895–1918) was a Russian avant-garde poet and artist. Only one line has survived from all her poetry, from the poem "Two in One Heart," which was dedicated to Vladimir Mayakovsky, with whom she had a brief affair: "Only about me, only about me, and let's not talk about others ..." Gumilina committed suicide at the age of twenty-three, throwing herself from a window, presumably under the influence of cocaine.

Jakobson: I was the first to write about it, but without mentioning her name, that's true. I wrote about it in my memoirs that came out in *The Literary Archive*.[58] If you could find her paintings or drawings, which I saw at her posthumous exhibit, that will be incredible material for Mayakovsky's biography, because he was always there.

Duvakin: Are you talking about Mayakovsky's drawings?

Jakobson: No, Gumilina's drawings and paintings. She drew Mayakovsky's portraits.

Duvakin: She drew pictures of him?

Jakobson: She drew him after they broke up. After she killed herself, there was an exhibit of her work, at the end of April 1919. It was a small exhibit, somewhere close to the Kuznetsky Most [Kuznetsky Bridge]. I went there with Khlebnikov. There was this big painting there, strangely realistic, but a kind of realism refracted through Cubism.

It depicted early morning light, a bed, and a girl, Gumilina herself, in a simple shirt, sitting on the bed. And you could see a forehead through the window – "my forehead melts the window glass" – Mayakovsky's forehead, and the rest of him, but without a coat or a tie.

The resemblance was striking, only instead of legs he had goat's legs; he was a faun. There were many other paintings, and there were even more that didn't make it into the exhibit. She married an artist, about whom you have probably heard already. He worked in the applied arts, a German. I believe Shklovsky wrote about him in his memoirs and somewhere else.[59] His last name was Schiemann.[60]

Duvakin: I have heard this name.

Jakobson: I think he died soon after the wedding. And she killed herself.

Duvakin: So she committed suicide shortly after they got married?

---

58 See "Russkii literaturnii arhiv," *Voprosy literatury* 8 (1956): 186–230.

59 Victor Shklovsky (1893–1984) was a pre-eminent Russian literary theorist and a Formalist. When Formalism came under attack for being too elitist after the revolution, many scholars associated with it were politically persecuted and had to emigrate. To avoid arrest, Shklovsky fled from the USSR in 1922 but returned for good later. A less known fact is that Shklovsky was also one of the most serious Russian film scholars. A close friend of Sergei Eisenstein, the Russian filmmaker, he wrote probably the most interesting study on Eisenstein (1979) and his method. Shklovsky died in Moscow.

60 Edward Schiemann (1894–1942) was a Russian artist, translator, and illustrator. He was married to Antonina Gumilina for one year and, after her death, organized an exhibition of all her work. Schiemann, being half German, was arrested in 1941 as a "German spy" and died in a concentration camp soon thereafter.

Jakobson: Yes. Her suicide is very clearly depicted in Mayakovsky's script *How Are You?*[61] It was about a suicide. I didn't know anything about the way Mayakovsky remembered this story back then. I only recall us having dinner in Pushkino:[62] Lilya Yurievna, Osip Maximovich, myself (I had also just arrived from the city), and Mayakovsky.

Osip Maximovich was telling us then: "So Schiemann came to me and said, 'You might be interested in buying some of these drawings – I have a whole lot of them here.'" Then he turned to Mayakovsky and told him that he was in some of them and that he was depicted very strangely.

Lilia, who didn't know any details, asked, "What happened?" "She killed herself." And Mayakovsky replied cynically, "With a husband like him, one has to commit suicide." Such scathing cynicism! Then the conversation turned to other topics.

It's very interesting that, when I was collecting materials and memories about Mayakovsky, Yakovleva told me[63] – do you know who she is? Anyway, she told me that in 1928, that is, eight years later, when she brought up the subject of Gumilina's suicide in front of Mayakovsky, she was stunned by the profound cynicism with which he talked about her. He seemed very agitated, she said.

Duvakin: Did he really have something to do with it?

Jakobson: Yes. I read her book, which was never published. She was a very talented poet. There was a poem there – half prose, half free verse – called "Two in One Heart."[64] It was about him.

Duvakin: "Two in One Heart." So that was after his relationship with Vera Feodorovna Shekhtel?[65]

Jakobson: Yes.

---

61 *Kak pozhivaete?* (*How Are You?*) was an experimental screenplay written by Vladimir Mayakovsky in 1926.

62 Pushkino got its name from Grigory Pushka, who owned the land on which the town was built. From the end of the nineteenth century onward, Pushkino, located only ten miles from Moscow, has been a fashionable place to have a country house. This is where the Briks had their *dacha* (country house), too.

63 Tatiana Yakovleva (1906–1991) was a French American fashion designer of Russian ancestry. Mayakovsky met her in Paris in 1928 and immediately fell in love with her. Tatiana felt flattered by the attention of this most famous Soviet poet. After their brief affair, which lasted just a few days, Mayakovsky returned to the USSR. Tatiana emigrated with her husband to the United States. They never saw each other again.

64 About "Two in One Heart," see note 57 to this dialogue.

65 Vera Shekhtel (1896–1958) was the youngest daughter of the architect Fyodor Shekhtel (1859–1926). In her youth she became fascinated with the Futurists and their poetry. She had a brief affair with Mayakovsky. Fyodor Shekhtel found peace and tranquillity in her little apartment during the last three years of his life, after his own home had been nationalized by the Bolsheviks.

4.10. Tatiana Yakovleva with an envelope, Paris, 1925–7. Photographer unknown.

4.11. Vera Shekhtel, Moscow, 1913–15. Photographer: Emil Bendel.

4.12. Fyodor Shekhtel, Moscow, 1900s–10s. Photographer unknown.

Duvakin: But before his acquaintance with Elsa?

Jakobson: In any case before Lilya.

Anyway, in the fall of 1916, in December, I think, Mayakovsky came to Moscow from Saint Petersburg. We were at Elsa's again. (That's a different occasion.) So, besides Elsa, there was also a man called Mar Levental.[66] I don't know if you know him. His name was Mark, but they called him Mar, Mar Levental.

He was mentioned in one of Elsa's early works, the novel *Wild Strawberry*.[67] Her relationship with him is all there. She said he was like a childhood illness: you had to go through Mar Levental. Then many years later, when she goes back to Moscow, she finds the man has turned into a monument.

So anyway, we didn't know what to do. There were some other girls there too.

---

66 Mark Levental (1894–1952) was the stepfather of Yuri Nagibin (1920–1944), a prominent Soviet writer. The writer's real father, Kirill Nagibin, had been executed by the Bolsheviks in 1920, and Levental took care of his pregnant wife and, when he was born, the son. Levental was exiled in 1927 to Komi Republic (a prison camp area), where he died in 1952.

67 After marrying the French officer Andre Triolet in 1918, Elsa Triolet left the USSR with him. In 1922 she turned to writing. She published two novels in Russian, *Zemlyanichka* (*Wild Strawberry*, 1926) and *Zashchitnyi tsvet* (*Camouflage*, 1928). In 1928 Elsa Triolet married the writer Louis Aragon. She won the Goncourt Prize in 1944.

Duvakin: So, he was very attracted to – what do you mean, exactly?

Jakobson: Women found him appealing, they liked him, and, if they did, he was ready to reciprocate.

Duvakin: And who was he, an actor?

Jakobson: No, I think he was a lawyer. A very sophisticated man, who at the time was also famous for winning, it seems, 100,000 rubles in the state lottery – money that he lost during the revolution. He later disappeared.

So, he was there, as was a beautiful Armenian woman who now, I think, lives in Paris; her last name was Begliarova. And Mar said, "The girls must go and see Vertinsky."[68] He was a big celebrity at the time, you know. We all went. We bought our tickets, in the first row. There were six of us.

And I witnessed there an incredible scene. When Vertinsky saw Mayakovsky, he couldn't speak, he couldn't recite his poems at all. He had to leave the stage. Then he came back after he had collected himself. Afterwards we went to have dinner with him, at the Arts and Literature Society, near the theatre.

Duvakin: Vertinsky already knew Mayakovsky then?

Jakobson: Yes.

Duvakin: What did he imagine would happen?

Jakobson: Mayakovsky was prone to angry outbursts back then. You know, I remember another amusing story. I think it happened at the Café Pittoresk,[69] but I am not sure.

---

68 Alexander Vertinsky (1889–1957) was a Russian and Soviet poet, singer, composer, cabaret performer, and actor. His original songs and performances were extremely popular in Russia, but following the revolution he decided to leave his homeland and work abroad. He toured Turkey, Poland, and Germany, then moved to Paris, where he performed before the Russian émigré clientele at Montmartre cabarets for nine years. Eventually he left France for the United States, where he had great success on the stage once again, but the Great Depression made him move to China and join the Russian expat community in Shanghai. In 1943 the Soviet government allowed Vertinsky to return to Russia. Although he was accepted with open arms at first, his concerts were closely monitored, and he soon found himself unable to have easy access to Russian audiences despite his immense popularity. Following his death from heart failure on 21 May 1957, his name was completely forgotten for several decades. Since the 1990s Vertinsky's songs have made a comeback and are now enjoyed by millions of fans in Russia.

69 Café Pittoresk was a popular Moscow café frequented by some of the most famous members of the Russian avant-garde movement. It was founded by one of the last Russian patrons of art, Nikolai Filippov. Its remarkable Modernist wall paintings by Georgy Yakulov (1884–1924) and, later, decorations and art by Alexander Rodchenko set it apart from similar establishments. After the revolution, the café was seized by the Bolsheviks and renamed the Red Rooster. For some time artists like Mayakovsky, Meyerhold, Bryusov, and even Lunacharsky continued to visit it, but the café soon lost its original charm and was officially closed in 1919.

Duvakin: Pittoresk – it must have been later.

Jakobson: Perhaps it wasn't Pittoresk yet then; maybe it was called Tramblet or something else. Somehow the three of us – Mayakovsky, Elsa, and I – ended up sitting together. And suddenly Mayakovsky decided to play his favourite game at the time: find himself someone new, a complete stranger, and throw at him all kinds of witticisms, puns, unexpected endearments. It was easy to lose your mind from all those conflicting messages.

I felt like I were transported back to the Lazarev Institute, where new guys were usually harassed, and you had to know how to act under the circumstances. Apparently I was able to keep my cool, and Mayakovsky liked that.

Duvakin: And you were the rookie then?

Jakobson: Yes, I was the new guy.

Duvakin: And this took place in the café?

Jakobson: It was the first time we had an actual conversation. Then he was also trying to get me to play a card game with him, chemin de fer [Russian, железка]. Do you know it? It's quite simple. But Elsa told me, "I forbid you to play. You only lose when you play with Mayakovsky."

Jakobson: And then … [*incomprehensible*] Mayakovsky left for Petersburg. Then it was called Petrograd.[70]

Duvakin: Did you live in Petrograd?

Jakobson: No, he lived in Petrograd. I have only lived in Moscow. This was the time – we are talking about January 1917 already – when I translated into French the first part of "A Cloud in Trousers," in verse. It was a decent translation, by the way. I still have it. I think it was pretty good. But I never tried to publish it. The thought never crossed my mind.

Lilya Brik

Jakobson: Around that time, I had a chance to go to Petersburg. Before I left, Elsa gave me an assignment, something to deliver to her sister, Lilya. She lived close to the train station, on Zhukovsky Street. I went to her place right after I got off the train.

I was unsure about what to think of Lilya. For one thing, I was upset that when I – she was five years older than me, and when I was a student at the

70 For the history of the names of the city, see note 92 to dialogue 1.

4.13. *From left to right*: Osip Brik, Lilya Brik, and Vladimir Mayakovsky, Moscow, 1928. Photographer: Alexander Rodchenko.

Lazarev Institute, she was always given to us as an example for her grades in writing and so on. Later, when I shared this with her, she told me, "Don't be angry with me. The writing teacher was in love with me back then."

There was another episode that upset me, although now Lilya doesn't remember it at all. It was something that happened at an event of the Society of Free Aesthetics,[71] in the beginning of 1914, before Marinetti's visit. Balmónt had just come back,[72] and the society had organized a celebration in his honour.

I was present too. By the way, secondary school students were not allowed to attend meetings at the society. So I didn't wear my uniform to the meeting. Since I didn't have plain clothes, I had to borrow them from someone. I sat in the first row, together with Lilya and Osip Maximovich, who very loudly applauded Balmónt and Bryusov.[73]

There were many who spoke. Then he [Mayakovsky] got up to give a speech, too. I must say this was the most effective speech I ever heard him give. He rose

71 About the Society of Free Aesthetics, see note 42 to this dialogue.

72 About Konstantin Balmónt, see note 49 to dialogue 3.

73 About Valery Bryusov, see note 16 to dialogue 1.

to his feet, leaned a little on the table in front of him, and said [*Jakobson imitates Mayakovsky's voice*], "Konstantin Dmitrievich, you heard speeches from your friends and admirers. Now listen to what your enemies have to say." And he continued, "Once, your poetry was heard in rocking chairs, on old estates, etc., etc., but now there is new poetry to listen to."

He recited something – I think one of his poems, "Sounds of the City," and some of Khlebnikov's poetry. Then Bryusov got up, furious, and said, "We are here to celebrate Konstantin Dmitrievich, not to insult him." At that point Balmónt pulled him to the side and talked wonderfully about how we could argue with each other as much as we wanted but that we were brothers in poetry, all bathed in "azure blue," so to speak. [*They chuckle.*]

By the way, he [Balmónt] gave Mayakovsky some of his poems with an autograph. Mayakovsky kept everything. And, since our interview is not for publication, I should share what Mayakovsky told me later: "It's such a pity… Sometimes you find yourself in the woods or in the fields, and you are in need of toilet paper, but all you have in your pocket are Balmónt's poems. You have to sacrifice them." He added something else, but I forget.

Duvakin: Roman Osipovich, other witnesses have said – Pertsov[74] claims that he read Balmónt's "Tishe, tishe sovlekaite s drevnikh idolov odezhdy" ["Quietly, Quietly Disrobe the Old Idols"]. Did that happen, or did he imagine it?

Jakobson: I don't think that's true.

Duvakin: Is it just an apocryphal story then?

Jakobson: Yes, apocryphal. I remember reading it and thinking, "That's not right."

Duvakin: The poem he read on behalf of the enemies, the recitation of "Sovlekaite s drevnikh idolov odezhdy" ("Disrobe the Old Idols") –

Jakobson: He wrote that for the occasion.

Duvakin: Who? Mayakovsky?

Jakobson: No, Balmónt.

---

74 Piotr Pertsov (1868–1947) was a Russian poet, publisher, editor, literary critic, journalist, and memoirist associated with the Russian Symbolist movement. A talented, intelligent, and very kind man, Pertsov was a lifelong friend of many prominent figures of the Russian avant-garde. After the revolution he resided in the Kostroma region and lectured at Kostroma University. His last years were darkened by solitude and a very difficult financial situation. Neither occasional publications nor lecturing brought Pertsov much money; he received no pension and lived in poverty. Only in 1942 did friends help him to become a member of the Union of Soviet Writers.

Duvakin: Aha, Balmónt. But still, Mayakovsky read that famous poem of Balmónt's, turning it against its author. "Disrobe. And in your prime, do not forget that death, as much as life, is beautiful, and that the cold grave is full of grandeur." That is, Balmónt is a corpse.

Jakobson: I can't be sure.

Duvakin: You don't remember it?

Jakobson: Not at all. I think it's unlikely. But maybe I just didn't notice, I was very nervous. What's kind of amusing is that Lilya Yurievna and Osip Maximovich were among those who hissed and yelled at Mayakovsky the most.

Duvakin: So they did not yet know each other then?

Jakobson: Not yet.

Duvakin: That's interesting.

Jakobson: Yes, it is. I remember that well. It turned me against them for a while. But I visited them later, in January 1917 more or less. If memory serves me right, it was 14 January. I was supposed to drop by, deliver the package, and then go away, but I ended up staying with them for ten days.

We became fast friends right away. Elsa had written to Lilya to ask me to read my translation, so I did. They loved it. We started talking, then Mayakovsky came and joined us. I was asked to read the translation one more time. Mayakovsky was so amusing.

Later, we were walking together in the street when he ordered me to recite my translation again. I did as I was asked. "Now translate it into Russian, word for word." He wanted to know how close to the original my translation was. You know, there were these lines there:

> You entered, swiftly, sharp as "Here!"
> punishing your suede gloves.
> And said, "You know,
> I'm getting married."[75]

I had that translated like this:

> Âpre, comme un mot dédein,
> tu entras, Marie,
> et tu m'as dit,
> en tournament tes gants de daim:
> "Savez-vous,
> je me marie?"

---

75 From "A Cloud in Trousers" (1914).

4.14. *From left*: Japanese journalist Tamidzi Naito, Boris Pasternak, Sergei Eisenstein, Olga Tretiakova, Lilya Brik, Vladimir Mayakovsky, Arseny Voznesensky, and Naito's assistant, Moscow, 11 May 1924. Photographer unknown.

He said, "No, no, I don't like that. It's the same word: 'Marie,' 'Marie'!" "No," I said, "it's Marie the first time, and 'married' the second." "That's no good." [*They laugh.*]

Duvakin: Was your translation ever published anywhere?

Jakobson: No.

Duvakin: Do you still have it?

Jakobson: I think I do.

Duvakin: Could you recite it to us? That's so fascinating!

Jakobson: I don't remember everything. I could recite the first few stanzas from memory. I don't remember all of it.

Duvakin: That's fine. Share what you remember, even if it's just a few lines.

Jakobson:

Vous pensez – c'est le délire de la maladie?
C'était,
C'était à Odessa.
"Je viendrai à quatre," Marie m'a dit.
Huit.
Neuf.
La onzième commença.
Voici le soir
Dans le froid nocturne
décembreux,
sinistres.
Vers le dos décrépit ricannent et hurlent les lustres.

There you have it. Volodya [Mayakovsky] and I became very close after that, I must say.

Duvakin: That's already …

Jakobson: That was in January 1917. It was the beginning of a close friendship. We somehow … the translation and everything … We used to stroll around and talk all the time. A lot. He was at a very dramatic point in his life.

Duvakin: How so?

Jakobson: In his personal life, things were not going well. His love life in particular.

Duvakin: His relationship with Lilya?

Jakobson: No. He was in a very difficult situation. [*incomprehensible*] We met several times … Then he came to Moscow again after the February Revolution, and from Moscow we went …

[THE RECORDING ENDS.]

Duvakin further comments in his voice that while he was changing the reel, they decided to have some tea. Jakobson started to feel a little nervous, tired, and promised to come to Moscow the following year and finish the conversation. Thus, here we have only memories of what happened before February 1917.

DIALOGUE 5
With Vladimir and Ariadna Sosinsky on 21 June 1969*

The second conversation that Duvakin recorded with Vladimir and Ariadna Sosinsky includes readings of letters by Marina Tsvetaeva, reminiscences about meetings with Boris Pasternak during the final years of the poet's life, and stories of their acquaintance with Isaak Babel in Paris. The interview ends with Vladimir Sosinsky's memories of his experiences in a German camp, his participation in the Oléron Island uprising, and his post–Second World War work for the United Nations.

Victor Duvakin: Let's start with you, Vladimir Bronislavovich, and Ariadna Viktorovna can join in. Do you have anything to add about Babel?

Vladimir Sosinsky: Last time I was telling you about Marina Ivanovna's love affair with the Vendée fishermen.[1] After you left, I was able to find the letter in which she wrote about them. I think it's worth recording it. Listen to this: "Dear Volodya!" (and the date is 26 May 1926). "We've been here for two months now. Do you want to know the most amazing development? The landlords absolutely adore me, he and she, one hundred and fifty years in total! Isn't that flattering? He is the perfect 'old man.'" Let me remind you that she loved the image of Casanova as an elderly man. In general, she loved old people, idealized old age, perhaps. So, you see, the talk about suicide and violent ending of one's life, that wasn't like her at all. She wanted to live long, as long as possible. "He is the perfect 'old man.' The two of them, and their love for me, are the most important events of the last month.

"Their affection represents ancient Vendée's love for me – no, more than that, the love of the whole old world to which they fully belong (perhaps it's the

* Length of interview – 2 hours and 20 minutes

1 About Vendée, see note 71 to dialogue 3.

discipline of the heart you can't find in the new world, I think, not until it grows old, too). It makes life beautiful again, erases its sharp angles, and warms the heart. I don't mean just good breeding – everything! For the first time since my childhood (Schwarzwald) I am enamoured by everyday existence.

"I also finally realized something else: I HATE the city. The only thing I love about it is the nature, the space where it ends. Here everything is nature. People's lives ebb and flow with the sea, and that's how time is measured as well."

In another letter, from a few weeks later, she writes that she sees the "sea as a wasted walking space. There's nothing I can do with it. Only the sailor or the fisherman can truly love the sea; the rest of it is the result of people's laziness, their love for rolling around on the beach. I am too old to play in the sand and too young to just lie on it. But it's still nice, overall. We have beautiful rocks here. And our landlords are wonderful, as if from a fairy tale."

And those same "wonderful landlords" turn into monsters by the end of summer: "Everything here is still marvellous ..." (just as it was before) "except for the hellish landlords, who hate us now, having been paid in full upfront, and want us to leave, threaten us with the local judge and police, for no reason at all." This is a good example of how she was: as quick to fall in love with as she was to quarrel with people.

Duvakin: They were just regular, gnarly Vendée peasants, who wanted to make some extra money but still possessed the kind of inherited culture I imagine everybody in France shares, right?

Vladimir Sosinsky: This next excerpt I am about to read is just for you, Victor Dmitrievich: "I have a big request. Could you please send me a few copies of proofs of [my poem about] Mayakovsky, I need them very much, especially to send to Pasternak and his family. (I have that opportunity now.)" If you remember, I was the secretary and editor of *Volya Rossii* (*Russia's Will*) in which "The Ratcatcher" was being published. "The second big request: please edit very carefully; those are not simple poems.

"I'll be criticized because of the content. Let's not give them reason to do so because of printing errors. Sending my corrections separately. Do pay special attention."

And, to finish talking about Marina Tsvetaeva, I want to share two entertaining pieces of writing we managed to preserve.

Here's an excerpt from a letter she wrote to my wife, Ariadna, whom she always called "Adia." "Adia, make sure to meet B." (She always used the initial, never wrote the whole name in her letters. Here she is referring to the Balmónts.) "Adia, make sure to meet the Balmónts. Mirra was a sweet thirteen-year-old; now she is a bit older than you. I beg of you, make his acquaintance. If he wants to kiss you (he sometimes does that!)" (there's an exclamation mark between brackets here), "tell him you have a fiancée, who's on a coffee plantation in Morocco at present."

Duvakin: Very charming! [*He laughs.*] She definitely knew Balmónt!

Vladimir Sosinsky: Yes. The second one is a whole letter written to Ariadna from Vendée. As she was thinking about the wedding between two people whom she wrote about in two different poems – Rodzevich and Bulgakova, the daughter of the priest-philosopher – she wrote the following: "St. Gilles" (that's a place on the coast in Vendée, where she used to go during the summer; she visited there several times, at least), "9 June 1925. Dear Adia! Bulgakova's wedding will take place on Sunday the thirteenth, at 93 rue de Crimée. Would be great if you find out in advance what time it is, and attend! ... Take Volodya and Doda and go. Then write to me about it. They picked a good day for it, ah? The thirteenth. Kisses, M. Ts."[2] I am that "Volodya," and "Doda" is Daniil Reznikov.[3]

Duvakin: So, he is the third.

Vladimir Sosinsky: That's right.

Duvakin: Who was Daniil Reznikov?

Vladimir Sosinsky: He was a poet, the recipient of the first award for best émigré poetry given by *The Latest News*. But he was very lazy and didn't produce much; that was the only prize he ever received. And now he works as a typography director at the same publication.

Duvakin: And why did she say that they "picked a good day for it, the thirteenth"?

Vladimir Sosinsky: It was always seen as an unlucky number.

Duvakin: I see, and that's the only reason? Not because she thought of this number as important to her?

Vladimir Sosinsky: Oh, no, no. It was just the unlucky number thirteen. Did you know that in America they don't have floors or hotel rooms numbered thirteen?

Duvakin: Really? How interesting. And the two poems are "Poema gory" and "Poema ..."

Vladimir Sosinsky: "Poema kontsa."[4]

---

2 The letters from Marina Tsvetaeva to Vladimir Sosinsky were published after the conversation took place.

3 About Reznikov, see note 84 to dialogue 3.

4 About these poems, see note 21 to dialogue 3.

Duvakin: "Poem of the End." Had she been in love with this Rodzevich for a long time?[5]

Vladimir Sosinsky: I think the affair lasted three years.

Duvakin: And they had regular rendezvous?

Vladimir Sosinsky: Yes.

Duvakin: I see. So one can look at this marriage with the daughter of the former Marxist who had turned philosopher and later a priest, Bulgakov, as – what's his first name and patronymic, do you remember?

Vladimir Sosinsky: No, I don't.

Duvakin: So she was right to view it as a cruel betrayal?

Vladimir Sosinsky: Yes. But "Poema kontsa" shows that they had already parted ways. She left us a few poems about this event in her life. Let me ask Ariadna if she can give us the exact titles.

[*There is a pause in the recording.*]

Duvakin: What's the title of this poem?

Ariadna Sosinsky: "Popytka revnosti" [Attempt at jealousy].

Duvakin: "Attempt at jealousy." Is it about Rodzevich then?

Ariadna Sosinsky: Yes, it is."How's your life there, how are you doing …?" [Russian, Как вам там живется, как вам можется …][6]

Duvakin: I remember it!

Ariadna Sosinsky: Of course you do. How did it go? Please don't record this. "A goddess … in place of Carrara marble …" No, I don't remember it.

Pasternak's Conversation with Stalin

Duvakin: All right, now that Ariadna Viktorovna has joined us, maybe we can, before we discuss Babel,[7] talk about your meetings with Pasternak and in general the topic of Marina and Pasternak.[8]

---

5 About Konstantin Rodzevich, see note 94 to dialogue 3.

6 This is an excerpt from Tsvetaeva's poem "Attempt at Jealousy," written on 19 November 1924. Sosinsky does not recite the poem correctly. It begins with the following lines: "Как живется вам с другою,- / Проще ведь? – Удар весла!" (How is life with her, the other, / Simpler, I guess? – A stroke of an oar!)

7 About Isaac Babel, see note 57 to dialogue 3.

8 About Boris Pasternak, see note 38 to dialogue 1.

Vladimir Sosinsky: I remember we met in the garden of his country house in Peredelkino,[9] and he was wearing a white tunic. We still have the colour film recording in which he told us about – we were shocked that he wanted to argue with us about the quality of *Sestra moya – zhizn'* (*My Sister, Life*) and *Temy i variatsii* (*Themes and Variations*).[10]

Ariadna Sosinsky: No, no, you are mistaken. He loved *My Sister, Life*! It was the *Themes and Variations* that he considered artificial, not an important book. On the contrary, *My Sister, Life* he felt was organic, while *Themes and Variations* seemed to him somewhat artificial, not true to life.

Vladimir Sosinsky: How do you remember Pasternak? Did you meet him too?

Duvakin: Yes, yes, several times.

Vladimir Sosinsky: He was such a great storyteller. For some reason he always made me think of organ music. His conversation sparkled and was as original as his poetry. I remember thinking I wished we had a way to record him then. He discussed many things with us then, but for some reason he especially told us in detail about his phone conversation with Stalin who called to discuss Osip Mandelstam.[11]

Duvakin: I have recorded memories about that, but I won't tell you what. You tell me. That's so interesting.

Vladimir Sosinsky: It's quite simple, really.

Duvakin: There were some discrepancies, all because of the ways he told it.

Vladimir Sosinsky: By the way, Elsa Triolet[12] shared with us around the time he was awarded the Nobel Prize, when everybody was annoyed with Pasternak, that –

Duvakin: Why?

---

9 Peredelkino is located about twenty miles southwest of Moscow. The creation of the village was Maxim Gorky's idea, who, in 1934, proposed to the government that some land be allocated to serve the needs of the Soviet literati. Surrounded by a dense pine forest, Peredelkino became famous for its very healthy air. Boris Pasternak, Konstantin Fedin, Ilya Ilf, Evgeny Petrov, and many other Russian authors had small cottages there.

10 *Sestra moya – zhizn'* (*My Sister, Life*) is a collection of Pasternak's early poetry, partially published in 1917. The book was inspired by Pasternak's romance with Elena Vinograd and was praised highly by many critics, and especially by Osip Mandelstam. *Temy i variatsii* (*Themes and Variations*) was another book of poems, written between 1916 and 1922.

11 About Osip Mandelstam, see note 72 to dialogue 1.

12 About Elsa Triolet, see note 51 to dialogue 4.

Vladimir Sosinsky: Because he refused to receive it. Anyway, Elsa Triolet also published her memories of that conversation, her version of her talk, with Pasternak about Mandelstam's case. We were all very confused because of the way he recalled everything; it was all very strange.

Duvakin: What was your impression of what had happened?

Vladimir Sosinsky [*turning to his wife, Ariadna Viktorovna*]: I'll start talking, but you can correct me any time.

Ariadna Sosinsky: Fine.

Vladimir Sosinsky: The phone rang. Stalin's secretary told Pasternak that Stalin himself wanted to speak with him. It all happened in the communal apartment, where there's always so much noise, commotion, and in general it was so difficult to have a serious conversation in such an environment. So Pasternak heard Stalin's voice, which he knew well from the radio speeches and so on. "I began complaining right away about my horrible living conditions, the communal apartment, how hard it was to hear the phone, and in general how terrible life was."

Duvakin: Did Pasternak say that?

Ariadna Sosinsky: Yes.

Vladimir Sosinsky: Pasternak told us: "Stalin didn't pay attention to any of my complaints, just asked me some questions, and I answered. Questions like, 'Do you know Mandelstam?' 'Yes, I do.' 'Tell me your opinion about Mandelstam? Is he a master? Is Mandelstam a master of his craft?' I replied, 'Never ask a ballerina or a poet about another ballerina or poet. They won't be honest in their assessment.' 'Fine, tell me then, are you friends with Mandelstam?' 'No, I wouldn't call him a friend.' Then Stalin said, 'You asked Bukharin to intervene on his behalf.[13] Why didn't you turn to me? Or the Writers' Union?'[14] 'The Writers' Union?' Pasternak replied, 'The Writer's Union doesn't concern itself with such things any more. And if I didn't turn to you – if I hadn't drawn attention to his fate, how would you have known anything? And you wouldn't be calling me right now.'"

---

13 Nikolai Bukharin (1888–1938) was a prominent member of the Bolshevik party. He was fluent in English, German, and French and was also a good economist. A close ally of Lenin (and initially Stalin), Bukharin advocated for the continuation of the New Economic Policy (Russian, НЭП) inaugurated by Lenin in 1921. He then used all his influence in 1929 to stop the process of the collectivization of peasant land. His resistance to Stalin's "reforms" resulted in his arrest; Bukharin was expelled from the party and sentenced to death. His wife, Anna, was also arrested and spent twenty years in labour camps. His son, Yuri, was placed in an orphanage, and his name was changed.

14 About the Union of Soviet Writers, see note 71 to dialogue 1.

So he behaved very admirably in this case because despite everything he still tried to help Mandelstam. There were other things Stalin said, like, "If he were my friend, a poet, if I were a poet, and my comrade was in trouble, I'd defend him better than you do." I don't remember the exact wording of Pasternak's response, but I think he replied, "I'd like to see you in person, Joseph Vissarionovich, and have a talk." "What about?" "About life and death." At which point Stalin hung up.

"After that conversation in the communal apartment had ended, I ran out into the street," Pasternak told us, "found a telephone booth, and called the Kremlin. I demanded to be put through to Stalin again. The same young man who had called me earlier replied that Stalin couldn't talk to me right now and asked what was bothering me. 'What am I supposed to do with this conversation? How would it fit into my biography? This was a historical call, after all! Can I talk about it with someone else? How am I supposed to live from now on?'"

We didn't understand then what he meant by that, "to live from now on." Well, Stalin called, he was trying to help Mandelstam, to show his humanity. Why would that call change anything? But it turns out that at the time, during the height of Stalinism –

Ariadna Sosinsky: How naive, how childish!

Vladimir Sosinsky: There was a certain kind of naïveté, childishness, an inability to comprehend simple moral obligations. Anna Akhmatova wrote in her memoirs that Pasternak should be given a B for his answers.[15] I disagree. He should be given an F!

Duvakin: I agree with you, Vladimir Bronislavovich.

Vladimir Sosinsky: He was too excited by Stalin's words.

Duvakin: Well, that's understandable.

Vladimir Sosinsky: He was agitated because Mandelstam had been arrested for writing anti-Stalin poetry. Did Pasternak know those poems?

Duvakin: I don't know.

Vladimir Sosinsky: He knew them.

Duvakin: You think he knew them? Maybe he didn't, after all.

---

15 Anna Akhmatova (b. Gorenko) (1889–1966) is considered to be one of the finest Soviet poets. She was also a seminal translator and literary critic. Akhmatova was a woman of incredible willpower. Her two husbands were arrested and sentenced to death. Her only son (Lev Gumilev, who later became a history professor) spent more than ten years in a concentration camp. She found the moral strength to continue her artistic activity to the end of her life and became a living legend for all who loved Russian literature.

5.1. Anna Akhmatova and Boris Pasternak, Moscow, 1946. Photographer unknown.

Vladimir Sosinsky: He was afraid he'd be saddled with something bad. He was afraid for his own life. Zinaida Nikolayevna put it nicely:[16] she told everyone, "My children were raised to love Stalin before anyone else, more than their own parents."

Duvakin: Zinaida Nikolayevna was Pasternak's last wife, right?

Vladimir Sosinsky: Yes.

Duvakin: His second?

Vladimir Sosinsky: Yes, his second wife.

Duvakin: Well, if we don't count Ivinskaya.[17]

16 Zinaida Neuhaus (Pasternak) (1897–1966) was the first wife of the pianist Heinrich Neuhaus. While still married, Zinaida met Boris Pasternak (who was also married at the time) and fell under the spell of his wonderful personality. The two decided to divorce their current partners, but the process proved to be more difficult than expected. In 1932 Pasternak even tried to commit suicide when Zinaida returned to her husband. After that, though, they finally married.

17 Olga Ivinskaya (1912–1995) was Boris Pasternak's last muse, from 1946 until his death in 1960. Many scholars insist that Olga was the prototype of Lara in his novel *Doctor Zhivago* (1955). Olga suffered considerably during her many years with and after Pasternak: she was arrested in 1949 – as a way of putting pressure on Pasternak – and spent a number of years in a labour camp. Even during the "thaw," the KGB found reasons to arrest her again, for using the royalty money from the sales of *Doctor Zhivago* abroad.

Vladimir Sosinsky: Right. We were shocked by this conversation with Pasternak and couldn't understand why he had told us about it in the first place. People usually try to defend themselves in such cases, while he denigrated himself completely in our eyes.

Ariadna Sosinsky: He told Triolet the same thing. Who asked him to?

Duvakin: I think he felt very guilty, and that was a sort of personal atonement for him.

Vladimir Sosinsky: Perhaps, though there was no atonement in the way he told the story – only enthusiasm for the historical moment, the fact that Stalin himself called.

He was concerned about what would be the importance of this conversation in his life, [what he was supposed to tell people about it]. Stalin's secretary was confused by that and told him, "Well, just say Stalin spoke with you." Because that was, so to say, somewhat flattering for Stalin.

Duvakin: He took on a noble role.

Vladimir Sosinsky: Yes, he did, in this case. He didn't execute the poet for those horrific poems he [Mandelstam] wrote against him.

Duvakin: Well, he did execute him, but later.

Ariadna Sosinsky: Yes, later.

Vladimir Sosinsky [*smiling*]**:** Later.

Duvakin: In an Oriental manner.

Vladimir Sosinsky [*sighs*]**:** In an Oriental manner.

Meetings with Pasternak

Duvakin: Can you tell me how is it that you met him in Peredelkino in 1957, when you came back only in 1961?

Vladimir Sosinsky: We came back home in 1960. It was 10 March. And he died on 10 May.

Duvakin: He died on 30 May.

Ariadna Sosinsky: We used to visit regularly. My husband worked for the UN, and, starting in 1965, we came back every two years.

Duvakin: When was the first time?

Vladimir Sosinsky: In 1955, and then in 1957. In 1958 I arrived from Geneva specifically to see [our son] Alyosha and find out how he was getting on.

Ariadna Sosinsky: That was in 1959.

Vladimir Sosinsky: Correct, 1959. And we returned for good in 1960.

Duvakin: I see. And that meeting in Peredelkino you were telling us about …

Vladimir Sosinsky: It happened in 1957.

Duvakin: Was that your first meeting with Pasternak?

Vladimir Sosinsky: No, it wasn't. We already knew each other.

Duvakin: That is, it wasn't something he'd share with a person he just met?

Ariadna Sosinsky: It was the second or third time we'd seen each other.

Duvakin: When did you first meet him? What did he know about you?

Vladimir Sosinsky: About us?

Ariadna Sosinsky: We wrote him a letter.

Vladimir Sosinsky: In 1955, during our first trip to the Soviet Union, we wrote him a note, telling him we wanted to meet him.

Ariadna Sosinsky: We told him we loved his poetry, that we knew Tsvetaeva, things like that.

Vladimir Sosinsky: And his response was quite long and original, along the lines of, "You can imagine how interesting it would be for me to meet you, you can tell me so much I don't know, how pleasant that would be," and so on. But it was actually a very polite refusal in the end. I don't know why.

Ariadna Sosinsky: He wrote about the novel he was working on.

Vladimir Sosinsky: And how precious time was for him then. He had heard about us from the Andreyevs too and in general knew of our existence, so to speak.

Duvakin: That happened in 1955 then?

Vladimir Sosinsky: Yes.

Duvakin: You didn't meet that time?

Vladimir Sosinsky: We did not. In 1957, when we called him on the phone, he spoke to us as if we already knew each other. Maybe that's how he talked to people, as if they were already friends, but, in any case, he was very chatty and pleasant. Not only did we make plans to meet, but he also got us tickets – for himself and the two of us, because he wanted to come along – to go see *Mary Stuart* at the Moscow Art Theatre.[18] He even "shocked" us at our first meeting with his tremendous "Bacchanalia," which we liked very much. Do you remember his poem "Bacchanalia"?[19]

Duvakin: For some reason I don't.

Vladimir Sosinsky: It wasn't published.

Duvakin: Then I simply don't know it.

Vladimir Sosinsky: Imagine, then, it was only our second or third meeting, and we were already friends.

Duvakin: After "Bacchanalia"?

Vladimir Sosinsky: Yes, and after *Mary Stuart*, and the delicious lunch we had with him, at which there was a lot of cognac. [*He smiles.*] He loved cognac.

Duvakin: Pasternak liked to drink then?

Ariadna Sosinsky: You see, he drank like a Georgian, not out of sadness or quietly, but joyfully, for fun.

Vladimir Sosinsky: I remember one time we met with Pasternak; it was at our going-away party – we were leaving for the United States again.

Duvakin: Did you come here for a couple of months?

Vladimir Sosinsky: Yes. And we were leaving for America again. He organized a party for us, and Evtushenko was there, too,[20] as well as some actors from the Moscow Art Theatre. That actor Levitov, one of the lead actors at theatre, had brought a group of actors from Leningrad. More than a dozen bottles of cognac were emptied that evening.

Duvakin: That was at Peredelkino?

---

18 About the Moscow Art Theatre, see note 105 to dialogue 1.

19 The poem "Bacchanalia" was written in 1957, in the midst of the Khrushchev's "thaw," when Communist ideals were debunked, and the country gradually fell under the spell of a universal "bacchanalia," driven by a new sense of permissiveness.

20 Evgeniy Evtushenko (1932–2017) was a prominent Soviet poet, writer, producer, actor, and literary critic. He rose to international fame during the period of spiritual stagnation that was characteristic of Leonid Brezhnev's leadership. Those who disliked him insisted that Evtushenko was a KGB agent, but that is doubtful. He just happened to be chosen to represent abroad the new image of an intellectually "free" USSR, and he took full advantage of it. Tired of his constant fighting with the system, Evtushenko left Russia in the 1990s and settled in Oklahoma, where he taught Russian literature until his death at the age of eighty-four.

Vladimir Sosinsky: Yes, Peredelkino.

Duvakin: So he organized a party in your honour then?

Vladimir Sosinsky: That's not what it was called officially, but it's really what it was. We were leaving in three days. It was an interesting evening. It turns out that was the first time Evtushenko and Pasternak had met.

Duvakin: Fascinating! And how were they?

Vladimir Sosinsky: Let me tell you something very interesting. People say Evtushenko brags too much, and so on. But on that occasion he was very modest, quiet, and shy. He came alive only when Pasternak read his poetry. He read to us "My Sister, Life" and "Bacchanalia," which very few people knew about then, and when he stumbled, thanks to all that cognac, Evtushenko fed him the next line. Evtushenko had to feed many lines to him. We were very impressed by that.

We were also impressed by something else, when he got to recite his own poetry. Boris Pasternak had told me earlier, when I had asked him about the new generation of poets, about Voznesensky,[21] and so on: "What is this new poetry? Imagine some new wallpaper: it may have a new pattern, but it's still just wallpaper and nothing more. That, too, shall pass."

That was his attitude towards the new poets, whom we were beginning to admire. We were bewildered by his attitude. But when Evtushenko read his poetry – by the way, he reminded us of Mayakovsky and Gorky for some reason.

Duvakin: Did he remind you of Yesenin, too?

Ariadna Sosinsky: No.

Duvakin: Really?

Ariadna Sosinsky: I knew Yesenin. No, not at all.

Vladimir Sosinsky: I thought that he read beautifully. His poetry was much better when he recited it himself than in print.

Duvakin: Yes.

Vladimir Sosinsky: And suddenly I noticed something. Boris Leonidovich [Pasternak] was searching for me.

---

21 Andrei Voznesensky (1933–2010) was one of the most notable Soviet poets. For his first published book of poems Voznesensky was heavily criticized, the editor lost his job, and Nikita Khrushchev urged him to leave the country. In the 1970s, however, Voznesensky was highly praised and well published, and his poetry was very popular and admired. All his life he cherished the memory of Boris Pasternak and twice a year read his own poetry in the Pasternak museum – a huge cultural event attended by many famous people from all over the world.

Duvakin: With his eyes?

Vladimir Sosinsky: Yes, with his eyes. And when he caught mine, he raised his finger, meaning "Listen to this!"

Duvakin: He thought that was something important, right?

Vladimir Sosinsky: He was showing me from a distance his admiration for Evtushenko's poetry. And when he finished, Pasternak started to heap compliments on Evtushenko, as only he could, and he was very sincere in his praise. And also, to finish about Evtushenko, something else left an impression on me that night: when he was leaving, he kissed Zinaida's hand.

A member of the Komsomol, yet he kissed the hostess's hand so politely, so fashionably! And he told her (I was sitting nearby, so I could hear him), "How lucky you are, Zinaida Nikolayevna! I spent three hours with Boris Leonidovich, and I feel full to the brim for many years ahead. While you've been with him for such a long time!"

Duvakin: Nicely put.

Ariadna Sosinsky: "And thank you for everything you do for him."

Vladimir Sosinsky: "Thank you …" He sounded so sincere. That's why I was so surprised to read, in French, Evtushenko's autobiography when it was published in the Parisian journal *Express*. There he described this same meeting very differently, not in the way you'd expect from someone who's supposed to be boastful. To the contrary. He was so modest in his recollections that he didn't even mention Pasternak's praise.

There was a little hint to that effect – he compared it to Derzhavin blessing Pushkin – but that was all; he didn't even say anything about Pasternak's admiration for his poetry. Evtushenko just wrote that "he shared his approval of my poems." He also didn't say anything about knowing Pasternak's poetry by heart and helping him to remember lines that evening.

I was very surprised by that, because people talked about it everywhere. But I should add that the explanation may lie in the fact that he thought Pasternak was a demigod, and he couldn't take any liberties in front of him.

Duvakin: Well, that speaks well of him, from a moral standpoint. Let's go back to Pasternak. That was the time you left, in 1957?

Vladimir Sosinsky: Yes.

Duvakin: But you also came in 1959?

Vladimir Sosinsky: Correct.

Duvakin: Did you see him that time too?

Vladimir Sosinsky: Of course. Several times.

Duvakin: Your meetings were also interesting?

Vladimir Sosinsky: Maybe it's not the right time to talk about this yet? The memories connected with *Doctor Zhivago*?[22]

Duvakin: Well, *Doctor Zhivago*, that's already history. Did he complain a lot?

Vladimir Sosinsky: Without a doubt. Zinaida Nikolayevna also took a big part in our conversations. But that's about all I can remember about our meetings in 1957.

Duvakin: In one of my recordings I have this memory of him running towards an almost complete stranger, an actor, and crying out, in total despair, even before all the later insults, when he found out that there was a political storm gathering over his head. He was very traumatized.

Vladimir Sosinsky: Yes, he was very traumatized, no question about that. He told us he was worried about his family, his fate, and that because of that – since we were going abroad, we had to make sure that he was not accused of somehow being responsible for sending the manuscript abroad.

Duvakin: Right. When was that? Before or after the Nobel Prize?

Vladimir Sosinsky: I think after, am I right?

Ariadna Sosinsky: No, I don't think so.

Duvakin: It happened before the Nobel Prize, around the time they were dragging him through the mud in the press: "A pig …"

Vladimir Sosinsky: I can't tell you the exact date, but those letters in *Novy mir* [The new world],[23] and Semichastny's article, had already been published.[24]

Duvakin: No, I'm thinking about the speech published in *Komsomolskaya Pravda*:[25] He was called "a pig," and that was horrible.

---

22 *Doctor Zhivago* (1957) is Boris Pasternak's most famous novel. When he was not permitted to publish it at home, Pasternak sent the manuscript to the Italian publisher Feltrinelli, who was more than happy to print it. Although Pasternak received the Nobel Prize for Literature in 1958, he was treated very poorly in his home country. Poverty-stricken, abandoned by almost all his friends, and humiliated, Pasternak died in his house in 1960.

23 About *Novy mir*, see note 103 to dialogue 3.

24 Vladimir Semichastny was the leader of Komsomol, the Communist Youth organization. He was one of Pasternak's most vicious critics. In 1958, before an audience of fourteen thousand people, including Khrushchev and other party leaders, Semichastny said, "If you compare Pasternak to a pig, a pig would not do what he did, because a pig never shits where it eats." Later (1961–7), Semichastny was the chair of the KGB.

25 *Komsomolskaya Pravda* (*The Komsomol Truth*) was Russia's most popular daily newspaper, founded in 1925. At its highest circulation point during the 1990s, it printed almost twenty-two million copies a day.

Vladimir Sosinsky: I can't be precise about the time, but he was very worried.

Ariadna Sosinsky: Very worried.

Vladimir Sosinsky: Worried and afraid.

Duvakin: Had his letter against the expulsion already been published?

Vladimir Sosinsky: He, by the way, claimed that by his own volition he ran to the post office to send the telegram refusing the Nobel Prize.

Ariadna Sosinsky: And the Writers' Union was not happy about it.

Vladimir Sosinsky: Yes, the Writers' Union was not happy about his decision.

Duvakin: That's confusing. Why? Khrushchev demanded that disciplinary action be taken against him.[26] So the Writers' Union actually defended him?

Vladimir Sosinsky: It seems they didn't want him to reject the Nobel Prize on his own. There were different opinions about that.

Duvakin: There was no consensus.

Vladimir Sosinsky: Correct, there was no consensus.

Duvakin: People were saying back then … (I can include this in the recording.) There was this rumour going around Moscow that, when the party congress took place (I don't recall which one; the XXI, perhaps), Khrushchev used to listen to Tvardovsky's opinion.[27]

You could buy *Doctor Zhivago* at the kiosk here; it was printed in a limited run in Russia – and also Pasternak's poems. Anyway, he [Khrushchev] asked Tvardovsky, "Do you really think Pasternak is an important poet?" And he replied, "Nikita Sergeevich, do you think of me as a good poet?" "Of course I do!" "Well," he says, "I can't hold a candle to him," or something like that. At any rate, he said that Pasternak was a much better poet than he was.

---

26 Nikita Khrushchev (1894–1971) served as first secretary of the Communist Party from 1953 to 1964, and as premier from 1958 to 1964. This time was marked by the end of repressions, a political "thaw" in the country, and the revival of cultural life. An impulsive and very stubborn person, Khrushchev managed to create significant tensions with many Western leaders and almost brought the world to the brink of a nuclear war. Still, the USSR's economic progress under his leadership is undeniable.

27 Alexander Tvardovsky (1910–1971) was a prominent Soviet poet. For many years he served as editor of *Novy mir*, and under his leadership many talented writers, including Alexander Solzhenitsyn, were allowed to publish their work. At the end of Khrushchev's "thaw," Tvardovsky angered the Communist Party leaders so much that he was forced to resign from his editorial post. He died from a stroke shortly afterwards, at the age of sixty-one.

And Khrushchev replied, very angry, "I will never forgive Surkov for this!"[28] Because Surkov had put him in this uncomfortable position. In general, we disgraced ourselves in the eyes of Europe in that case. What can you do, it was a mistake. Now you can read about *Doctor Zhivago* in the *Literary Encyclopedia*.[29]

Vladimir Sosinsky: Without a doubt.

Duvakin: It's included in Paperny's article.[30] One cannot omit that. Personally, when I read *Doctor Zhivago*, I was not …

Vladimir Sosinsky: I was also not particularly impressed.

Duvakin: If there had been a more rational response, there wouldn't have been such uproar. They should have written a comprehensive interpretation. Instead, there was that wild sensation. Kind of similar to Veresaev's *Deadlock*.[31] Not the same, of course, but there are certain parts …

I think it pales in comparison with Pasternak's poetry. He thought it was his greatest achievement, though, just like in the case with *Selected Passages*.[32]

Vladimir Sosinsky: Yes, he was genuinely upset when we shared our opinion of *Doctor Zhivago*.

---

28 Alexey Surkov (1899–1983) was a minor Soviet poet, remembered for the 1941 song "Zemlyanka," which became famous throughout the country during the Second World War. The song is about a soldier writing a letter to his wife after a battle, telling her that Death is always just a few steps behind.

29 The *Literary Encyclopedia* was an ambitious project begun in 1929 by Anatoly Lunacharsky, then the minister of education in the Bolshevik government. The best literary critics were invited to participate, and by 1937 the ten volumes of the encyclopedia consisted of more than five thousand articles, many of which were brilliant. The eleventh volume was stopped from publication by the censors. That encyclopedia could not have had an article about *Doctor Zhivago*; therefore Duvakin is obviously referring to later, different Soviet encyclopaedias of poorer quality, of which there were many.

30 Zinovy Paperny (1919–1996) was a Soviet literary critic who wrote an article about Pasternak in 1968 (*Kratkaya literaturnaya entsiklopedia*, vol. 5, cols. 617–21), in which *Doctor Zhivago* was mentioned.

31 Vikenty Veresaev (Smidovich) (1867–1945) was a Russian/Soviet writer. A doctor by training (like Anton Chekhov), Veresaev loved literature and started by writing about his medical experiences. His first book, *Memoirs of a Physician*, had a tremendous success. After travelling to Greece, Veresaev began translating *The Iliad* and *The Odyssey* into Russian. His novel *Deadlock* (1923) is among the most faithful depictions of the Soviet revolution.

32 Duvakin means *Vybrannye mesta iz perepiski s druzyami* (*Selected Passages from Correspondence with Friends*, 1847) by the famous Russian writer Nikolay Gogol (1809–1852). It was a sermon-style book and very different in tone from Gogol's previous satirical writings. The book damaged his reputation among the progressive members of the Russian intelligentsia. The indignant letter sent by the literary critic Vissarion Belinsky to Gogol in July of 1847 was triggered by *Selected Passages*.

Duvakin: Ah, so you told him.

Vladimir Sosinsky: Yes. He gave us the manuscript to read on our journey from Moscow to Rostov on the ship *Ukraine*. Was it in 1957?

Ariadna Sosinsky: Yes.

Vladimir Sosinsky: Could it have been in 1957?

Ariadna Sosinsky: Yes, yes. Alyosha was about to enter the university.

Vladimir Sosinsky: That was before the Nobel Prize, before it was published abroad.

Duvakin: I think it was published by Ivanov's son?

Vladimir Sosinsky: No, Feltrinelli, an Italian.[33]

Ariadna Sosinsky: An Italian.

Duvakin: I see. An Italian. But he brought something or visited ...Vyacheslav Ivanov[34] was working at the Vatican Library[35] in Italy at that time – Vyacheslav Ivanov, the poet.

Ariadna Sosinsky: Yes, I've heard. Maybe it's wrong, and it wasn't Feltrinelli after all.

Duvakin: Was he a Communist publisher?

Vladimir Sosinsky: Yes, he was a member of the Italian Communist Party.

Duvakin: It's not known how he got the manuscript.

Vladimir Sosinsky: Pasternak himself gave it to him.

Duvakin: Do you think so?

---

33 Giangiacomo Feltrinelli (1926–1972) was an Italian publisher and political activist. In spite of the pressure exercised by the Italian Communist Party and the Soviets, Feltrinelli, who always prided himself on being independent of all political movements, published *Doctor Zhivago* in 1958.

34 Vyacheslav Ivanov (1866–1949) was a prominent Russian poet, playwright, scholar, and literary theorist associated with the Russian Symbolist movement. He lived abroad between 1886 and 1905 but then returned home, only to leave again – this time for good – in 1924 after he came into conflict with the Bolshevik government. After travelling around for a while, he finally settled down in Italy.

35 The Vatican Apostolic Library, better known as the Vatican Library, is the library of the Holy See, located in Vatican City. Formally established in 1475, although it is much older, it is one of the oldest libraries in the world and contains a significant collection of historical texts.

Vladimir Sosinsky: Yes. Alexey Surkov sent a telegram to Feltrinelli in which he said, "On behalf of the union, and Boris Leonidovich, who gave you the manuscript, I ask that you return it." There was such a telegram.

Duvakin: And did he return it?

Vladimir Sosinsky [*laughing*]**:** The manuscript? No way! He held on to it tightly.

Duvakin: That's understandable.

Vladimir Sosinsky: So we read it, and then he wanted our opinion, of course. We were in a difficult position because he obviously gave it tremendous importance.

Duvakin: A disproportionally great importance in the context of his work.

Vladimir Sosinsky: That book was disproportionally important to him, yes. He said it was the best thing he had ever written.

Duvakin: Yes, yes, yes!

Vladimir Sosinsky: He believed *Doctor Zhivago* was the reason for his existence. And it wasn't just a book but an embodiment of Russian philosophy as a whole.

Ariadna Sosinsky: And that the epoch spoke through him, in his voice. He thought he was representing the era. But that was not true at all.

Vladimir Sosinsky: We couldn't agree with him, unfortunately.

Duvakin: I liked it better when I read it the second time around. The first time I rushed through it and didn't understand everything. Now I could read it slowly, carefully, and completely legally.

Vladimir Sosinsky: From a formal standpoint it's not very good: the ending about the time following the cult of personality feels rushed, hastily added.

Duvakin: I'd call the book uneven, even eclectic.

Vladimir Sosinsky: Uneven, yes, but the love story is good.

Duvakin: Perhaps.

Vladimir Sosinsky: It really is.

Duvakin: Maybe.

Vladimir Sosinsky: The civil war, which fascinated the Americans so much – we had students come up to us to tell us very enthusiastically how incredibly well the civil war was depicted in *Doctor Zhivago*. We have other, much better depictions of the civil war in Russia.

Duvakin [*with excitement*]: Of course!

Vladimir Sosinsky: In the beginning of our Soviet literature ...

Duvakin: Of course, but he didn't know that.

Vladimir Sosinsky: Yes.

Duvakin: That's literature about literature.

Vladimir Sosinsky: We noticed that some Americans – we were living in the United States then – were also disappointed in the book, but everyone tried not to show it. There was something else, too. You were expected to have read *Doctor Zhivago*. It was in vogue, back then; you wouldn't be well received in certain cultural circles if you hadn't read it. And everyone was disappointed. I didn't meet a single person who spoke of it enthusiastically. They were all quite subdued.

By the way, that was an interesting time in America, 1958, 1959, 1960. There were two major bestsellers then. They were competing for the most attention. One was by a Soviet author, and the other by an émigré: Vladimir Nabokov's *Lolita*[36] and Boris Pasternak's *Doctor Zhivago*. They took turns heading the bestseller list for two years.

Duvakin: I know about Vladimir Nabokov only from Struve's book *Russian Literature in Exile*,[37] which I borrowed from Gudzy.[38] He was my go-to person for such things. I borrowed *Doctor Zhivago* from him, too. I don't know what happened to that edition. Gudzy passed away. He introduced me to so many works. I borrowed Remizov's books from him as well, autographed by Remizov himself.[39]

Vladimir Sosinsky: He gave us two notebooks with his poetry. I still have one of them; the other I gave as a present to Vadim Leonidovich Andreyev.[40] They were –

36 About Vladimir Nabokov, see note 61 to dialogue 3.

37 Gleb Struve (1898–1985) was an émigré Russian poet and literary historian. He worked in Europe and later in the United States. Among his numerous works is the book *Russian Literature in Exile* (1956).

38 Nikolay Gudzy (1887–1965) was a professor at Moscow State University who specialized in early Russian literature. He was also an expert on the works of Leo Tolstoy.

39 About Alexey Remizov, see note 43 to dialogue 3.

40 About Vadim Andreyev, see note 74 to dialogue 3.

Duvakin: Original manuscripts?

Vladimir Sosinsky: Yes.

Duvakin: And what else?

Vladimir Sosinsky: Doctor Zhivago's poetry.

[*There is a pause in the recording.*]

Duvakin: I have it in my hands: *Kogda razgulyaetsya.*[41] It's typed on a typewriter, correct?

Vladimir Sosinsky: Yes. They are not handwritten.

Duvakin [*reading*]:

> Во всем мне хочется дойти
> До самой сути.
> В работе, в поисках пути,
> В сердечной смуте.
>
> [In everything I want to find
> Its proper essence.
> In work, in searching for the way,
> In heart's turmoil.]
> That's all.[42]

Vladimir Sosinsky: We also have his autobiography, which was published in *Novy mir*. As for *Doctor Zhivago*, I refused to take it abroad with me, in accordance with Zinaida Nikolayevna's wishes.

Duvakin: I see, Zinaida Nikolayevna …

Vladimir Sosinsky: She asked me not to take it.

Duvakin: Right, she didn't want to add more fodder to the fire.
[*Duvakin recites:*]

> Состав земли не знает грязи.
> Все очищает аромат,
> Который льет без всякой связи
> Десяток роз в стеклянной вазе.

---

41 This last book of Pasternak's poetry was published only after his death, in 1961. The book itself was written in 1956.

42 This is an excerpt from "Во всем мне хочется дойти до самой сути" ("In Everything I Want to Get an Essence"), one of the most known poems in the collection. The poem was written in 1956.

[The composition of the earth knows no grime.
The all-cleansing aroma
Of a dozen roses in a glass vase
Pours out, free of any ties.][43]

[*There is a break in the recording.*]

The Meeting of Pasternak and Tsvetaeva

Duvakin: Now I will ask you if you would please talk about Pasternak and Tsvetaeva.

Vladimir Sosinsky: Yes, we have to. It happened in …

Duvakin: You mentioned the conversations about *Zhivago* from 1957–9, then in 1960 you arrived a few weeks before his death, so you couldn't have seen him then; he was in the hospital.

Vladimir Sosinsky: I don't recall if it was the same time he told us about the phone call from Stalin about Mandelstam, or on a different occasion, but I remember it happened in the garden, and he was wearing a light summer suit, all white. For some reason his mannerisms, the way he spoke, reminded one of a horseman and an Arabian horse at the same time. (I don't know why I am remembering this.) Anyway, he told us about his meeting with Marina Tsvetaeva. First of all, he was very upset that all the letters she had sent him from abroad had been lost.

Duvakin: During the evacuation?

Ariadna Sosinsky: No, he was afraid –

Duvakin: And did he destroy them himself?

Ariadna Sosinsky: No, no, he gave them to a certain woman (I don't know who), and she kept them with her at all times. But once she travelled by train late at night and left them in the car.

Duvakin: Oh, no!

Ariadna Sosinsky: She couldn't find them again. Not too long ago someone told us that the letters still existed somewhere. I don't know if that's true or not.[44]

---

43 This is an excerpt from the poem "Вакханалия" ("Bacchanalia") written in 1957, during Khrushchev's "thaw."

44 Marina Tsvetaeva's letters to Pasternak have been lost, but some drafts remain. They were published for the first time in 2004. See Evgeniya Korkina and Irina Shevelenko, eds., *Marina Tsvetaeva, Boris Pasternak: Dushi nachinayut videt'. Pisma 1922–1936* (Moscow: Vagrius, 2004).

Duvakin: It's very possible.

Vladimir Sosinsky: It is.

Ariadna Sosinsky: That's one of the legends told by the same woman who insisted she had found Tsvetaeva's grave not in an Orthodox cemetery but in a cemetery of some sect. In a word, total rubbish! Nonsensical stories!

Vladimir Sosinsky: In one of the conversations we often had with him – it was just the three of us, no other guests, not even Zinaida Nikolayevna was there.

Duvakin: The two of you and him?

Vladimir Sosinsky: Always just the three of us. He took us out into the garden, and we had a wonderful conversation. At that time, as I was weighing the pros and cons of returning home for good, and the friendship with Pasternak was a major reason for considering a life in Russia. I dreamed of talking with him forever.

Duvakin: And then you arrived, and he died a week later.

Vladimir Sosinsky: Yes. I wanted to say that he really regretted it, even more so than in the case with Mandelstam. He told us that, first of all, he was put off by the way she [Tsvetaeva] looked: "It was my fault, of course, because she didn't look like the ideal I used to imagine. She looked old. We looked at each other and were scared of looking at each other; it was all quite unpleasant.

"We were at a loss for words, and I didn't give her the kind of attention, warmth, I should have given her during our first meeting. All in all, there was no real meeting. She retreated – from herself and from me. And that's the worst part – it was a catastrophe, and I knew it, but all my attempts to change the situation, find the commonality between our souls, which without a doubt existed ..."

Duvakin: Because of their correspondence?

Vladimir Sosinsky: Yes. "... but I just couldn't do it. I kept stepping into it. She noticed my lack of tact and was upset about it, almost crying. And that was it." He said the following: "I didn't do anything for her, none of us did; we didn't give her the chance to live and work here, nobody helped her, and so we are all responsible for her death, especially me."

He spoke with profound sadness about what happened with her and felt it all very deeply. "If we only knew what was going on, what would happen ... We had examples from the past, we knew how we had to treat people!"

Duvakin: There were many examples.

Vladimir Sosinsky: Plenty.

Ariadna Sosinsky: He read us then his poem, the one dedicated to Tsvetaeva. When I read it again later, I didn't find this line he shared with us: "No, you are not the Queen of Spades!"[45] As if she'd come back from the dead, and he was scared of her, the Queen of Spades.

Duvakin: She was a ghost, we might say.

Ariadna Sosinsky: Yes, from the afterlife. But I didn't find this line anywhere ever again. I don't know if it was a different poem.

Duvakin: Is it recorded somewhere?

Vladimir Sosinsky: He probably crossed it out.

Ariadna Sosinsky: It's possible that he did. But it really left an impression on me; there was a certain feeling of horror in it: "No, you are not the Queen of Spades!"

Duvakin: When did he read it to you? In 1957 or 1959?

Vladimir Sosinsky: 1957.

Duvakin: When you visited him.

Vladimir Sosinsky: Right, in 1957.

Duvakin: Yes, he must have felt guilty. You're also saying her death was the result of a certain …

Vladimir Sosinsky: … lack of attention. You must note that her fame only came after the Second World War, during the 1950s, after her poetry collections had been published. In truth, her fame came only recently.

Duvakin: Was she famous abroad?

Vladimir Sosinsky: Without a doubt. The first poetess, the first Russian émigré poet. Who else was there?

Duvakin: Of course, one cannot compare her to Gippius.[46]

Ariadna Sosinsky: Not at all.

Vladimir Sosinsky: Gippius didn't write during the time we were in emigration.

Ariadna Sosinsky: There was a very small group of people who understood her then. But I should say that wasn't the only reason she was forgotten. Then there

---

45 "The Queen of Spades" ("Пиковая дама," first published in 1834) is a short story by Alexander Pushkin with supernatural elements. Hermann, the main character, hopes to extract from an old countess the secret of winning at cards, but she dies from fright when he appears in her room late at night. She then comes back as the Queen of Spades to haunt him and takes her revenge by making him lose all his fortune, as well as his sanity, at the end of the story.

46 About Zinaida Gippius, see note 29 to dialogue 3.

was also the tragedy with her son. He was very rude, and she felt – or maybe he told her that she was a burden to him, that it would be easier for him to live without her.

Vladimir Sosinsky: We should add here something that got lost in the previous recording: Marina Ivanovna loved Boris Leonidovich [Pasternak] not only as a poet but also as a man. She loved him passionately.

Duvakin: Without ever having met him?

Vladimir Sosinsky: Yes. And she expected so much from their meeting. She dreamed of having a child with him, which she wrote about many times in her letters.

Duvakin: She shared that?

Vladimir Sosinsky: Yes. She first wanted to call her son Boris but changed her mind out of consideration for Sergei Efron's feelings.[47] She called him Georgi, or Mur, which is what she called him at home. She truly, wholeheartedly, from the bottom of her female heart believed that it was predestined: Pasternak and Tsvetaeva had to meet and fall deeply in love with each other.

Similarly to the way Dante imagined a special place for those who didn't meet each other on earth, she thought they had to meet in Russia, when she finally returned home. This is why their encounter turned out to be even more difficult – terrifying and tragic – for her, because it ended up being just a mundane comedy.

Duvakin: What he saw when they met, as you were describing her …

Vladimir Sosinsky: She was all sharp angles, jutting out at everybody, him included, and life itself.

Duvakin: He saw sharp angles, I see.

Vladimir Sosinsky: Yes. And he was shocked by her appearance. She looked much older than her age. Of course, she was no longer so young as when they had first met in Berlin.

Duvakin: Ah, so they had already met?

Ariadna Sosinsky: Yes, they had, but she wasn't his type even back then.

Vladimir Sosinsky: He didn't like sharp angles. He preferred softness.

Ariadna Sosinsky: Softness, femininity.

Duvakin: Ovals.

---

47 About Sergei Efron, see note 19 to dialogue 3.

Vladimir Sosinsky: Ovals. [*They smile.*]

Ariadna Sosinsky: And cheerfulness, right?

Vladimir Sosinsky: Correct.

Duvakin: Well, let's end our conversation about Pasternak with that. One more thing: you mentioned that Mur didn't die at the war front but somewhere else.

Vladimir Sosinsky: That should be confirmed properly. We heard rumours. We knew the type of person he was. He was a selfish, extremely proud, arrogant boy. He thought he was a genius, not sure of what kind, but he did think very highly of himself and didn't allow anybody to treat him without the proper respect he thought he deserved.

They said army life was very difficult for him because he was surrounded by people who didn't understand him. And once there was a knife fight that ended tragically for him.

Duvakin: He was stabbed? That's horrible, of course, but it happened after her death, correct?

Vladimir Sosinsky: Yes, after her death.

Duvakin: She was no longer among the living then. Well, let's end here, as far as Pasternak and his relationship with Marina is concerned, and about Tsvetaeva in general.

Vladimir Sosinsky: Yes.

Meeting Mayakovsky

Duvakin: Now, let's talk about – for you this may be something small, but for me it's of utmost importance. Did you ever meet Mayakovsky?

Vladimir Sosinsky: Yes.

Duvakin: Did you meet in person?

Vladimir Sosinsky: I saw him only once. He was performing on stage.

Duvakin: Were you interested in him before?

Vladimir Sosinsky: Very much so!

Duvakin: When did you become interested [in him]?

Vladimir Sosinsky: Let me tell you about this day because it was actually a curious one for both my wife and me. We liked only the early Mayakovsky, from the first part of his life. We liked his "Backbone Flute,"[48] his super-Futurist poetry – so full of sharpness. I was remembering this when visiting Burliuk in New York.[49]

He [Burliuk] read some poetry that reminded me of the spirit of those times, and I told him, "David Davidovich, your poems reveal Mayakovsky's influence." "What!" He was appalled. "It's the other way round: he was influenced by my poetry!" He was offended that I said Mayakovsky had influenced his poetry. It turns out Mayakovsky was the one who was influenced by Burliuk.

I must say we liked Mayakovsky, the early Mayakovsky. The poems that came to us later, during the Soviet times, didn't seem as interesting to us. Maybe it was a matter of not having the right attitude to appreciate them, or maybe it was something else. So what happened that night when we heard Mayakovsky in Paris? All the Russian émigrés were there; the place was packed. And it was a huge hall, I can't now remember which one.

Duvakin: Was Georgy Ivanov there?[50]

Vladimir Sosinsky: Yes, Georgy Ivanov was there, as were many others. There was shouting, and notes being sent to him, but the most important thing was that we suddenly realized that Mayakovsky was a great poet, a completely new kind of poet, not the one we used to know, and he influenced our views. In the sense that he revealed to us who he really was then – a poet of the Soviet era – because we, like Khodasevich,[51] used to appreciate him only as a pre-Soviet poet.

Duvakin: What do you mean "like Khodasevich"?

Vladimir Sosinsky: Khodasevich also thought that Mayakovsky wrote real poetry in his youth and that his later work was worthless.

Duvakin: Did he change his mind after that evening, too?

Vladimir Sosinsky: No, Khodasevich continued to view him the same way.

Duvakin: He later wrote a very negative article –

Vladimir Sosinsky: Very negative.

Duvakin: – about Mayakovsky, and I think he even wrote a very bad obituary.

---

48 About "The Backbone Flute," see note 53 to dialogue 3.

49 About David Burliuk, see note 13 to dialogue 4.

50 Georgy Ivanov (1894–1958) was a Russian poet. His poetic talent flourished in emigration; in France he acquired the reputation of being the best Russian émigré poet. Ivanov also became an influential literary critic. His last years were darkened by a difficult financial situation and health issues.

51 About Vladislav Khodasevich, see note 75 to dialogue 3.

Vladimir Sosinsky: It was horrible indeed. He called him "a mare decked out in a bridal dress." These were terrible articles!

By the way, about Mayakovsky's reading: I got the impression – I remember the way Mandelstam described how one of his friends read Tyutchev's Alpine poetry: "It's as if he drew in a breath of Alpine air himself. The poems were rolling off his tongue!"[52]

Similarly, when Mayakovsky read his poetry, we could hear the noise of the crowds, the flags flapping, and we could picture in front of us a podium in a great square, surrounded by a million listeners. Mayakovsky revealed that to us. His reading was incredibly powerful.

I remember something else. We used to argue a lot about different styles of poetry reading, but I think Mayakovsky was among the most impressive readers of his own poetry. Pasternak's voice, for example, sounded very weak, and he raised it a bit, like a howl, at the end of each line, which took away from the impact of his poetry. Tsvetaeva also didn't do her poetry any favours when she read it out loud. Mayakovsky, on the other hand, made his poems sound exceptional, a work of genius.

Remizov put it so well (I remember his words exactly): "Blok read his poetry best.[53] He had the amazing ability to express its inner music. It was unpleasant to listen to actors reciting his work. Rhythm is the soul of music. And rhythm has such an important role in Mayakovsky's art. That's where poetry comes from! Poems are not meant to be understood. You don't need to comprehend them." (I don't agree completely with Remizov on that.) "Poetry must be heard with the heart. Like music. The professional actors didn't have the right rhythm, expression.

"Verbal expression is needed for proper understanding, to help those who don't have the ear for it. I'd rather read Blok's poetry for myself and not listen to others recite it. You wouldn't hear them right, unless, of course, the actor doesn't get it into his head that poetry is different from talking; but it often falls on deaf ears."

I must say Mayakovsky was an ideal example for us of how to read poetry. Just as Remizov was our model for how to read the prose of Pushkin,[54]

---

52 About Fyodor Tyutchev, see note 42 to dialogue 1.

53 Alexander Blok (1880–1921) was one of the best Russian Symbolist poets, as well as a capable publicist, playwright, translator, and literary critic. Born into an aristocratic family, Blok accepted the Bolshevik Revolution in 1917, a move that surprised many of his admirers and friends. While he could see the "downfall of humanism" (a phrase he used in a 1918 article) in Soviet Russia, he felt that this new stage was inevitable in the history's march onward. His conflicting feelings about the revolution are captured well in his famous poem "The Twelve" (1918). He became disillusioned with the Bolsheviks very quickly and stopped writing poetry for the remainder of his life. In 1921 he became ill and needed treatment abroad, but the official permission to leave Russia came three days after his death.

54 About Alexander Pushkin, see note 40 to dialogue 1.

Gogol,[55] Leskov,[56] his own. Nobody could read like him! Bunin read like an actor, of course.[57] He acted out the parts – the peasant, the nobleman. He read his stories like an actor, and so did Zaytsev,[58] and everybody else. Remizov, on the other hand, revealed the rhythmic nature of his prose, the soul of every object mentioned in it.

Duvakin: Like Mayakovsky …

Vladimir Sosinsky: The same way Mayakovsky read his poetry.

Duvakin: [Revealing] the inner content of his poems.

Vladimir Sosinsky: The inner content, and against the background of large crowds and thundering noise, fireworks, if you'd like, great rumble, the letter R and other letters, too, breaking ice blocks – it was the most amazing thing! And there's something else that should be noted: afterwards, at the end of the reading, there were notes being passed around, and people were yelling against the Soviet Union and against Mayakovsky. Yet his clever responses to the émigrés' negativity earned him a round of applause by those same émigrés. [*Duvakin chuckles.*] So, it was ultimately a complete victory over the listeners.

Duvakin: He had many similar victories, but that one was certainly one of the hardest to achieve.

Vladimir Sosinsky: One of the hardest, I think, and it stayed with me all my life. From that moment on I loved everything Mayakovsky wrote, and especially his Paris cycle of poems. We read, and walked around with those poems,

55 About Nikolay Gogol, see note 54 to dialogue 2.

56 Nikolai Leskov (1831–1895) was a prominent but, for a long time, unappreciated Russian writer, playwright, and journalist. Praised for his unique writing style and innovative experiments in form, and held in high esteem by Tolstoy, Chekhov, and Gorky among others, Leskov is credited with creating a comprehensive picture of contemporary Russian society, using mostly short literary forms. His major works include *Lady Macbeth of Mtsensk* (1865) (which was later made into an opera by Shostakovich), *The Cathedral Clergy* (1872), *The Enchanted Wanderer* (1873), and "The Tale of Cross-Eyed Lefty from Tula and the Steel Flea" (1881). During his lifetime he was constantly attacked by contemporary critics, who did not approve of his critical views of Russian society. Soviet literary propaganda, too, found little of use in Leskov's legacy, often labelling the author "reactionary," and it was only in the 1990s that his work finally began to garner the attention it so richly deserved.

57 About Ivan Bunin, see note 44 to dialogue 3.

58 Boris Zaytsev (1881–1972) was one of the last authors associated with the silver age of Russian literature. A talented writer, playwright, and literary translator, Zaytsev was uncompromising in his attitude towards the Bolsheviks. In 1922 he emigrated to France, where he spent the rest of his life. A close friend of Chekhov, Bunin, Korolenko, and Leonid Andreyev, Zaytsev was one of the few who, while in emigration, managed not only to preserve his own literary talent but also to develop it to the fullest.

and took his poetry all around Paris, and we read these amazing poems not only in our circles but also in various public forums, on stages.

Duvakin: And at literary soirées, too?

Vladimir Sosinsky: Yes, yes.

Duvakin: You were reading Mayakovsky's poetry in emigration?

Vladimir Sosinsky: Yes.

Duvakin: Of course, you were most touched by the last lines: "Подступай к глазам разлуки жижа, сердце мне сентиментальностью расквась …" [Come to my eyes, tears of parting, break my sentimental heart …].[59]

Vladimir Sosinsky [*continuing*]: "Я хотел бы жить и умереть в Париже, если б не было такой земли – *Москва*" [I would want to live and die in Paris if there were not such a place as Moscow].

You remember, by the way, how Elsa Triolet, when she came to Moscow and wrote about it in *Lettres françaises*, ended with the same lines: "I would want to live and die in Moscow if there were not such a place as Paris."

Duvakin: Yes. Another French woman left me exactly the same note, too.

Vladimir Sosinsky: You see, that's already commonplace. Well, this is all I can tell you about Mayakovsky. It's not much. You have to know more in order to tell more.

As for Alexander Kibalnikov's monument,[60] I must say that's not how I remember Mayakovsky. First of all, Mayakovsky was much more handsome and more magnificent than the way the statue presents him.

Duvakin: Really? How interesting!

Vladimir Sosinsky: I am certain of it. Now I understand Ehrenburg,[61] who used to tell me, "Every time I pass by it, I don't recognize Vladimir Vladimirovich." There's something too –

Duvakin: Grounded?

Vladimir Sosinsky: Yes, it's hard to express. I have the impression that through his travels abroad and through his poetry he was able to accomplish a lot more than all of our official cultural ambassadors put together.

---

59 About this short poem called "Farewell," see note 55 to dialogue 3.

60 Sosinsky refers to the famous monument to Vladimir Mayakovsky, which was erected in Triumfalnaya Square in Moscow in 1958 by Alexander Kibalnikov (1912–1985), a prominent Soviet sculptor.

61 About Ilya Ehrenburg, see note 114 to dialogue 3.

Duvakin: In the sense that – that's important!

Vladimir Sosinsky: But of course.

Duvakin: It was proof that there was culture in the Soviet Union.

Vladimir Sosinsky: Real culture. That was always the case, and it was blatantly, violently obvious. We always felt it, and, of course, the Russian émigrés were seen as experts about all things Soviet, and our opinions were sought by the French, the English, and the Americans.

Duvakin: Were you around in 1928 when Tsvetaeva wrote the "You have a choice" letter to Mayakovsky?

Vladimir Sosinsky: Yes, but we didn't pay much attention then; we were busy with other things. We were in Paris at the time, yes.

Duvakin: It came out that "Mayakovsky got permission, while Milyukov didn't."[62] She sent the letter to *Poslednye Novosti* (*Latest News*), but they didn't publish it. It was published here. I'd like Ariadna Viktorovna do add something now. [*There is a pause in the recording.*] Ariadna Viktorovna, could you tell us anything else?

Ariadna Sosinsky: Hardly. The only thing I could add is how strange Mayakovsky's behaviour was on stage. You got the feeling that he felt very much at home there, a daily occurrence, totally normal for him. It seemed that nothing stood between him and the audience; he seemed oblivious to the fact that everyone was watching him. He acted and moved as if he was born to do this, as if it was his natural state of being.

Duvakin: He was in his element.

Ariadna Sosinsky: His element, yes. So I can't even imagine him in his everyday life. He left such an impression on me.

Vladimir Sosinsky: That's very true. He walked around on stage the same way you'd imagine him pacing alone back and forth in his own private room.

Ariadna Sosinsky: He had something that many actors often lack: a feeling for the stage and a certain calmness, a complete lack of awareness of the fact that there were others watching, while at the same time he was capable of quick, brilliant, original retorts to anything coming from the audience. He was so quick on his feet! You get that from his poetry as well. After all, his poems do not feel like words written on paper; it's as if he is talking to you, don't you think?

---

62 About Pavel Milyukov, see note 48 to dialogue 3.

Duvakin: Do you remember what he recited that night?

Ariadna Sosinsky: I don't.

[*There is a pause in the recording.*]

Isaac Babel

Duvakin: Vladimir Bronislavovich, now we'll turn to our next topic: Babel.[63] But as that's a part of your overall narrative – you told us a lot about the beginning of your life. Now I'd like you to turn to the period after 1929: how and when you left Paris, when you came to the Soviet Union – just the big picture; no details are necessary.

Vladimir Sosinsky: Yes. But I have to start earlier, before 1929, because Babel came to Paris first in 1927–8. Ariadna Viktorovna and I had just become engaged.

Duvakin: In our first conversation we got as far as your wedding.

Vladimir Sosinsky: Yes.

Duvakin: And you remained in Paris?

Vladimir Sosinsky: Yes. When Babel came for the first time, we were living in Clamart. It's one of Paris's suburbs, which is now very famous in literary and philosophical circles because Nikolai Aleksandrovich Berdyaev,[64] one of the greatest philosophers of our time, used to live there. Clamart attracted as many people as Leo Tolstoy's Yasnaya Polyana did.[65] I must tell you that we liked Babel right away, from the moment we met. I don't remember how and why we met.

Ariadna Sosinsky: I can tell you that: it was through Olga Forsh.[66]

Vladimir Sosinsky: That's right! I can show you a little note I have saved; it's somewhere around here. He wrote, "If you don't mind, Olga Dmitrievna Forsh and I will visit you around 8:30 p.m." I still have the note. Back then Babel lived on Villa Chauvelot, 15.

63 About Isaac Babel, see note 57 to dialogue 3.

64 About Nikolai Berdyaev, see note 18 to dialogue 3.

65 About Yasnaya Polyana, see note 63 to dialogue 1.

66 Olga Forsh (1873–1961) was a Russian/Soviet writer working in the genre of historical fiction. During the Soviet times she was tremendously popular, but after Perestroika her name fell into oblivion, and her novels were forgotten.

So we liked Babel's appearance and his books, which we found very moving back then, especially *Odessa Tales*.[67] He seemed to me to be someone who loved life, people, who was interested in everything happening around him.

He was a short, stocky, broad-shouldered man, whose eyes always seemed on fire, burning with curiosity, and who had the ability to reveal the essence of everything. He was so amazing, joyful, an uncommonly happy man. I see him as he was, fully alive, as if we parted only yesterday. And I must add that this impression coincides with everything I've ever heard or read about him.

Babel charmed us from the start. I should note that the Russian émigrés met him with hostility. First of all, his first appearance in the Rotonde in 1927 caused a scandal,[68] which was picked up by all the newspapers, but especially the evening news. Valentin Goryansky[69] (a former member of *Satiricon*[70] and a good friend of Arkady Averchenko,[71] Teffy,[72] and other émigré writers) greeted him [Babel] with a slap in the face by yelling "*Chekist* [Cheka officer]!"

The thing is, a book of Soviet authors' autobiographies had just been published and had made its way to Paris, in which Babel had written that he had been a *chekist* in Odessa. That was the reason why he was greeted with such animosity by the émigrés, for whom that was a horrible word. Babel, of course, responded to the insult right away.

---

67 *Odesskie rasskazy* (*Odessa Tales*, 1931) is a collection of short stories by Isaac Babel. They are notable for their sharp observations of human nature. Published individually in magazines throughout 1923 and 1924 and collected into a book, they deal primarily with a group of Jewish gangsters from the Moldavanka, a section of Odessa. Their leader is Benya Krik, known as "the King."

68 Café Rotonda (French, Café de la Rotonde) was a famous Parisian literary café frequented by the likes of Kazimir Malevich, Marc Chagall, Diego Rivera, Jean Cocteau, Aristide Maillol, Maurice Ravel, and Ilya Ehrenburg.

69 Valentin Goryansky (1888–1949) was a Russian poet. He left Russia after the revolution and lived in France, where, during the German occupation, all his sons except for one were executed by the Nazis.

70 *Satiricon* was a Russian satirical journal published weekly between 1908 and 1914. Its publication was halted by the beginning of the First World War. The journal was named after *Satiricon*, the classic example of Menippean satire written by Petronius in 1 AD.

71 Arkady Averchenko (1880–1925) was a brilliant Russian satirist. His talent as a writer flourished when he was the chief editor of *Satiricon* (1908–14), but after the revolution Averchenko was forced to emigrate because Vladimir Lenin had ordered his arrest. He eventually settled in Prague, where he died at a fairly young age (forty-five) after an unsuccessful glaucoma operation.

72 Teffy (Nadezhda Lokhvitskaya) (1872–1952) was often called "the first Russian female satirist," or "the queen of Russian humour," but she herself was much more modest about her own literary talents. In emigration she published extensively and was among the most popular writers of the Russian émigré circle. She managed to meet or be a close friend of many notable people of the twentieth century, including Grigori Rasputin, Vladimir Lenin, Alexander Kerensky, Ilya Repin, Ivan Bunin, and Vsevolod Meyerhold.

Duvakin: He did?

Vladimir Sosinsky: Of course. There was a fight. There was a big, serious scandal. He was met with great hostility.

Babel himself treated the émigrés with an amazing – I'd say not just sympathy but also wise tenderness. I remember how eager he was to go to Milyukov's lecture. We warned him, told him, "Why? What is so interesting about it?" But he had to do it anyway. He came back in awe: "If only I were a chairman of the Supreme … a leader of the Soviet government –" (or whatever that was called).

Duvakin: It was called chairman of the Central Executive Committee of the USSR back then.

Vladimir Sosinsky: "– I'd, of course, invite him to come to the USSR. He would be able to do so much there. Such brilliance! What he said was so interesting!" and so on. Don-Aminado,[73] whom we didn't care for that much –

Duvakin: Who?

Vladimir Sosinsky: Don-Aminado was a satirist writing for the *Latest News*, who had also worked for *Satiricon* earlier. We didn't care for him very much. We preferred Zoshchenko,[74] Ilf, and Petrov.[75] Anyway, he [Babel] liked Don-Aminado.

He [Babel] spoke very highly of Remizov and visited him. I seem to remember him talking about Vladimir Nabokov, who is now very fashionable abroad; we knew him then as Sirin.[76] Of all the young Russian authors abroad,

---

73 Don-Aminado (Aminad Shpolyansky) (1888–1957) was a Russian writer, satirist, and lawyer. After the revolution he emigrated to France, where he continued to publish books, some to great acclaim. Aminado's work was prohibited in the USSR for almost seventy years, and the Russian reader had to wait until 1990 to finally become acquainted with his books.

74 About Mikhail Zoshchenko, see note 48 to dialogue 1.

75 Ilya Ilf (1897–1937) and Evgeny Petrov (1903–1942) were two Soviet prose writers, both natives of Odessa. They are most remembered for two humorous novels, *Dvenadtsat' stulyev* (*The Twelve Chairs*) and *Zolotyoy telyonok* (*The Golden Calf*). In 1935–6 they were allowed to travel to the United States. They journeyed in a Ford car from New York to San Francisco, taking countless pictures along the way. During this trip they met Ernest Hemingway, Henry Ford, and many others. Upon their return to the Soviet Union, they published a book called *Odnoetazhnaya Amerika* (*One-Storied America*), in which, despite the oppressive political situation at home, they highly praised many aspects of the American way of life. Unfortunately, Ilya Ilf died in 1937 of tuberculosis that he had contracted during his long (twelve-week) trip around the United States. Petrov, seriously depressed by the death of his colleague and best friend, wrote nothing of any significance afterwards. He became a frontline reporter during the Second World War and was killed in 1942, near Sevastopol, during a German air strike.

76 Sirin was Vladimir Nabokov's literary pseudonym.

5.2. Mikhail Zoshchenko in the office of the journal *Smekhach*, Moscow, 1923. Photographer: Boris Ignatovich.

he [Babel] singled out Sirin and Gazdanov.[77] About Sirin he said the following: "Incredible! He is sitting under a glass bell, with no earth and air, and writing about nothing, nowhere – and yet he makes it all so interesting!"

That's very curious, by the way, that Babel was able to understand and see through Sirin so well. To this day we are amazed by all the clamour and glamour of his writing, when it's all actually so empty. Such desolation! He keeps sliding over brilliant surfaces without getting to the depths of anything, the way Dostoevsky could.

Duvakin: Now he is writing in English, right?

Vladimir Sosinsky: He wrote his novel *Lolita* in English, and now it's a world bestseller. It's an incredible work but still all superficial brilliance and noise.

77 Gaito Gazdanov (1903–1971) was a prominent Russian émigré writer. After the revolution he lived in Paris, where, in addition to writing, he had to work as a taxi driver for many years in order to support his family. During the Nazi occupation Gazdanov stayed in Paris and risked his life to help the Jews hide or escape Nazi persecution. After the war Gazdanov, for many years, worked for Radio Liberty and gave lectures on Russian literature.

Duvakin: Where does the action take place?

Vladimir Sosinsky: In America. In the United States of America. What else? We had many meetings. For example, among the surviving letters from him you can read the following: "My Sunday trip to see you in Clamart (that's where we lived then) ended in a misfortune: not knowing my way around, I lost a whole hour looking for the right tram, and found myself at Chatelet at nine o'clock. Remember, I am near-sighted. I was told the trip to Clamart would take about an hour, maybe even an hour and a half. It would have been too late to come then, so it turned out I couldn't keep my promise. I am so sorry we couldn't see each other. Please forgive me! I got sick, my old respiratory tract illness has come back. Today I am going south. I'll be in touch as soon as I get back to Paris."

My brother –

Duvakin [*surprised*]: Do you have a brother?

Vladimir Sosinsky: Yes, he was a taxi driver in Paris, had his own car. By the way, not too long ago we learned –

Duvakin: So it was possible to have your own car and drive it as a cab?

Vladimir Sosinsky: Yes, you could use your own car to drive clients. By the way, some Frenchman made a witty remark about that. He said that having come to Moscow from Paris, he saw a big similarity between the two cities: in both places taxi drivers spoke Russian. [*Duvakin laughs.*] That's how it was then: half of the taxi drivers in Paris were Russian.

Duvakin: What years are we talking about?

Vladimir Sosinsky: The 1920s; there were fewer later.

Duvakin: We didn't have taxis at that time; you could hire a horse cab.

Vladimir Sosinsky: Not too long ago there was a book published, by Yuri Pavlovich Annenkov,[78] a marvellous artist; his sketches were especially wonderful. He is the painter of some famous portraits of the leaders of the October Revolution, and also of writers, and so on. His portraits of Boris Pasternak and Anna Akhmatova are incredible.

Duvakin: He was also an illustrator.

78 Yuri Annenkov (1889–1974) was an important figure in the Russian avant-garde movement. He was an excellent graphic illustrator and portraitist who made portraits of Trotsky, Pasternak, Gorky, Akhmatova, and many others. In France, Annenkov worked on the sets of more than sixty ballets and fifty films, and in 1955 he was nominated for an Oscar in the category of Best Costume Designer. By the end of his life Annenkov had illustrated the books of Alexander Solzhenitsyn and Mikhail Bulgakov and written penetrating memoirs about meeting many notable people of the twentieth century.

Vladimir Sosinsky: For example, his picture of Blok lying in state is one of his most powerful works. Yuri Annenkov published two volumes of memoirs, which are less reminiscences about his own life and more memories of meetings with other people. He confused me with my brother there, by the way.

Annenkov made other mistakes as well. It was with one such big mistake that I'd like to begin my story about Babel. He said that Babel often tried to dissuade people from returning to their home country. That's an obvious lie. Not only do I have clear memories that contradict that idea, but I also have noted in my diary that – for example, when Natalia Kedrova was visiting …

I'm talking about the famous Kedrov Quartet[79] that Chaliapin[80] took part in, the one that became so famous around the world. She was the main Kedrov's daughter. Natalia Kedrova sang some Russian songs for us. I remember well how he went up to her and told her: "Natasha, how can you stay here? You are Russian, you sing Russian songs so beautifully, your voice must be heard at home."

In general, every time we met, he tried to convince us to go back home. "Do not be afraid of anything. Nothing will happen to you. We can live together." He talked about the amazing new generation of Soviet youth. I remember how he enjoyed telling us about Soviet girls and how he often mentioned a particular "metro builder," an "engineer metro builder." Antonina Nikolayevna, his widow, who now lives in Moscow and who once shared so many wonderful stories about Babel, is writing her memoirs about him now.[81]

I have to tell you that Babel was devoted to his country, loved it unconditionally, and was proud of all that had been achieved there. But it's also true that he was friends with people who were singled out by Stalin. He was friends with Tukhachevsky and many other important figures of the times.[82]

---

79 The Kedrov Quartet was founded by Nikolay Kedrov (1871–1940), a famous and very talented Russian opera singer. This first all-male Russian quartet performed Russian folk songs, romances, and opera arias to great public and critical acclaim. Fyodor Chaliapin called it "a miracle of vocal art," and the English king George V invited the quartet to perform in London in 1923.

80 About Fyodor Chaliapin, see note 49 to dialogue 1.

81 Antonina Nikolayevna Pirozhkova-Babel (1909–2010), the wife of Isaac Babel, was a civic engineer and writer. For almost fifteen years she did not know that her husband, arrested in 1939, had been executed, and she only found out the truth in 1954. Babel's precious manuscripts, confiscated by the NKVD, disappeared forever, but Antonina Pirozhkova scrupulously collected everything related to her husband, and in 2001 in the United States she published the book *Sem' let s Isaakom Babelem* (*Seven Years with Isaac Babel*). (At the time of this conversation [1969], Antonina Pirozhkova was still in the Soviet Union, surviving on a small pension, and without hope that her memoirs would ever be published.)

82 Mikhail Tukhachevsky (1893–1937) was a brilliant Soviet military commander of exceptional bravery, competence, and initiative. He was referred to as "the Red Napoleon" in the foreign press. In 1920–1 he was in charge of the Soviet western front in the Polish-Soviet war. Soviet forces under his command successfully pushed the Polish forces out of Western Ukraine, driving them back to Poland. He served as chief of staff of the Red Army from

Duvakin: He was a good friend of Mikhail Koltsov.[83]

Vladimir Sosinsky: That's true. [*There is a pause in the recording.*] The place where we lived was known as Le Plessis[84] during Maupassant's times.[85] Later they added "Robinson" to the name, in honour of Robinson Crusoe, because during the age of Maupassant there was a café consisting of interconnected tiny tree houses there, and the clients would climb up to those huts by ladders. We enjoyed visiting this area as well. Isaac Emmanuilovich [Babel] loved it there and laughed a lot.

Duvakin: Excuse me, could you clarify.

Vladimir Sosinsky: The café up in the trees was called "Robinson," after Robinson Crusoe. There are, by the way, many novels –

Duvakin: So you could get a cup of coffee there?

Vladimir Sosinsky: Coffee, wine, whatever you liked. The poor waiter had to run up and down the ladders. If anyone up there wanted something, they had to turn on a small light. It was such a fun period because so many of Maupassant's novels took place in those trees. So his [Babel's] first wife and daughter, Natasha, used to live right there in Le Plessis-Robinson. Natasha came to Moscow not too long ago and visited with her other blood sister –

Duvakin: Half-sister.

Vladimir Sosinsky: – Lydia Babel,[86] who is a very talented designer here in Moscow.

1925 through 1928, as assistant in the People's Commissariat of Defence after 1934, and as commander of the Volga military district in 1937. He was awarded the rank of marshal of the Soviet Union in 1935. The Soviet authorities falsely accused him of treason and had him shot during Stalin's military purges of 1937–8. His status was rehabilitated in the late 1950s.

83 Mikhail Koltsov (1898–1940) was a famous Soviet journalist and the founder of many interesting and popular magazines such as *Ogonek*, *Krokodil* (*Crocodile*), and *Za Rulem* (*Behind the Steering Wheel*). *Ogonek* and *Za Rulem* sold up to five million copies every week. During his short life Koltsov wrote more than two thousand magazine articles and brought the genre of the feuilleton (the short satirical article) to its height. In 1938, unexpectedly, Koltsov was arrested in his own office, brutally tortured, and then sentenced to death by Stalin. His body was cremated, and the ashes buried in an unknown place.

84 Le Plessis-Robinson is a small old town about seven miles south of Paris. It was indeed renamed in honour of the tree-house cabaret (established in 1848) because of a tree-house described in *The Swiss Family Robinson* (1812), a novel by Johann David Wyss.

85 Guy de Maupassant (1850–1893) was a prominent nineteenth-century French novelist, a master of the short story form, and a representative of the Naturalist school. Maupassant considered the Russian novelist Ivan Turgenev to be one of his most influential teachers. During his short life, which ended tragically at the age of forty-two, Maupassant wrote about three hundred short stories, six novels, and a collection of poems.

86 Lydia Babel (b. 1937) is the youngest daughter of Isaac Babel. She became an architect and since 1996 has been living in the United States.

Duvakin: And Babel's first wife?[87]

Vladimir Sosinsky: She didn't want to return to the USSR.

Ariadna Sosinsky: He didn't want to leave her. There was the daughter. He wouldn't leave her. But since she refused to go, and he couldn't live abroad, they divorced.

Duvakin: Forgive me, I may not be aware of something here. Did his wife always live abroad?

Vladimir Sosinsky: Yes, since after the October Revolution.

Duvakin: She emigrated then?

Vladimir Sosinsky: She did.

Duvakin: How about him? He was in the Budenny's army and so on …

Vladimir Sosinsky: Yes.

Duvakin: When was that?

Vladimir Sosinsky: That was when he lost her.

Duvakin: So they got married before the revolution?

Vladimir Sosinsky: Correct, before the revolution.

Duvakin: I see. She left, and he stayed behind.

Vladimir Sosinsky: Yes.

Duvakin: Later he came to visit his –

Vladimir Sosinsky: When he came to Paris, he got together with her again, and they continued for a while to live as husband and wife; that's how Natasha was born.

Duvakin: And his behaviour was accepted back home?

Vladimir Sosinsky: It was.

Duvakin: So later he went back to Russia, and she stayed behind?

Vladimir Sosinsky: Yes, she stayed behind.

Duvakin: And he married a metro builder?

Vladimir Sosinsky: Yes, she was an engineer, an actual engineer with a college degree, a specialist in building tunnels. So he married Antonina Nikolayevna, who should be seen as his real widow.

---

87 Babel's first wife, Yevgenia Borisovna Babel, emigrated to France in 1925 and never returned to the USSR.

Duvakin: So the other one [Yevgenia] didn't die, but …

Vladimir Sosinsky: She didn't want to live in the Soviet Union.
He wanted to go back, and so he did.

Ariadna Sosinsky: He came [to Paris] several times; he got permission to travel, and then he always came back. He was never an émigré, not even for a day. But he came and tried to convince her to go with him. She refused, and that's how they parted.

Vladimir Sosinsky: So they separated in 1932, correct?

Ariadna Sosinsky: Correct. But in any case, I must tell you that when we talk about Yevgenia Borisovna, as was her name, we must say that –

Duvakin: His first wife?

Ariadna Sosinsky: Yes. We must say that he had a very ironic, sarcastic attitude towards this sweet Yevgenia Borisovna, whom we called "the red-haired beauty." He used to say: "There's always one beautiful daughter in a Jewish family. And when I came along –"

Duvakin: Was she also Jewish?

Vladimir Sosinsky: Yes, of course. So, as Babel was telling us: "When I arrived in Odessa as a provincial tutor, my future mother-in-law did not approve of me and my attempts to court Yevgenia Borisovna. Still, we got married. My mother-in-law was very unhappy. But when my name began to appear in various newspapers, and I became a writer, she –

Ariadna Sosinsky: She almost lost her mind.

Vladimir Sosinsky: – she almost lost her mind from indignation that the lousy Isaac suddenly became someone important. Her daughter was always someone –

Ariadna Sosinsky: They were a rich, bourgeois family.

Vladimir Sosinsky: A rich, bourgeois family. And then he also climbed up to the top. That was a great insult that she barely survived. Besides this, he made fun of her. She had a very elaborate hair-style, and it always seemed like her hair took up all of the room she was in: "You can't get past that hair; it has taken over the room!"

He also joked that she didn't want to go to the Soviet Union because she was in love with French commodes. At first, we were not sure what he meant. It turns out her brother, who supported them financially, worked as a representative of a toilet-making factory. So she couldn't leave the foreign commodes and therefore didn't want to go back home. [*They laugh.*]

He always made fun of that. He was very interested in the smallest, tiniest thing that happened around Yevgenia Borisovna. The first time we heard that story, my brother, who was also there, didn't get it, couldn't understand why we were laughing, what was so funny. He taught Yevgenia Borisovna how to drive, somewhere between Nice and Saint-Jean-de-Luz in the south of France. So once he said the following: "Yevgenia Borisovna presses so gently on the gas pedal." And Isaac Babel never forgot this and used to whisper during conversations, "Yevgenia Borisovna presses so gently on the gas pedal."

Duvakin [*laughing*]: He loved those kinds of stories.

Vladimir Sosinsky: He loved to joke around.

Ariadna Sosinsky: He always made fun of those he loved.

Vladimir Sosinsky: Yes, even those he loved. That's how he was.

Duvakin: And what about his second wife, Antonina …?

Vladimir Sosinsky: Nikolayevna.

Duvakin: Nikolayevna. What's her last name?

Vladimir Sosinsky: She was very different from Yevgenia Borisovna. First of all, she is ethnic Russian, and, second, we cannot compare her qualities to the other wife. She is an important person. While Yevgenia Borisovna was simply… comparing the two would be …

Ariadna Sosinsky: She was very bourgeois, that's all.

Vladimir Sosinsky: Too bourgeois. She loved all kinds of material comforts too much. And that was obvious in her behaviour.

Duvakin: He found someone who was similarly creative, a lot more like him.

Vladimir Sosinsky: Theirs was true love, a meeting of the minds. That was reflected in their daughter as well, Lydia Isaacovna, who resembled her father not only physically – she is a pretty girl, despite the likeness.

Duvakin: How is that possible? He was such a monkey!

Vladimir Sosinsky: It turns out it's possible. Besides, she is very talented and interesting as a person.

Perhaps the most important of my meetings with Babel took place in the émigré restaurant the Bear.

I have to tell you that Babel and I liked the same things: we loved it all, the music, the vodka, the dirty jokes, everything. So our meeting was incredible, and not just that one but many others, too. It was easy for us. I'll tell you about one evening at the Bear. It must have been at the beginning of the 1930s, probably '32 or '33, when Hitler was already rising in power. Ariadna, was Hitler already in power?

Ariadna Sosinsky: Yes, yes.

Vladimir Sosinsky: He must have come one more time then.

Duvakin: Hitler took power in 1933.

Vladimir Sosinsky: I mean, did Babel come to Paris one more time?

Ariadna Sosinsky: I think so.

Vladimir Sosinsky: Well, simply put, our conversations were extremely interesting. The more vodka we drank, the more music we heard and appetizers we consumed, the chattier Babel became, and the more fascinating stories he shared with us. I must say I remember especially the freedom of thought and expression we had, because it was a very difficult time then in Russia. He told us, for example –

Duvakin: Tell us everything.

Vladimir Sosinsky: – a story about Lenin. Once there was a party at Kamenev's, a drinking party. Kamenev had an open bottle of vodka on the table,[88] and then all of a sudden Trotsky showed up. He took the scene in and quickly turned around, mumbling to himself, "You can't have a proper conversation with such scoundrels!" and left the room.

There was another drinking party at Karl Radek's. Karl Radek was a jokester and a cynic.[89] So one day Lenin was walking down a street, and a Red Army guard accosted him and told him: "Vladimir Illych, isn't that awkward? Many people have nothing to eat, yet they are drinking there!" The next morning, when Lenin saw Karl Radek, he scolded him, "You, my dear, next time pull down the shutters, close the windows, so nobody can see you!"

Here is the difference between Lenin's and Trotsky's approach to things. "Not once during the revolution," Babel lamented, "did Trotsky drink even a bottle of vodka!"

Duvakin [*surprised*]: You are kidding!

Vladimir Sosinsky: No, it's true.

88 Lev Kamenev (b. Rosenfeld) (1883–1936) was a prominent Bolshevik revolutionary, a friend of Lenin, and a member of the Politburo. In 1936 he was arrested and sentenced to death for his support of Leon Trotsky.

89 Karl Radek (b. Carol Sobelsohn) (1885–1939) was a Marxist revolutionary, active in the Polish and German social democratic movements before the First World War, and an international Communist leader in the Soviet Union after the Russian Revolution. Lenin did not respect him but valued his talent as a journalist and propagandist. In 1936 Radek was arrested and expelled from the party. His daughter and wife were also arrested and exiled. Radek was sent to a labour camp, where, in 1939, he was killed by one of his cellmates who may have been a special NKVD agent.

Duvakin: Did Lenin drink?

Vladimir Sosinsky: He approached such things very differently. [*He smiles.*] He was not as strict in applying his principles as Trotsky was. I remember what he [Babel] said very well: when Lenin spoke, it seemed that you could see inside his head and admire the workings of his brain – similar to watching an engine and seeing all of its parts move. You could see his thoughts forming in his head. And that difficult, wonderful work really impressed his listeners.

He [Babel] remembered Stalin very differently. For example, he told me the following story. Once there was an official lunch at the Kremlin, and he was amazed at how Yagoda behaved himself at the table.[90] That same Yagoda, who was in charge of so many people's lives, their fate, on the White Sea–Baltic Canal and elsewhere.[91] Babel kept staring at him, wondering how it's possible for him to speak so calmly, normally, while thousands of people's future depended on his will; how terrifying that man was – this Yagoda – a real wolf!

But just as Babel was thinking about that, Stalin entered the room, and all of a sudden Yagoda turned into a snivelling, reverential footman, bowing down to Stalin. And Babel realized something: "Now you could see who the real wolf was! The truth revealed itself!"

Then he added, deep in thought, "That's so interesting from a historical perspective: when that beast came to life in Munich,[92] we had someone else here to stand up to him, our own beast. We've let our own wolf loose! And you'll see that he'll be victorious." We remember those words because they turned out to be prophetic.

Duvakin: Yes, but not exactly, of course.

Vladimir Sosinsky: That's correct, not completely, but still, such conversations you can't … He told many funny stories, too. "I went to the university – but

90 Genrikh Yagoda (1891–1938) was a secret police official who served as director of the NKVD, the Soviet Union's security and intelligence agency, from 1934 to 1936. Like many Soviet NKVD officers who conducted political repression, Yagoda himself became ultimately a victim of the purge. He was demoted from the directorship of the agency in 1936 and arrested in 1937. Charged with the crimes of wrecking, espionage, Trotskyism, and conspiracy, Yagoda was a defendant at the Trial of the Twenty-One, the last of the major Soviet show trials of the 1930s. Following his confession at the trial, Yagoda was found guilty and shot.

91 The White Sea–Baltic Canal (1931–3), which connects the White Sea with Lake Onega, is 180 miles long and was built in twenty months, without any machinery, by the forced labour of Gulag prisoners. According to official records, between twelve thousand and twenty-five thousand labourers died during the construction of the canal, but historians put the figure much higher, at two hundred and fifty thousand deaths.

92 Vladimir Sosinsky refers to Adolf Hitler here, whose early career started in Munich, Bavaria. Hitler was born in Braunau am Inn, a small town in Austria at the border with Germany, thirty-seven miles from Munich.

unlike anyone else, I went to Samara to study[93] – nobody else did that. I rented rooms from an old woman, who was deaf-mute; we had to communicate through written notes. The morning after I moved in, I wrote the following to her: 'Where is your lavatory?' And she wrote back, 'My darling, I don't understand foreign languages.'"

Duvakin: Whom did he write this to?

Vladimir Sosinsky: His landlady, the one who was deaf and mute, from whom he was renting a room in Samara.

Duvakin [*laughing*]: I see!

Vladimir Sosinsky: He told us many stories, which should have been included in his *Red Cavalry*.[94] I remember the one about the Cossack, the commander of the regiment, a very desperate man, who once received a letter from his father in his home village: "You should be ashamed of yourself! The whole village is laughing at you: you fought so much, killed so many innocent people, yet somehow never managed to receive the Order of the Red Banner!"[95] [*Duvakin chuckles.*] So he moaned and groaned in front of Babel, then said, "I need to think of something all will remember." One day he mounted his horse and, breaking through the door, he galloped into the local movie theatre, which put an end to the show. He was demoted to a soldier after that.

Duvakin: What was he before?

Vladimir Sosinsky: Commander of the regiment. I remember also this sentence, not sure why; I even wrote it down in my diary: "If I were a poet, I'd write a wonderful poem about Mandelstam. He served poetry so selflessly, magnificently!"

Duvakin: That's very well put.

---

93 Samara is an ancient Russian city located on the Volga River. Today Samara's riverfront is considered to be one of the favourite recreation places for both local citizens and tourists, but during the Soviet period it was mostly developed as an industrial centre.

94 *Red Cavalry* is a collection of thirty-five short stories by Isaac Babel written between 1923 and 1925. The stories take place during the Polish-Soviet War and are based on Babel's diary, which he kept when he was a journalist assigned to the Semyon Budyonny's First Cavalry Army. The book openly reveals the brutality of war and the heroism of the common men, yet it was not well received by many Soviet military commanders who insisted that everything described in it was a lie. When Babel was arrested in 1939 and executed in 1940, his works were removed from all Soviet libraries, and his name was never mentioned again for many years. It was only in the 1990s that his books were reintroduced to the Russian reading public and are now widely appreciated both at home and abroad.

95 The Order of the Red Banner was established in 1918. It remained the highest order of the Soviet Union until 1930, when it was superseded by the Order of Lenin.

Vladimir Sosinsky: He even loved Georgy Adamovich,[96] despite his claims that he was the greatest Russian critic. If you remember, Georgy Adamovich was a member of the younger group of Acmeists.[97]

Duvakin: I remember.

Vladimir Sosinsky: Georgy Adamovich, Georgy Ivanov,[98] and even Nikolay Otsup.[99] Babel thought that Tukhachevsky stood out. He saw him not only as a brilliant military mind and an incredible human being but also as a genius tactician and strategist. It was because of Tukhachevsky that Babel believed Hitler would ultimately be defeated, because it was already clear there would be a war.

Duvakin: That must have been before Tukhachevsky was executed?

Vladimir Sosinsky: Yes, before that.

Duvakin: How terrifying!

Vladimir Sosinsky: So, in that sense ... Babel said that there were, of course, some difficulties around our return home, but they were not unsurmountable. So you could never argue, the way Yuri Annenkov did, that Babel conducted anti-Soviet propaganda in emigration. That's simply not true, pure slander!

Duvakin: That's what Annenkov wrote in his book?

Vladimir Sosinsky: Yes, published and translated into English. Another interesting thing I find in my notes: he talked to us about two books he was writing at the time. One was a story about beggars travelling all around Russia, which would give him the opportunity to discuss every aspect of life in the country. What? [*He turns to Ariadna Viktorovna.*]

---

96 Georgy Adamovich (1892–1972) was a Russian poet associated with the Acmeists. After the revolution he emigrated to France, where he became one of the most influential literary critics in the Russian émigré circle.

97 Acmeism was a poetic school that emerged in Russia around 1910–12. Nikolay Gumilev and Sergei Gorodetsky are considered its founders. The most prominent poets of the school were Anna Akhmatova (in her early years), Osip Mandelstam, and Mikhail Kuzmin. The group often met in the Brodyachaya Sobaka (Stray Dog) café in Saint Petersburg. Most of the Acmeists, except for Akhmatova, Gorodetsky, and Kuzmin, fell victim to Stalin's purges.

98 About Georgy Ivanov, see note 50 to this dialogue.

99 Nikolay Otsup (1894–1958) was a Russian poet and translator. After the revolution he was invited to work at World Literature Publishing House, where he became friends with Nikolay Gumilev and Alexander Blok. After Gumilev's execution in 1921, Otsup decided to leave Russia. He served as a volunteer in the French army during the Second World War and was awarded a medal for his bravery. In 1951 he defended his doctoral dissertation on Nikolai Gumilev at the Sorbonne; it was the first serious academic work on the poet. Otsup died unexpectedly from heart failure in 1958.

Ariadna Sosinsky: They are searching for food.

Vladimir Sosinsky: Yes, they are looking for food. In that way he could capture life on the collective farm, the revolution in the villages – and it was all to be done very bravely. Antonina Nikolayevna confirmed his plans, too. The second book was about horses. When he told us about it, he lived near Zvenigorod;[100] there was a stud farm there, which he visited often because he was very interested in horses.

Similarly, during one of his trips he and I went to see a stable in Le Plessis-Robinson. He had a particular love for horses. I remember he so wanted me to arrange a meeting with the famous Count Urusov[101] – not the one who wrote a book about horses – but his son, who also shared his father's passion for the Orlov Trotter.[102]

He was involved in the racehorse business in France at the time, naturally. I remember Babel writing to me: "Of course, we don't need to have a special meeting; we could tell each other much of interest. I have programs and pictures from Moscow and so on. On the other hand, I would like to know more about the horse-racing business in France if the occasion presents itself."

Besides that, he badly wanted me to introduce him to the Kuban, and Don Cossacks who worked at the Renault automobile factory at the time.[103]

Duvakin: Really!

Vladimir Sosinsky: Yes. I drove him around Boulogne-Billancourt. Those are the Parisian suburbs where you could find the different buildings of the Renault factory; I used to work there and knew all the cafeterias where the Russians went – because people ate dinner there. They'd have dinner in the cafeteria and take a sandwich with them to work for lunch. He had such wonderful

---

100 Zvenigorod is an old town near Moscow, dating back to the twelfth century. The natural environment of hills and forests made the countryside around Zvenigorod a favourite retreat for many famous Russians, such as Alexander Herzen, Anton Chekhov, Maxim Gorky, and Pyotr Tchaikovsky. At present it remains a popular tourist attraction.

101 Prince Sergei Urusov (1859–1915) was an expert on horse husbandry and the author of a fine book about horses, *Vse o loshadi* (*All about Horses*, 1898). Babel wanted to meet his son Peter.

102 The Orlov Trotter is a famous horse breed noted for its incredible stamina and speed. It was developed in Russia by Count Alexei Orlov, the commander of the Russian navy during Catherine the Great's rule.

103 The Renault auto group was founded by the three Renault brothers in 1898 and has been extremely successful ever since. Their cars are very popular all around the world. A lesser known fact is that the brothers also created the FT-17 tank, whose shape and design became the blueprint for all future tanks. The Renault tanks were considered to be among the best during First World War.

conversations with them! Nobody knew that he was Babel or that he was a Soviet citizen, and he learned so much about their life.

Duvakin: How could they not recognize him?

Vladimir Sosinsky: You know, you couldn't even tell he was Jewish.

Duvakin: On the contrary, it was impossible not to see that.

Vladimir Sosinsky: No, it was easy to take him for a gentile. I have the proof, am I right, Ariadna? I have recorded the following story. Once a Cossack was giving water to his horse, and Babel reached out for the bucket. "All of a sudden an ancient Jewish sorrow came over me," he told me, "and I felt very thirsty, but the Cossack snapped at me, 'Keep away, Jew, I won't give you anything!' That was the only time I was taken for a Jew while I was in the army." He was bold, if you remember, and just a little bit snub-nosed.

Anyway, that was all true. And it was, by the way, very typical of him. Yes! He also shared this great story with us: "Natasha is so stingy!" (That was his daughter.) "Just like my grandma! You see," he said, "she is so stingy, doesn't want to share her toy with the other kid!" He was talking about his daughter.

"As a young boy, I was very small and frail. Everybody worried about me because I was so thin, and my grandma always tried to fatten me up. And I would run away to play with my friends and give them my meat sandwiches and all the bread and sausages, which I didn't eat. When she noticed that, she ran after the children who had taken the sandwiches, and snatched them away forcefully, even pulling the food out of their mouths with her own hands."

Duvakin: My goodness!

Vladimir Sosinsky: There was such a big food fight. Well, as I noted in my diary then: "Perhaps there was no such grandma. He simply loved to shock people with his stories so much." Right, I think that's all.

Duvakin: How about some other stories he told you? There's so little that's been written about him.

Vladimir Sosinsky: You know, I can tell you that most of his stories, which he told us in the restaurant the Bear, were very similar in style to "My First Honorarium," his last short story, if you have read it.

Duvakin: I haven't.

Vladimir Sosinsky: I remember he was very interested in the Whites and even went to some of their meetings, a celebration of some regiment.[104]

---

104 About the Whites, see note 34 to dialogue 1.

I remember he made a special trip to the Sainte-Geneviève-des-Bois Russian cemetery where many generals, colonels, and captains were buried.[105] The remarkable thing was that they were buried according to their rank, division, and regiment. There was the grave of the captain of the regiment or the division, followed by the grave of the leader of the battalion, then that of the company commander. There were spaces left for those still living to be buried there eventually as well. It's the only cemetery of this kind I am aware of. He found it very impressive, this famous cemetery.

Well, I'd like to end here, with those notes from my diary. They are the reason why I can tell you such stories, since they were able to survive. And the things that were not recorded properly, let them remain in my memories. [*He smiles.*]

Duvakin: That's too bad! Well, that's fine. In any case, our conversations won't be censored.

Vladimir Sosinsky: I understand, but still, I don't want to – I can't bring myself to talk about that.

Duvakin: His language could be pretty dirty, couldn't it?

Vladimir Sosinsky: A lot, but only at parties, of course. He told stories so masterfully that the naughtiness – no, he was just a very skilful storyteller, and everything had its purpose, its psychological value, only in that sense, you see …

Duvakin: Right, I see.

Vladimir Sosinsky: It was excusable.

Duvakin: In the name of literature?

Vladimir Sosinsky: Yes. But this literariness was not important in and of itself, as in the other art forms he expressed. He loved to tell stories about overheard conversations between lovers, about trysts at hotels somewhere, about things that happened in the room next door, about heartfelt conversations with a certain man or a woman – all thrown together. There were many such stories like "My First Honorarium." I recommend it to you.

Duvakin: Was it published in the latest two-volume edition?

---

105 The Sainte-Geneviève-des-Bois Russian cemetery is part of the Cimetière de Liers and is called the Russian Orthodox cemetery. Since its establishment in the late nineteenth century, it has become the most important necropolis of Russian émigrés in the world. Many notable Russians – such as Ivan Bunin, Boris Zaytsev, Zinaida Gippius, Dmitry Merezhkovsky, Alexey Remizov, Nadezhda Teffy, and Andrei Tarkovsky – are buried there. Now the cemetery is closed, and its future is unclear because it is not officially considered a landmark and has no legal protection, although the French Ministry of Culture and Communication recognizes its importance as a historical monument.

Vladimir Sosinsky: I don't think so. Am I right, Ariadna?

Ariadna Sosinsky: Yes.

Duvakin: He used jargon, a colourful Odessan language,[106] when he narrated his stories, didn't he?

Vladimir Sosinsky: Absolutely! He was so good at it! Now when I read something from Odessa,[107] I always think of Babel. It's horrible …

Ariadna Sosinsky: My mom studied in Odessa. And he [Babel] always talked to her so passionately about Odessa. Do you remember?

Vladimir Sosinsky: Yes, they found common ground right away and even travelled to the south together.

Ariadna Sosinsky: No, you are mistaken. They travelled along the Loire together.

Vladimir Sosinsky: Yes, they visited the castles on the Loire.[108] By the way, those are some of the most interesting sites in France – all the medieval castles that managed to survive, one more beautiful than the next. That's an incredible tour, somehow underappreciated by tourists.

Duvakin: May I stop you here? Did Olga Eliseevna accept Babel,[109] so to speak?

Ariadna Sosinsky: Yes.

Vladimir Sosinsky: Oh, they were good friends.

Ariadna Sosinsky: She loved his stories passionately and read everything related to Babel, and to the Soviet Union in general.

Duvakin: Did she move back with you? When did she pass away?

Ariadna Sosinsky: She died here, at home.

---

106 The Odessan language is a Russian dialect heavily influenced by the Yiddish language and Ukrainian grammar and phraseology.

107 Odessa was founded in 1794 by the order of the Russian empress Catherine the Great. A beautiful city on the Black Sea, Odessa is presently in Ukraine and has more than one million residents. It is known for its unique culture that combines humour and natural intelligence – qualities that every "Odessite" is expected to possess.

108 The châteaux of the Loire Valley are part of the architectural heritage of the historic towns of Amboise, Angers, Blois, Chinon, Montsoreau, Nantes, Orléans, Saumur, and Tours along the Loire River in France. As many French kings before Francois I (1494–1547) preferred the beautiful and flowering banks of the Loire to Paris, they and their nobility built palaces along them. The Renaissance and Enlightenment majesty of these castles continues to attract tourists.

109 Olga Eliseevna Chernova-Kolbasina (1886–1964) was Ariadna Sosinsky's mother.

Duvakin: I see, she died here.

Vladimir Sosinsky: In the next room.

Duvakin: She came back with you?

Vladimir Sosinsky: Yes.

Ariadna Sosinsky: She followed a little later because we didn't have an apartment when we first came back. [*She turns to Vladimir Sosinsky.*] You can finish about …

Duvakin: Yes. What were you doing in Paris?

Vladimir Sosinsky: Right. I can tell you that our conversations with Babel about Russia, about the Soviet Union, were like seeds falling on fertile land and undoubtedly played an important role in our desire to go back home. This desire became very strong on 22 June 1941.

Life in Paris during the 1930s

Duvakin: That's understandable. What about the 1930s? Did you live in Paris proper?

Vladimir Sosinsky: Yes, Paris proper.

Duvakin: What did you do in Paris?

Vladimir Sosinsky: As I told you already, I worked as a secretary for the editorial board of the journal *Russia's Will.*[110]

Duvakin: It was still going?

Vladimir Sosinsky: And even as director of typography. But the printing press published many other things. There was also a French section. I think I mentioned already (I'm not sure if it was recorded) that some famous people often came there – Vaillant-Couturier (the famous French Communist)[111] and Louis Aragon[112] – and we spent many nights working together urgently on the publications …

---

110 See note 2 to this dialogue.

111 Paul Vaillant-Couturier (1892–1937) was a journalist and one of the founders of the French Communist Party. He admired the Bolshevik Revolution and visited the USSR in 1921 to meet Vladimir Lenin.

112 Luis Aragon (1897–1982) was a prominent French writer, an active member of the French Communist Party, and the husband of Elsa Triolet. He visited the USSR many times, but he grew more and more concerned about freedom of expression in the Soviet Union. He actively protested against Sinyavsky-Daniel's trial (1966) and then wrote a personal letter to

Duvakin: I see.

Vladimir Sosinsky: Then there was a war in Spain.

Duvakin: Yes, I know: 1936, 1937, 1938.

Vladimir Sosinsky: During that period I didn't have time to focus on my own creative writing, because I had to do this kind of intensive typographical jobs and make a living somehow.

Duvakin: In publishing?

Vladimir Sosinsky: In publishing. It was typographical work. I had almost stopped publishing my own writing by the end of the 1920s.

Duvakin: What did you publish earlier?

Vladimir Sosinsky: Short stories, articles. Mostly in *Russia's Will*.

Duvakin: So you didn't publish a separate book?

Vladimir Sosinsky: No, there was just the small book about Makhno,[113] with three short stories about him.

Duvakin [*very surprised*]: Was Makhno then in …

Vladimir Sosinsky: Yes, he was in Paris at the time.

Duvakin: Ah, you met there?

Vladimir Sosinsky: We met in Paris. He came to complain to me that I had depicted him poorly in my stories, made him seem like a bandit, while he was a pure anarchist, a follower of Kropotkin.[114]

Duvakin: I see.

Leonid Brezhnev (the leader of the Communist Party in the USSR at the time) requesting the release of the film director Sergei Paradzhanov, one of the first notable persons in the country to receive a prison sentence for being gay. After that, Aragon's visa to the USSR was permanently revoked.

113 Nestor Makhno (1888–1934) was an anarchist and the commander of an anarchist army located in Ukraine. He started as an ally of the Bolsheviks, but they soon betrayed him, and Trotsky even issued an order for his arrest. Makhno left Russia and, after a long period of wandering around Europe, finally settled in Paris, where he soon died from tuberculosis.

114 Prince Peter Kropotkin (1842–1921) was a Russian scientist, a prominent geographer and geologist, and the "father" of Russian anarchism. His reputation as a scientist was so high that, while living in London, Kropotkin was invited to contribute a series of articles for the *Encyclopaedia Britannica* (1902). In Russia he was offered a ministerial position in the provisionary government headed by Alexander Kerensky, but he declined. Disillusioned by the results of the Bolshevik Revolution, Kropotkin quietly died in his little house near Moscow, refusing to accept help from the Bolshevik government.

Vladimir Sosinsky: This dark, short, snub-nosed, pockmarked man with darting eyes came in.

Duvakin: You're describing him so well.

Vladimir Sosinsky: I took his picture. He gave me this whole lecture but couldn't convince me anyway. Later he brought me a book he had published, which I gave to the library here.

So my life went in that manner until 1939 when I joined the fight against the Fascists. For me, Hitler's emergence took on a very personal significance, absolutely personal. I volunteered to serve in the French army.

Duvakin [*very surprised*]: So you were part of the French Resistance?[115]

Vladimir Sosinsky: Yes, I was. And I was very disappointed by Ribbentrop's trip to Moscow.[116]

Duvakin: You don't say!

Vladimir Sosinsky: But after I was wounded in the Ardennes, when Guderian's[117] tanks were sent against us, the Foreign Legion,[118] we were – because I didn't want to become a French citizen ….

Duvakin: Were you already a Soviet citizen?

Vladimir Sosinsky: No, I was stateless. I should note that when I was in Berlin, in 1922–3, Germany was the first to recognize the Soviet Union as a country, I think.

---

115 The French Resistance (1940–4) was a movement against the occupation of France by Nazi Germany.

116 Joachim von Ribbentrop (1893–1946) was the Nazi minister of foreign affairs from 1938 to 1945. A successful businessman (he was selling German wine worldwide), Ribbentrop became interested in politics and soon gained Hitler's attention and trust. In 1939 he visited Moscow and signed the infamous Molotov-Ribbentrop Pact (the Nazi-Soviet non-aggression pact). In 1945 Ribbentrop was arrested by American troops and then sentenced and executed as a war criminal in 1946.

117 Heinz Guderian (1888–1954) was a Nazi general, the commander of the German motorized troops, and an early proponent and the main advocate of the so-called Blitzkrieg method of warfare. In 1945 he was arrested by American troops, but at the Nuremberg trial he was only a witness, not one of the accused. After the war he participated as an expert consultant in the rebuilding of the German economy and wrote his memoirs, *Erinnerungen eines Soldaten* (*Panzer Leader*, 1951). He died in 1954 from liver failure associated with persistent alcoholism.

118 The French Foreign Legion is a military infantry branch within the French regular army. The legion was established in 1831 to allow foreign nationals to serve in the army for a fixed salary. The number of the enlisted has varied over time, but at its peak the legion reached forty thousand soldiers. Today the French Foreign Legion counts about ten thousand soldiers from more than one hundred countries.

Duvakin: Yes, that happened in 1922.

Vladimir Sosinsky: Right. I didn't want to miss my chance and lose my citizenship so I registered with the embassy. Afterwards in Paris I worked for three years for the trade representation offices and once again didn't miss the registration period for getting citizenship. But every time I made inquiries about going back home, I received a brief letter informing me that the Central Committee had responded with the following: "As you were born in (such and such year), you must serve in the Red Army." I replied that I was ready to serve in the Red Army,[119] even though I was already engaged to this beautiful lady here. And I got an answer after a while that "the Central Committee has reviewed your request for receiving citizenship and denied it." It was an official, printed letter.

Duvakin: So that's what happened.

Vladimir Sosinsky: Yes. I don't know why, but they had clearly decided not to allow us to return: Vadim Andreyev and me. When Gorky spoke with Stalin about Vadim Leonidovich [Andreyev], Stalin said, "Let him in!"

Duvakin: True, but that was already later.

[*There is a pause in the recording.*]

Participation in the Second World War

Duvakin: You mentioned that you volunteered to serve in the French army.

Vladimir Sosinsky: Yes. I should clarify that as a non-French citizen I couldn't serve in the French army, only in the Foreign Legion. Actually, that wasn't the Foreign Legion per se but a special volunteer regiment – foreign volunteer regiment as it was called then. It inherited the traditions of the Foreign Legion. There I served as a platoon commander and was wounded in the same village where Joan of Arc was born[120]; that's where I was captured by the Germans.

Duvakin: Oh, my goodness!

---

119 The Red Army was formed on 23 February 1918 by the decree of Vladimir Lenin. In 1946 it was renamed to the Soviet Army.

120 Joan of Arc (1412–1431) is a French national hero. She was born in a small village, Domrémy, at the time of the Hundred Years War (1337–1453) between France and England. At the age of sixteen, Joan arrived at the court of the dauphin of France, Charles (the future King Charles VII), and requested that his army be put under her command, claiming that she had been sent by God. Hesitant, Charles gave her a few regiments, and in four days the siege of Orléans (located about seventy miles from Paris) ended. But Charles betrayed Joan in battle: she was captured by the Burgundian forces. Philippe, Duke of Burgundy, sold Joan to England for ten thousand French livres, where she was executed by burning at the stake.

Vladimir Sosinsky: No matter how hard I tried to escape, I was captured on four separate occasions on the same day.

Duvakin: Where could you escape to? They had already taken all of France.

Vladimir Sosinsky: Yes. That was the beginning of the horrible period of captivity. For me, the worst day was 22 June 1941, when I saw countless trains passing by our camp in Potsdam, going east, and loaded with such weapons, such machinery, so many soldiers and officers, that it seemed to me that no country in the world – let alone France! – would be able to withstand it. And the first news was very sad.

Duvakin: Yes.

Vladimir Sosinsky: The first news was so terrible, I thought it was a nightmare we were experiencing, not life. The first time I exhaled with relief was when a German Communist worker brought the news of –

Duvakin: Moscow?

Vladimir Sosinsky: – the military parade in the Red Square.[121]

Duvakin: Yes, that was Stalin's idea, not a bad one.

Vladimir Sosinsky: This was the first good news we got. By the way, not just us, the prisoners of war, but also many Germans wanted to see Hitler destroyed as soon as possible.

Duvakin: You don't say! There was such an internal opposition?

Vladimir Sosinsky: Without a doubt, there was. It wasn't an actual resistance movement, nothing organized, just conversations. We had to wear overalls with a sign on the back, "Französische Kriegsgefangene" [French prisoner of war]. They felt they could speak openly with the Frenchmen. After all, France had already been conquered by the Germans. The French and us, we shared similar hatred for the Germans. So I found myself taking part in the French Resistance.

Duvakin: I'm sorry but how …? Were you imprisoned in Potsdam?

Vladimir Sosinsky: Yes.

121 The military parade honoured the twenty-fourth anniversary of the Bolshevik Revolution (7 October 1941). This parade was unique in many ways: it took place during the battle for Moscow; the German army was standing just ten miles away from the capital; all those who participated in the parade were going straight to the front, and many of them would never return; and Stalin, who never was very talkative, delivered a long speech to cheer up the soldiers and the whole country – to show that the country was still capable of defeating the enemy.

Duvakin: That meant you were in the centre of Germany, the centre of Berlin. How could you see the trains from the concentration camp? The military echelons were not …

Vladimir Sosinsky: I was not held at Luckenwalde,[122] but at a different, smaller camp, where there were about three hundred of us. It was not exactly a concentration camp, though we were surrounded by wire fences. Although we were part of Luckenwalde officially, we actually lived in a much smaller camp.

Duvakin: Was it a part of the Buchenwald?[123]

Vladimir Sosinsky: No, Luckenwalde.

Duvakin [*thoughtfully*]**:** Never heard of it.

Vladimir Sosinsky: So the trains and everything else went past us; there was no secrecy about any of it.

Duvakin: Were there any Soviet prisoners of war?

Vladimir Sosinsky: There were some. I saw some horrifying scenes. For example, I saw Polish policemen patrolling the wire fences, whips in hand, and all you had to do was throw a cigarette to a Russian, a Soviet prisoner, and you'd see him immediately fall down, either shot by a bullet from the watch tower or struck with a whip by a Pole. They played different nationalities against each other. For instance, they'd put Poles or Ukrainians in charge of the Russians. They did such things all the time and didn't themselves get involved.

Duvakin: That must have been at the beginning of the war. Later, of course, things changed.

Vladimir Sosinsky: Yes, later, as you say.

Duvakin: And you received news of the first Soviet victories.

Vladimir Sosinsky: Yes, through a secret radio transmission.

Duvakin: In the concentration camp?

Vladimir Sosinsky: No, you see …

Duvakin: And how did you get out of Potsdam?

Vladimir Sosinsky: How did I manage to get from Potsdam to France?

---

122 The concentration camp Stalag III-A was located in Luckenwalde, about forty miles from Berlin. It was one of the first prisoner-of-war camps built as a model for many future camps.

123 The Buchenwald concentration camp was the first camp established in Germany, in 1937. Over time it added 139 smaller sub-camps under the same authority. More than 250,000 prisoners went through it until it was liberated by American troops in 1945.

Duvakin: Yes.

Vladimir Sosinsky [*smiling*]: That's quite interesting. I received official papers as a participant in the First World War. Our ladies were able to secure them for me, even though I had only taken part in the civil war, not the First World War. And, as a married man, a father with a child, I was set free.

Duvakin: As a French prisoner of war?

Vladimir Sosinsky: Yes, I passed for a Frenchman.

Duvakin: I understand.

Vladimir Sosinsky: So, finally, I was allowed to go home.

Duvakin: How many years did you spend there? One, two, three?

Vladimir Sosinsky: Of course, about two years had already passed. But we had a problem in the camp. There was a search in the Soviet part of the camp, and they found letters in Russian, written by the same hand and sent from the French section. It was my handwriting. I was the only one who knew Russian.

Duvakin: You wrote letters for …

Vladimir Sosinsky: Correspondence between some Frenchmen and the Russians. So I was arrested and thrown into the disciplinary unit, and my departure fell through. I had to stay there an extra year and a half. But later they forgot about this. I was even sentenced to death and spent several days awaiting execution. But that's not important. What matters is that I was freed in the end, and towards the middle of 1943 I was able to get to Oléron Island,[124] so it took less time than I told you at first. The war in France started earlier, you see.

Duvakin: For you it started in 1939. Almost four years.

Vladimir Sosinsky: Yes. So I ended up on Oléron [Island]. There were, by the way, a lot of Soviet citizens working on the construction of the Atlantic Wall.[125] They joined the French Resistance and helped capture the island. We tell this

124 Oléron Island is located in the Atlantic Ocean and is the second-largest French island. In April of 1945 the German-occupied Oléron was liberated by French military forces; more than eight thousand soldiers were deployed to the island. Their assault was supported by the internal French opposition.

125 The Atlantic Wall was a system of coastal fortifications built by Nazi Germany in 1940–4. It was supposed to protect Germany from the invasion of the Allied forces through France, Belgium, and the Netherlands. Although German propaganda proclaimed it to be invincible, in reality the wall was poorly built and poorly defended. Still the myth of the unassailable wall helped Nazi Germany to postpone the Allies' invasion of Europe because the Allies were afraid that they would be unable to deal efficiently with the wall.

story in *The Heroes of Oléron*, a brochure that we have just published here with Vadim Leonidovich Andreyev.

Duvakin: Ah, I remember reading something about it. And where is that island?

Vladimir Sosinsky: In the Atlantic Ocean.

Duvakin: Near the coastline?

Vladimir Sosinsky: Near La Rochelle.[126]

Duvakin: Is it a small island?

Vladimir Sosinsky: Quite small: thirty kilometres [twenty miles] in length and five kilometres [three miles] in width.

Duvakin: And you were able to capture it?

Vladimir Sosinsky: Not exactly. [*He smiles.*] When the French army was attacking from without, the Soviet men within were blowing up all the batteries and guns around – which helped the French army a lot. But that's a long story and not very important.

[*There is a pause in the recording.*]

The Return to the USSR

Vladimir Sosinsky: I should tell you that after the war I was invited to work as an editor for the secretariat of the United Nations. That's how I spent thirteen years there.

Duvakin: In New York?

Vladimir Sosinsky: In New York. I travelled all over the world but never stopped asking to be allowed to return home. Never!

Ariadna Sosinsky: Though he had a Soviet passport.

Vladimir Sosinsky: I did have a Soviet passport.

Duvakin: Since when?

---

126 La Rochelle is an old port in western France on the Atlantic Ocean. The city was founded in the tenth century by the Knights Templar, also known as the Order of Solomon's Temple. For the next five hundred years La Rochelle was the largest and most active French port. The Nazis build a special bunker for their submarines near the city, and it was the last French city to surrender to the Allied forces, on 8 May 1945.

Vladimir Sosinsky: Since 1946.

Duvakin: So, after the amnesty given to émigrés?[127]

Vladimir Sosinsky: Yes. Those of us who lived in France and Yugoslavia and who had not dishonoured ourselves by collaborating with the Germans, received Soviet passports. Unfortunately, every time I raised the question of going back, I ran into an obstacle. I was finally able to resolve the matter when I was working in London in the Disarmament Commission and happened to meet –

Duvakin: So, you also worked in London?

Vladimir Sosinsky: Yes, in London and in Geneva and in Paris.

The person who most helped me come back – that is, the only one to send a telegram on my behalf to Moscow – was the [Soviet] ambassador to London at the time, Yakov Alexandrovich Malik, with whom I became close in the course of my work. I recorded his speeches in my capacity of serving as chair of the Russian stenography department at the UN, as well as editor-in-chief, which meant I was present at all meetings of the Security Council, the First Committee, the General Assembly, and the Disarmament Commission.

Duvakin [*laughing*]**:** One had to stand up and salute you when you entered the room!

Vladimir Sosinsky: It was a fairly important position. I was one of twenty-five people whose names were on the special list.

Duvakin: So you had a pretty good life, more or less.

Vladimir Sosinsky: The kind of life where you get a thousand dollars a month, which now would be a thousand rubles – a nice salary, to be sure![128]

Duvakin [*whistles, with surprise*]**:** Yes, for sure!

---

127 On 14 June 1946 the Soviet government issued a decree that guaranteed all former citizens of the Russian empire, and those who had lost their Soviet citizenship for any reason, the reinstatement of their Soviet citizenship as long as they formally applied for it at the Soviet consulate in France. Many émigrés, mostly members of the intelligentsia, welcomed the news and returned to the USSR. Immediately they were bitterly disappointed in their decision: at the port of entry their passports were taken away, and their French citizenship was revoked; many were immediately arrested and send to labour camps; families were split apart and forced to live in different places. But some – mostly doctors, engineers, and scientists – were well received and successfully integrated into Soviet society.

128 For comparison, at the time of the Sosinsky interview, a university professor in the USSR received a salary of 550 rubles per month. In the military a major received 350 rubles per month; a colonel, 500 rubles; and a general, 800 rubles. But engineers earned only 150 rubles; doctors, 200 rubles; and school teachers, only 110 rubles.

Vladimir Sosinsky: It was thanks to that salary, in dollars, not rubles, that I was able to buy this apartment we are sitting in now. I bought it when we arrived in 1958.

Duvakin: It's a nice apartment, indeed.

Vladimir Sosinsky: Yes. When I went to Washington and asked to go home, I was told very kindly, "You know, we need you here, you're irreplaceable," and so on, "and there are no apartments there!" Back then, apartment construction was not on the same scale as it is today.

Duvakin: Yes.

Vladimir Sosinsky: "It would be hard to find a job there. You know languages, so that would help, but getting an apartment is another matter – very hard." I managed to trick my bosses in Washington, though. When I arrived here, I went to the president of Mosstroi [a Moscow construction company], and he put me in touch with co-operative housing.

I remember he asked, "Would a building with Soviet medical workers be fine with you?" I replied, "Very much so! If I get sick, the neighbours will take care of me."

He laughed and then opened an account for me at the Foreign Trade Bank because I had to transfer some dollars here, and I paid ten thousand dollars for this apartment.

Duvakin: Did you move here right away or had to live somewhere else first?

Vladimir Sosinsky: We lived in a village in the Moscow outskirts for two years while the apartments were being built. The apartment cost me ninety thousand rubles at the time. A dollar was worth ten rubles then. I transferred nine thousand dollars.

Duvakin: Well done.

Vladimir Sosinsky: I also bought the Volga that you saw.[129]

Duvakin: So, are you now getting your retirement cheque from the United Nations?

Vladimir Sosinsky: No, I am receiving a Soviet pension.

Duvakin: As a Soviet writer?

Vladimir Sosinsky: As a Soviet citizen.

Duvakin: Oh, that's good!

[*There is a pause in the recording.*]

---

129 The Volga used to be a luxury Soviet car whose production started in 1956 and was discontinued only in 2010. It served as a symbol of status and success during the Soviet period.

Meeting French Writers

Duvakin: You also mentioned that you met some French writers.

Vladimir Sosinsky: Right. I met people like Louis Aragon and Vaillant-Couturier. But, overall, it's true that there weren't many authors in our circles.

Ariadna Sosinsky: There was Kessel.[130]

Vladimir Sosinsky: Kessel? He is not well known here, but there he is really big. His best novel is *L'Équipage*, the first book – well before Saint-Exupéry[131] – about planes and plane crews. It came out in 1914, or maybe 1915, or 1916. Of course, I moved mostly in Russian literary circles. Once I got to the United States, I switched to a Soviet environment because the people working for the United Nations there were Soviet citizens and representatives of the Soviet government, envoys from Park Avenue.[132] But only one of them was willing to help me.

Duvakin [*sighs*]: I understand.

Vladimir Sosinsky: Yes.

Duvakin: And when you left Paris, the Russian émigrés – what was left of them anyway; most of them had already gone – were very hostile towards you.

Vladimir Sosinsky: The émigrés were still very much there, and I was anathema to them. There's this very talented young writer, Vladimir Varshavsky.[133]

---

130 Joseph Kessel (1898–1979) was a French journalist and writer, whose novel *Belle de Jour* (1928) was turned into a famous film of the same name by Luis Buñuel. Kessel served as an aviator during both world wars and wrote about his experiences in the book *L'Équipage* (1923). He was elected to the Académie française in 1962.

131 Antoine de Saint-Exupéry (1900–1944) was a renowned French writer and aviator. His most famous book, *The Little Prince,* was written and published first in English in New York in 1942, before it was published in his own language. By now his book has been translated into nearly 250 languages and has sold close to 150 million copies. For a long time the cause of his death remained unknown, but in 2000 the remains of his aeroplane were discovered in the sea near Marseille.

132 The USSR representatives at the United Nations at that time lived and worked on Park Avenue.

133 Vladimir Varshavsky (1906–1978) and his family left Russia after the revolution. During the Second World War he participated in the French Resistance. He later emigrated to the United States. There he published his memoirs *Nezamechennoe pokolenie.* The book appeared in a Russian language edition with the English title *The Lost Generation* in New York in 1956 and brought him well-deserved fame and financial independence. Near the end of his life, Varshavsky moved to Switzerland where he continued to work part-time for Radio Liberty.

His book *The Lost Generation* is quite well known and even translated into several languages. We were good friends, but the Russian émigrés arranged for a visa for him to work for the United Nations in America, with the provision that he was not to meet with me, because I was –

Duvakin: Did he receive the visa as a White émigré?

Vladimir Sosinsky: Correct.

Duvakin: So he was not allowed to communicate with Sosinsky, who had discredited himself, so to speak.

Vladimir Sosinsky: Yes, yes, yes. So he never spoke to me, but he did wink at me from a distance when we ran into each other in an elevator or somewhere else. [*Duvakin chuckles.*] They could have pulled him out right away. Thanks to that, we had many such funny encounters.

Duvakin: Did you ever meet Elsa Triolet?[134]

Vladimir Sosinsky: Not me. Ariadna Viktorovna's sister knew her. But their relationship was not very good.

[*There is a pause in the recording.*]

Duvakin: How about you, Ariadna Viktorobna, do you want to add anything else? About Babel, for example?

Ariadna Sosinsky: No, I don't think so.

Duvakin: All right, we can be satisfied with what we've got, though I know your memories are truly inexhaustible.

Vladimir Sosinsky: I think we could say more about Remizov,[135] who is not very highly regarded here for some reason.

Duvakin: He's simply not very well known here.

Vladimir Sosinsky: That's true.

Ariadna Sosinsky: Of all the writers abroad, he was the one who had the most positive attitude towards the Soviet Union and Soviet culture. After all, he received a Soviet passport at the same time we did.

Vladimir Sosinsky: We know so little about him.

Ariadna Sosinsky: He read all the Soviet books he could find. Spent a lot of money. His financial situation was very dire, but he spent all the money friends

134 About Elsa Triolet, see note 51 to dialogue 4.

135 About Alexey Remizov, see note 43 to dialogue 3.

gave him on such books and quarrelled with his benefactors because of that. He loved Soviet culture! When my older son entered the university in 1957 – we arrived in 1960, but he had already started his studies at the Moscow University a few years earlier.

Duvakin [*surprised*]**:** Here?

Ariadna Sosinsky: Yes. Alexey Mikhailovich [Remizov] was so happy about that; he almost considered him his grandson. It brought him such joy!

Duvakin: We'll have to devote a separate meeting to Alexey Mikhailovich.

Vladimir Sosinsky: We must. It's our responsibility towards the future.

Duvakin: Of course!

Vladimir Sosinsky: I am certain that this situation will be reconsidered in the future, and he will be given the respect he deserves.

Duvakin: Of course, of course. Thank you so very much.

[THE RECORDING ENDS.]

Afterword

Caryl Emerson

The modern period knows three contrasting perspectives of historical commentary, each with its own truths and illusions. The first position is the objective outsider's ideal: a narrative compiled after the fact with the benefit of hindsight, dependent on the material traces that survive. The second position is that of the subjective insider: the story of events recorded in process (a diary, a personal letter) or in retrospect (a memoir). A third position, exemplified by the taped discussions translated in this volume, is both the oldest and nowadays the most innovative: an oral history. Its realization requires at least two living people, an interviewer and a subject. Since they react to each other's verbal prompts in a shared context, the testimony is hyper-subjective. But the goal is not authority or factual accuracy. A previously unknown historical fact might indeed surface, but what matters are the personal impressions and associations offered up in an aura of trust. In live oral-history scenarios we learn simultaneously about the person speaking and about those being spoken of. Both are porous moving objects of study. Distinct layers of memory can coexist uneasily in a single person, linked by facial gestures or intonation. Consider dialogue 2 held on 19 August 1974 with Viktor Ardov, and his self-correcting memory of Vsevolod Meyerhold. Early in the interview he identifies with a progressive group of theatre people who praised Meyerhold, criticized all academic theatres, and believed that Meyerhold "represented the real, revolutionary Soviet art. [*He sighs.*]" By the end of the hour, that sigh has been made good. Fifty years have passed, Ardov notes, and he has changed his mind: "I still believe that he [Meyerhold] had great talent, but it was completely wild, unchecked." Which Ardov – the young or the old – should be engaged and encouraged? When both currents are flowing, how does the interviewer point the way and then get out of the way? Oral history is an ocean. Truth, such as emerges in these dialogues, is always a palimpsest.

Viktor Duvakin was a master at negotiating these waters, and this afterword will suggest some of the reasons. In terms of his own education and training, he was more qualified to speak to some interlocutors than to others, but all agree that his success was as much a matter of temperament as a matter of conscious policy. Duvakin was not a dissident. His scandalous defence of Andrei Sinyavsky in 1967 was an act of courage on behalf of a gifted former student, not a rejection of the regime. Born in 1909, Duvakin was wholly formed by the Soviet epoch and its educational system, absorbing its utopian values, enthusiasms, required reading lists, and constant summons to higher norms of cultural work. His public energy and life force were legendary. "It was as if Viktor Dmitrievich Duvakin had been a locomotive in some earlier life," the literary critic Vladimir Radzishevskii wrote in a 2004 commemorative essay on Duvakin titled "The Outcast with an Antediluvian Tape Recorder: Life after the Disaster."[1] "Either he was puffing with impatience, heated up and shrouded in smoke and steam, or else he was rushing ahead, with a roar and a whistle. He was always in a hurry and always late." With refreshing candour, Duvakin never lied about references he did not recognize or about pan-European events that had been obscured or distorted by party-minded curricula. Nor did he ever conceal the centre of own personal fascination, Vladimir Mayakovsky (1893–1930). The lifespan of that poet defined for him the avant-garde era, the domain of his oral-history project, stretching from the Great War through to the First Writers' Congress of 1934. The most savage years of Stalinism were bracketed out. This was a good thing because acts of remembering are called up not from some open pit but from behind a protective shield. Or as Radzishevskii put it in the aforementioned essay, even when witnesses want to co-operate and tell the truth, "memory is generally oriented not towards self-disclosure, but towards self-defence." As in dialogue 4 with Roman Jakobson (taped on 21 August 1967, during his sixth visit to the USSR), Duvakin's opening assurance to his subjects was routinely in this spirit: "Tell me everything you remember … in as much detail as possible. You should rest assured that whatever you choose to share will not be published ... I'm working for the twenty-first century … I am not planning to write a biography [of Mayakovsky]; I don't have time for that right now … You will not be tied down by anything, and I will not bombard you with questions ... [But] I have plenty of tape." Duvakin, smiling eagerly into the face of his elderly subjects, aimed to open the dikes.

He hewed strictly to the biographical line. Political or economic history came in only to the extent that his subjects chose to address it. Duvakin wanted to learn from these people, not just exhaust them. His every move made it clear

1 See Vladimi Radzishevskii, "Izgoi s dopotomnym magnitofonom:zhizn' posle katastrofi," *Znamya* 12 (2004): 200–1.

that even though their testimony would not be made public in their lifetime, they were doing him (as well as history) an irreplaceable favour, and he stood personally in their debt. This method, a mix of the interviewer's intensely subjective appetites and a distant, objectively unknown horizon ("the twenty-first century"), was not born from scratch in 1967. Duvakin had been actively involved in phonographic documentation since the 1930s, gathering information about Mayakovsky for literary museums. By the 1960s, however, on the far side of the Stalinist night, he was dealing with a more traumatized clientele. Most of his interviewees were septuagenarians. Aging brains can be fertile and tenacious, clearer on events that occurred a half-century earlier than on the breakfast the interviewees ate that morning, but their memories are delicate. They rise, sink, and wander. Even though several of the interlocutors in the present volume – Roman Jakobson, Vladimir Sosinsky, and Ariadna Sosinsky – spent much of their life in emigration and thus were spared the horrific memories of those who stayed at home, everyone was cautious. They were being asked to speak freely in a country that until quite recently had shot its artists and poets and continued to censor the rest. In any event, Duvakin as interviewer preferred the trivial daily detail over any political commentary: what people lived by, be it a habit, a revered line of verse, a bawdy joke, or random mundane recollection. "Viktor Dmitrievich pressed his interlocutors on trifles," Radzishevskii remarked, "and they never attempted universal generalizations. But it would sometimes happen that these trifles would open up on an abyss."[2]

The Duvakin method has been variously described. Of highest priority was putting his aging, memory-laden clients at their ease. Dmitry Sporov, now chair of the Department of Oral History at Moscow State University, has written eloquently of Duvakin's heroic pursuit of the "living word" during a sclerotic and repressive era (the "long seventies," 1967–82), when no one trusted an officially printed text, and only the spoken utterance had a semblance of honesty. But speech too was not wholly safe, especially into a microphone as part of an officially sanctioned project. What is more, the most elementary recording equipment could be hard to come by in Russia's chronically deficit economy. Duvakin secured the continuing support of the rector of Moscow State University, Ivan Georgievich Petrovskii, who could not overturn the Communist Party's directive to fire the immensely popular Duvakin from his teaching duties but who could respond to the outpouring of protest by creating, and standing by, his colleague in this new academic archival post. Duvakin's tape recorders were gradually upgraded: in March 1967 he secured a stationery Tembr with a guaranteed supply of tape, and in 1968 he was supplied with a portable Tesla. Early in 1967, when Duvakin was informed that no interviewing space was available on the university

2 Radzishevskii, "Izgoi s dopotomnym magnitofonom:zhizn' posle katastrofi."

premises, he responded with alacrity and sound sense. He would conduct his interviews in the apartments and homes of his interlocutors. This arrangement would be easier for his elderly clientele – not only physically. Psychologically, this was a generation for whom "being called in for questioning" was hardly a positive thing, however benignly repackaged it was. Interviewees were visited at home and urged to share impressions outside their specialty; "professional" topics were discouraged. Of course, mutual knowledge of a Russian poem was not considered professional. Loving Russian poetry, and being able to ignite it at any moment in a spontaneous joint recitation, is a trademark of Duvakin's method. No matter how many years are spent abroad, and no matter how polyglot the interviewee might be, being a Russian brings with it this love and this capacity.

Sporov has noted other aspects of the Duvakin approach to oral history. For all the richness of those fifteen years of work and interviews with three hundred individuals, the collected cassettes remain a single person's prism, a pool limited to Duvakin's personal acquaintances and contacts. At the time, only personal networks were trustworthy. It is easy to forget the darkness of the 1960s to 1970s, when no one dreamed that "the twenty-first century" for which Duvakin was compiling his testimony would arrive so abruptly – at the end of the 1980s. Although Sporov was certain that the state security organs knew about Duvakin's activities, he could not say how interested the authorities were in them. So one personal contact led covertly to another, usually along a poetic or dramatic seam. Soviet linguist Vyacheslav Ivanov arranged the meeting with Roman Jakobson during Jakobson's penultimate trip to Russia. The satirist and cartoonist Viktor Yefimovich Ardov (dialogue 1), whose Moscow apartment was a refuge for non-conformist writers and poets over decades, provides fascinating testimony about the rivalry of Moscow theatres in the 1920s, far exceeding any details about the production of Mayakovsky's plays that was Duvakin's initial point of entry. Duvakin's former seminar student Vadim Kozhinov, a disciple of Mikhail Bakhtin, introduced him to that aged and ailing thinker, and, among the astonishing things we are learning from the recently published translation of Bakhtin's conversations with Duvakin, is Bakhtin's deep and loving knowledge of poetry, a trait obscured in his more novelistic essays. Whether by instinct or design, Duvakin pulled the evidence of this love out of all his interviewees, even though he had promised not to badger them with leading questions and not to "tie them down."

Many potential (and priceless) candidates did not materialize. It would happen that at the most inopportune moment the equipment would fail, or health would break down, or caution would prevail. Other desirable candidates circulated in spheres too distant from the Duvakin network. Sporov notes that in all the cassette tapes – a total of 1,200 – there is not a single reminiscence about Aleksei Losev, an immensely important classicist and philosopher "whom Duvakin could not have failed to know about, but that was an entirely other environment, alien to him."

To these observations of Radzishevskii and Sporov, I add one of my own. In the early 1990s, as independent (non-Marxist) philosophy was rapidly acquiring a footprint in post-Communist Russia, Duvakin's six conversations with Bakhtin (conducted in March 1973) were serialized in the Russian humanities journal *Chelovek*. When these transcripts were annotated, issued, and then reissued in book form, Bakhtin scholars in Russia began to register their unease. In the same year that Vladimir Radzishevskii published his glowing tribute to Duvakin's oral-history project (2004), Vitalii Makhlin spoke up, on behalf of Bakhtin's legacy, in the literary journal *Voprosy literatury* (*Literary Questions*).[3] Without engaging the virtues of the larger Duvakin enterprise, Makhlin argued that these lengthy taped sessions might have some ethnographic value (on how the world of Soviet philology thought and functioned in the stagnant decades before the end), but they were "not Bakhtin." They were one long, embarrassing demonstration of an intellectual and generational gap between the riches of nineteenth-century Europe and the poverty of Soviet-Stalinist thought. Not only did the monolingual Duvakin fail to recognize the names, terms, and poetic movements in pre-war Germany and France, but, more damaging, in Makhlin's view, was that Duvakin proved incapable, hour after hour, of picking up on Bakhtin's philosophical asides and threads of thought. These threads never unwound in a Soviet direction. All of Bakhtin's categories had been formed before the revolution. At times Duvakin and Bakhtin meant opposite things by the same phrase. Analysing exchanges in the transcripts where such mismatchings occurred (much as Bakhtin had analysed micro-passages of Dostoevsky's dialogues), Makhlin acknowledged Bakhtin's "speech tact" in the face of Duvakin's "congenial obtuseness." What discussions there might have been had Duvakin been up to the task! But ultimately – Makhlin asked his readers – what did it mean to be on opposite sides of a paradigm shift? It meant that you were not even aware that you had misunderstood the question. The Duvakin interviews, Makhlin concluded, might have been structured as a *beseda* (colloquy) in the formal sense, but they were not a *razgovor* (conversation) – and never a dialogue. We might ask whether the same "culture gap" mars the Jakobson and Sosinsky interviews in the present volume. Duvakin undertook these with sophisticated polyglot émigrés, whose experience of European culture was immeasurably deeper than his own. Should this matter?

Soon after his review had appeared, I wrote to Makhlin. As one old Bakhtin hand to another, I commiserated with the missed opportunity to record a real dialogue among equals with a complex, shrouded, carnivalized, and often contradictory interviewee, who had only a year left to live. But it occurred to me, back then in my note to Makhlin and recently, that there are robust advantages

3 V. Makhlin, "Toje razgovor," *Voprosi literaturi* 3 (2004): 3–45.

to the Duvakin method, which apply to all levels of education and cultural exposure. Duvakin did not arrive as an official academic, with his tape recorder and a resolve to footnote the abstract schema in the written texts of his interlocutors. He resolved to put them at their ease. As an enabling conduit for personality, he welcomed everything. He wanted to hear (and record) the *surviving voice* – whatever it remembered, however faultily – and he prompted this voice with every tool at his disposal. Although some titbit about Mayakovsky was always eagerly received, the session was not a lesson, and there was no script. Perhaps his interviewees would not have relaxed and spoken (or wandered) so freely had they thought that everything would be understood and further interrogated. This point is worth pondering. The 2017 biography of Bakhtin by Aleksei Korovashko in the ZhZL (Lives of remarkable people) series, something of a scandal in its own right, opens with a frontal attack on the Duvakin interviews, claiming that Bakhtin lied to Duvakin about his family history – and about much else, too.[4] Korovashko misses the point. Bakhtin could have easily misremembered some details, and he might have been misinformed about his genealogy, but the interest and value of his voice do not rest there. Duvakin's interviewing skill lies is his ability to delight in whatever he hears, to join with it, and amplify it. He draws on a huge (if homegrown) base. My own impression of Duvakin as interlocutor is that of an extraordinarily resourceful learner, who wastes no time posing, showing off, or apologizing. He does what we all do in real living dialogue: he seeks to add something of his own to whatever he hears from the other party. Whenever it is remotely relevant, he links this comment to a poem or a poet. In the Duvakin-Bakhtin volume there are many lovely moments between these equals in poetry. At the end of the second interview Bakhtin notes approvingly to his younger colleague:

Bakhtin: I see you know poetry pretty well.

Duvakin: I do.

Bakhtin: And not just the older poetry . . .

Duvakin: Yes, I know poetry. Right. Well . . . It's nice that you can feel that.[5]

One senses Duvakin smiling as he says this – not for himself but for the Russian literary tradition.

---

4 Alexei Korovashko, *Mikhail Bakhtin* (Moscow: Molodaya gvardiya, 2017), esp. 5–10. Korovashko, whose disrespect for his biographical subject takes one's breath away, calls Bakhtin an imposter and a Khlestakov in his interviews with Duvakin.

5 *Mikhail Bakhtin: The Duvakin Interviews, 1973*, ed. Slav N. Gratchev and Margarita Marinova, trans. Margarita Marinova (Lewisburg, PA: Bucknell University Press, 2019), 93.

The garments of the themes that recur in this present volume – trivial details, eccentricities, emotions, attitudes, lines of recited poetry – remain with us far more vividly than would any ideological or philosophical pronouncements. Duvakin responds to each detail gleefully, with genuine excitement: "I didn't know that!" "That's so interesting!" Chuckling, he relishes the occasional off-colour joke. Food in the cafés is a favourite theme, as is the way people looked; both themes tap into the visual-emotional memory of the very old. Ardov (in dialogue 1) lingers for a while on the sight of Blyumkin's cleft lip and overall ugliness and makes much of Yesenin's irresistible pinkish-blonde hair and Ivan Aksenov's long dense beard. We are delighted to learn that Zoshchenko is a "fire fan" – that he attends fires in the way that some people attend the theatre. But the Sosinskys' recollection of Tsvetaeva (dialogue 3) is excruciating: that her husband, Sergei Efron, defended her genius and forgave her excesses, and that everyone loved Marina Ivanovna but she was "thirsty for people, especially for men who were younger, and this was noticeable in her behaviour, and we didn't like it." Her long-anticipated meeting with Pasternak was a failure on cruelly physical grounds: she was too old, and because she fuelled herself on erotic fantasies, she blamed herself and the world for this failure. One is struck throughout the volume by the obnoxious or infantile behaviour of poets and performing artists that is all taken for granted and tolerated: Yesenin's egoism, Meyerhold's narcissism and pursuit of novelty at all costs, and Mayakovsky's calculatedly rude outbursts. The exception here is the luminous Isaac Babel in Paris – shrewd, life affirming, curious. To Babel we owe the difference between Lenin and Trotsky (dialogue 5): Lenin was funny, flexible, and knew how to drink vodka when it was appropriate, whereas Trotsky was cruel, doctrinaire, and did not drink at all. And then, running through domestic and émigré interlocutor alike, is the implicit theme of power: those who despised it and those who admired, worshipped, and feared it. Tsvetaeva, with tremendous naïveté, pride, and personal courage, ignored power and lived arrogant and self-assured in her own world. Pasternak (as the Sosinskys portrayed him) worshipped power; apparently, like Mikhail Bulgakov, he never outgrew Stalin's telephone call in June 1934. But, remarkably, none of these behaviours, indiscretions, or petty vices of poets compromises the hero of this book, which is poetry itself.

This worship of poetry (and of its creators) is, I believe, the quintessence of the present volume that we can carry away. The book builds on the earlier Duvakin-Bakhtin collection and is a worthy companion to it. This adoration of poetry pulsates throughout the book, but an example from the first and last chapters will suffice. In the opening dialogue (Viktor Ardov on Yesenin and Mayakovsky), the English-language reader is treated to two pages on the rhythmic structure of Russian poetry recited aloud, with a passionate aside on the peculiar guttural pronunciation of a single consonant in the mouth of a single poet (Yesenin). Although none of this detail can persist in translation, the editors are utterly correct in not deleting it. To Russians, how poetry is relayed is a deep and vital matter. To the American ear, the conventional Russian recitation style, akin to a trance, can sound bombastic and artificed; English poetry has not done that for centuries. But this rhythm electrifies, mesmerizes, and unifies a Russian audience. On its behalf, bottomless behavioural licence is granted to poets, and their products are adored. None of the three layers in the Duvakin conversations (interviewer, interviewee, recalled characters) challenges its truth. In the final dialogue Vladimir Sosinsky discusses Mayakovsky's poetry readings in Paris in November–December 1924. He quotes Aleksei Remizov on how "poetry must be heard with the heart. Like music," and how the inner content of poems is rhythmic and aural and "not meant to be understood" cerebrally. These same rules apply to the prose of the great Russian writers Pushkin, Gogol, and Leskov. A single rhythm infuses their works, and this texture must be reproduced. That rhythm is the birthright of the poet, even when one writes in prose. But professional actors, when reading Russian literature aloud, often fail to grasp this fact, that "poetry is different from talking," as Remizov affirms. On that point, Sosinsky speaks for the entire Duvakin oral-history project, which is shot through with such ecstatic, unifying poetic moments. In addition to its homy everyday detail and the unforgettable image remaining from a distant encounter, the present book should be appreciated for this approach to the task of testimony. An act of verse could always catch, transform creatively, and transcend the traumatic chaos of the Soviet years.

Notes on the Photography Collection

Ekaterina Snegireva

The photographs that appear in this book belong to Mayakovsky State Museum, Moscow, Russia. To this day, it is the only museum dedicated to the life and work of the most futuristic poet of the Soviet time, Vladimir Mayakovsky. The museum's extensive and diverse collection contains about fifty thousand items, including the poet's personal items, his manuscripts, letters, the rare books he owned, and his paintings and graphic works.

After Mayakovsky's tragic death in April 1930, his family and friends decided preserve his heritage by founding a museum dedicated to his life and work. That was not an easy task during the Soviet times, especially while Stalin was still in power, but luck was on their side: in 1937 a small museum, which also served as a library, opened in the same building where Mayakovsky had lived with Lilya and Osip Brik from 1926 to 1930.

The Briks were not only close friends of Mayakovsky but also his most dedicated followers: they helped recreate the authentic atmosphere of the apartment in which the three of them had lived together, by donating furniture, household items, clothes, and other personal items of the poet. For the next thirty years the museum continued to grow, and in1967 the entire building was given to the museum to accommodate its unique collection.

Mayakovsky's notebooks have a special place among the museum holdings; they are filled with his handwritten rhymes, quatrains, drafts of future poems, and drawings. They are not only invaluable to any scholar who studies Mayakovsky's creative process – his "secret laboratory" of poetry making – but also fascinating to anyone interested in literature as a whole. The museum owns sixty-eight of Mayakovsky's known seventy-two notebooks.

Vladimir Mayakovsky's creative drive found realization in literature, but he also produced many interesting paintings, drawings, advertisements, and propaganda posters. Vera Shekhtel, the daughter of the famous architect Fedor Shekhtel, and

Mayakovsky's short-term lover, donated to the museum a series of his drawings – the famous "Giraffes" created by Mayakovsky during his studies at the Moscow School of Painting, Sculpture, and Architecture. But the real highlight of the museum's collection is, without a doubt, the painting *Chemin de fer* (*Roulette*) executed by Mayakovsky in 1915. This work is one of very few examples of futuristic painting, and it continues to be included in avant-garde art exhibitions around the world.

The Mayakovsky State Museum also contains materials related to the life and work of many of Mayakovsky's contemporary writers, poets, artists, actors, and playwrights, all of whom are now considered representatives of the Russian avant-garde. Visitors delight in the extensive collection of works by David Burliuk, Natalia Goncharova, Olga Rozanova, Elena Guro, El Lissitzky, Mikhail Matyushin, Kazimir Malevich, Mikhail Larionov, Gustav Glutis, and Piotr Miturich.

Another important part of the museum collection – arguably the most exciting one – is the collection of photographs taken by Vladimir Mayakovsky himself, which consists of more than three hundred and fifty professional and amateur photographs. In addition, the museum owns a significant number of pictures of the poet's friends and acquaintances; there are rare photographs of David Burliuk, Vasily Kamensky, Boris Pasternak, Elsa Triolet, Vera Shekhtel, Tatyana Yakovleva, and many others.

There are pictures from every period in Mayakovsky's life, from early childhood to his last day. These are portraits of different times, depicting the poet as he was in everyday life; among friends, acquaintances, and colleagues; and at work (giving speeches and reading his poetry). Many of the photographs exemplify the exceptional skills of the photographers who took them; some have become a part of other works of art, such as photomontages and collages. They all help us reconstruct not just the chronicle but also the geography of Mayakovsky's life.

Today the museum continues to grow and diversify its collection with new acquisitions, such as works of contemporary artists inspired by Mayakovsky, or personal artefacts related to the poet. One of the most recent acquisitions was the private archive of Helen Patricia Thompson, the daughter of Vladimir Mayakovsky and the Russian émigré Elli Jones, who had spent all of her life in the United States. After her death in 2016, her son donated to the museum a wealth of materials related to her book about her parents, their love, and their relationship and a number of photographs.

For this book we decided to illustrate the entire history of the Russian avant-garde by providing rare pictures of Vsevolod Meyerhold with his wife, Zinaida Raikh; rehearsals led by Meyerhold; Sergei Yesenin, together with Isadora Duncan and her daughter Irma Duncan; Mayakovsky with his lifelong lover, Lilya Brik, and her husband, Osip; groups including Boris Pasternak and Sergei Eisenstein; and many others. Some of the photographs will be completely new to the Western reader. We are pleased to have the opportunity to share these special materials from the collection of the Mayakovsky Museum.

About the Contributors

Caryl Emerson is an A. Watson Armour III professor emeritus of Slavic Languages and Literatures at Princeton University. Her work has focused on the Russian classics (Pushkin, Tolstoy, Dostoevsky), Mikhail Bakhtin, and Russian music, opera, and theatre. Recent areas of interest include the Russian Modernist Sigizmund Krzhizhanovsky (1887–1950), the allegorical, historical novelist Vladimir Sharov (1952–2018), and the co-editing, with George Pattison and Randall A. Poole, of *The Oxford Handbook of Russian Religious Thought*.

Irina Evdokimova is a lawyer, who has worked in Russia as a criminal prosecutor in the office of Attorney General for five years. She has a fondness for the silver age of Russian poetry and literary criticism and plans to write about the period. She co-edited the book *Dialogues with Shklovsky: The Duvakin Interviews, 1967–1968* (2019) and contributed to the volume *Viktor Shklovsky's Heritage in Literature, Arts, and Philosophy* (2019).

Slav N. Gratchev is an associate professor of Spanish at Marshall University. He is the author or editor of six books: *The Polyphonic World of Cervantes and Dostoevsky* (2017); *Don Quixote: The Re-accentuation of the World's Greatest Literary Hero* (2017); *Bakhtin's Heritage in Literature, Arts, and Psychology* (2018); *Dialogues with Shklovsky: The Duvakin Interviews, 1967–1968* (2019); *Viktor Shklovsky's Heritage in Literature, Arts, and Philosophy* (2019); and *Mikhail Bakhtin: The Duvakin Interviews, 1973* (2019). In addition, Slav Gratchev has published articles on Cervantes, Dostoevsky, and Bakhtin in various journals including *Cervantes, College Literature, The South Atlantic Review, Comparative Literature and Culture, The Russian Review*, and *The Nabokovian.*

Margarita Marinova is an associate professor of English and Comparative Literature at Christopher Newport University, Virginia. She has published three books to date: *Transnational Russian-American Travel Writing* (2011), *Mikhail Bulgakov's Don Quixote* (2014), and *Mikhail Bakhtin: The Duvakin Interviews, 1973* (2019). Margarita Marinova has also published articles about Russian and Soviet literature and culture, Cervantes in Russia, contemporary Bulgarian literature, and travel studies, in scholarly collections and journals such as the *Slavic and East European Journal*, *Studies in Travel Writing*, *The Comparatist*, and *Tulsa Studies in Women's Literature*.

Ekaterina Snegireva is a historian. She is head of the photo archive of Mayakovsky State Museum, and an author of numerous articles about Vladimir Mayakovsky and the representation of his life and works in photographs. Ekaterina Snegireva is one of the pre-eminent contemporary Russian scholars specializing in the avant-garde photography of the 1920s–1930s.

Dmitry Sporov is a historian, and for the last ten years he has been the chair of the Department of Oral History at Moscow State University's Science Library. He is also the president of the Russian Foundation for Research in the Humanities. Dmitry Sporov is the editor of the book series Let's Remember Moscow. They represent a unique and invaluable collection of oral memoirs about Moscow in the 1930s and 1940s. He contributed to *Mikhail Bakhtin: The Duvakin Interviews, 1973* (2019).

Index

Note: Due to the frequency with which they are mentioned, Vladimir Mayakovsky, Marina Tsvetaeva, Boris Pasternak, and Sergei Yesenin do not have separate entries in the index.

www.ingramcontent.com/pod-product-compliance
Lightning Source LLC
LaVergne TN
LVHW041114090826
844660LV00062B/903/J

* 9 7 8 1 4 8 7 5 2 7 2 5 9 *